Understanding Lifestyle Sports

What makes a lifestyle sport distinctive?

Skateboarding is now more popular than many traditional team sports in the USA. Is sport culture, and the identities that emerge from it, being transformed in the twenty-first century?

The past decade has seen a tremendous growth in the popularity of activities like skateboarding and snowboarding; sports that have been labelled as 'extreme' or 'lifestyle' and which embody 'alternative' sporting values such as anti-competitiveness, anti-regulation, high risk and personal freedom. The popularity of these activities goes beyond the teenage male youth that the media typify as their main consumers.

This book examines the popularity, significance and meaning of lifestyle sport, exploring the sociological significance of these activities, particularly as related to their consumption, and the expression of identity and difference. The edited collection includes unique ethnographic research work with skaters, surfers, windsurfers, climbers, adventure racers, and Ultimate frisbee players. The central themes explored in *Understanding Lifestyle Sport* include:

- How might we describe lifestyle sports?
- What influence do commercial forces have on lifestyle sports?
- Do lifestyle sports challenge the hegemonic masculinities characteristic of traditional sport environments?

Belinda Wheaton is a Senior Research Fellow at the University of Brighton's Chelsea School where she lectures in the sociocultural study of sport and leisure, and sport journalism. She is an active windsurfer, surfer and snowboarder and also writes for a range of 'lifestyle sports' magazines.

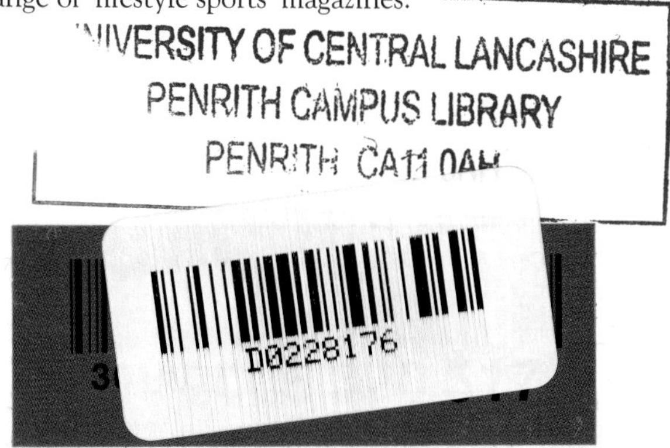

Routledge Critical Studies in Sport

Series Editors

Jennifer Hargreaves

Brunel University

Ian McDonald

University of Brighton

The Routledge Critical Studies in Sport series aims to lead the way in developing the multi-disciplinary field of Sport Studies by producing books that are interrogative, interventionist and innovative. By providing theoretically sophisticated and empirically grounded texts, the series will make sense of the changes and challenges facing sport globally. The series aspires to maintain the commitment and promise of the critical paradigm by contributing to a more inclusive and less exploitative culture of sport.

Understanding Lifestyle Sports

Consumption, identity and difference

Belinda Wheaton

Routledge
Taylor & Francis Group
LONDON AND NEW YORK

First published 2004
by Routledge
2 Park Square, Milton Park, Abingdon, Oxon, OX14 4RN

Simultaneously published in the USA and Canada
by Routledge
270 Madison Ave, New York, NY 10016

Reprinted 2005

Typeset in Goudy by
GreenGate Publishing Services, Tonbridge, Kent
Printed and bound in Great Britain by
TJ International, Padstow, Cornwall

British Library Cataloguing in Publication Data
A catalogue record for this book is available from the British Library

Library of Congress Cataloging in Publication Data
A catalog record for this book has been requested

ISBN 0-415-25954-1 (hbk)
ISBN 0-415-25955-X (pbk)

Contents

Contributors

Becky Beal is an Associate Professor of Sport Sciences at the University of the Pacific in Stockton, California. She teaches courses in the sociology of sport and ethics. Her research interests include 'alternative' sport culture and the construction of those participants' sporting identities. She has been an active member of the North American Society for the Sociology of Sport, and has served on the editorial board for the *Sociology of Sport Journal*.

Douglas Booth is a Professor of Sport and Leisure Studies at the University of Waikato, New Zealand. His primary research interests cover the study of sport as a form of popular culture with a particular emphasis on political relationships and processes. Within this broad framework, specific areas of investigation have included racism in South African sport, the Olympic movement, and the beach. He currently serves as an executive member of the Australian Society for Sport History and on the editorial boards of several journals including *Journal of Sport History* and the *International Journal of the History of Sport*.

Kyle W. Kusz is Assistant Professor of Kinesiology at the University of Rhode Island in Kingston, RI. His work has centred upon critically examining the cultural politics of the white masculinities produced in sport formations, sport celebrities, and sport films of 1990s' America. His forthcoming book entitled: *Reality Bites?: White masculinity, sport, and contemporary American culture* will be published by Peter Lang Publishing, Inc. in 2005.

Joanne Kay holds a PhD in Sport Sociology from the Université de Montréal. She is currently a senior policy analyst and sport policy research coordinator with Canada's federal government. Kay's research has examined new sport culture, specifically in relation to corporate, media and gender dynamics. Kay's work on adventure racing has been published in *International Review for the Sociology of Sport and Sociology of Sport Journal*. Kay's work as a freelance journalist has been featured in local and national media. As an athlete, Kay was a member of Canada's national triathlon team.

Suzanne Laberge is a Professor in the Department of Kinesiology at the Université de Montréal where she teaches sociology of sport and physical activity. She has published on gender relations, cultural issues in physical activity participation, extreme sport, and social theory in journals such as *Men and Masculinities*, *Sociologie et Sociétés*, *Sociology of Sport Journal*, *International Journal for the Sociology of Sport*, and *Society and Leisure*. She is mainly known for her expertise in the use of Pierre Bourdieu's social theory applied to physical activity and sport practice.

Neil Lewis was a Teaching Fellow in Sociology at Lancaster University until 2003 where he lectured upon the anthropology of modernity. He is currently teaching geography at a secondary school in Blackpool and sometimes writing a book entitled *Dying to Stay Alive: An Ethnography of Adventure Climbing* when time allows. His research interests include the anthropology of the body, tourism/leisure, environmental sociology, and existential philosophy.

Catherine Palmer is a lecturer and researcher in the Department of Public Health, Flinders University of South Australia, where she teaches courses in anthropology and public health and research methods. Her sports research background is extensive, and includes sport and identity making in the global arena, drugs, gender, sport in cross-cultural contexts, risk and danger, sport and social inclusion and physical activity and locational disadvantage. Current research is examining physical activity and locational disadvantage in suburban Australia. Forthcoming research will examine the sporting experiences of newly arrived migrants in Australia.

Victoria Robinson is a Lecturer in Sociology at the University of Sheffield/University of Newcastle. Her work on climbing will be the focus of a book currently in preparation entitled *A Different Kind of Hard: Everyday Masculinities, Identity and Rock Climbing*, due to be published by Berg in 2005. She is also working, with Diane Richardson, on the third edition of *Introducing Women's Studies: Feminist Theory and Practice* (2nd edition 1997), published by Macmillan.

Andrew Thornton is Senior Lecturer in the School of Life and Sport Sciences at Roehampton University of Surrey (London, UK). His PhD thesis (Toronto) was Ultimate Masculinities: An Ethnography of Power and Social Difference in Sport. His main interests are cultural studies of sport and leisure. He is particularly interested in how race, identity and difference are at work within sport and popular culture. He has published in the areas of critical race theory, gender and cultural studies. Andrew is currently carrying out research on the sporting body in popular film and is co-editing the forthcoming anthology, *Leisure, Media and Visual Culture: Representations and Contestations* (LSA Publication No. 83). He also continues to 'chase plastic' around the Ultimate field on a regular basis.

Charlene Wilson is Program Director for a student YMCA in Stockton, California. She began assisting Becky Beal with skateboarding research in the summer of 2001 after receiving her bachelor's degree in sociology from

University of the Pacific. She plans to attend graduate school in the Autumn of 2004.

Belinda Wheaton is a Senior Research Fellow at the University of Brighton's Chelsea School. She lectures in the sociocultural study of sport and leisure, and sport journalism. Her research and publications have focused on the sociological significance of lifestyle sport cultures, and qualitative methodologies. She is writing a book on the *Cultural Politics of Lifestyle Sport* also to be published by Routledge. Belinda remains an active windsurfer, surfer, and snowboarder, and still writes – occasionally – for windsurfing, kite surfing and other sporting magazines.

Series editors' foreword

Dramatic changes and controversial developments are transforming the ways in which sport is experienced and understood. Many of the old ideas about sport embracing 'noble' and 'educational' values, offering disadvantaged peoples 'a way out', bringing nations closer together, or creating healthy bodies seem increasingly to lack credibility. In particular, there are widespread concerns that economic and political forces are becoming too influential and are distorting the role and place of sport in societies across the world. Further, there are anxious and often confused debates about the impact of new technologies and cultures of consumption on the integrity of sport. In short, as we move through the twenty-first century, sport faces serious and important challenges since its emergence in its modern form in the nineteenth century. Can we say with any confidence, for example, that sport as we now know it today, still recognisable from the beginning of the last century, will be equally recognisable at the end of this century?

These observations about sport today and the key questions raised above provide the impetus for this new Routledge Critical Studies in Sport series. Our intention as editors of the series is to tackle some of the big questions facing sport and society, to question assumptions about sport, to critique established ideas, and to explore new ones. Books in the series will investigate the changing features of 'old' sports and the distinguishing characteristics of 'new' ones; they will examine the social, political, environmental and technological dimensions of sport; they will interrogate theoretical procedures and issues which are the focus of controversy; and they will expose uncertainties that pose important questions about present trends and future predictions. They will also be empirically grounded and socially relevant, challenging and innovative, in particular through their engagement with issues concerning relations of power and discriminatory practices. The series as a whole aims to challenge complacency and encourage reflection and should assist students, researchers, policy-makers and professionals to make sense of the changes, challenges and crises facing sport globally. The guiding philosophy for the series can be summarised as:

- Interrogative: challenging common-sense ideas and exposing relations of power in the world of sport

- Interventionist: highlighting the relationship between theory and practice and providing arguments and analyses of topical and polemical issues
- Innovative: seeking to develop new areas of research, and stimulating new ways of thinking about and studying sport.

The Routledge Critical Studies in Sport series is particularly timely as sport studies continue to expand within higher education. As sociological analyses of sport in particular mature and become more sophisticated, the new insights that emerge need to be expressed and debated and it is expected that the series will become a key forum for such debate. As editors of the series, we are concerned to promote a more inclusive and less exploitative culture of sport practice and analysis, thus reviving what we call the 'social criticism of sport'.

The emergence and rapidly growing popularity of 'lifestyle sports' has been one of the most significant developments in recent years, to which the sport sociology community has given little attention so far. This has served to reinforce the marginal status of lifestyle sports and reveals one way in which scholars can be implicated in reproducing dominant relations of power in sport. We are delighted therefore that one of the first books in the series is *Understanding Lifestyle Sports*. This collection will certainly provide students with an invaluable resource about a burgeoning culture of sport that many of them will already be familiar with. What are known variously as 'action sports', 'extreme sports', 'postmodern sports', or what Belinda Wheaton has called 'lifestyle sports', represent a phenomenon that poses many questions that this series is designed to address. For example: 'To what extent do lifestyle sports offer an alternative culture to dominant sporting practices?' 'Do they offer more egalitarian and empowering gender identities than other sports?' 'Do lifestyle sports offer a counter to the commercially exploitative world of mainstream sport? 'In what ways has the media industry specifically, and the culture industries in general, sought to embrace lifestyles sports?'

One of the hidden features of Belinda Wheaton's book about lifestyle sports is that through this study of alternatives, of subcultures or the subaltern comes knowledge also about how the dominant is reproduced. Importantly, *Understanding Lifestyle Sports* is not merely an exploration of a range of alternative, emergent, subcultural practices, but is also a critique of mainstream sport and an insight into relations of power between the two. We would argue, therefore, that this collection makes relevant and important reading that has implications far beyond the insular world of one or other of the lifestyle sports featured in the book. The flamboyant world of these new 'other' sports are understood only in relation to 'established' ones embodying quite different social relations, meanings and values. This book should therefore be a key reading not only for all devotees of lifestyle sports, but for everyone else concerned with the culture of modern sport in general.

Jennifer Hargreaves (Brunel University, London)
Ian McDonald (University of Brighton)

Acknowledgements

Firstly I'd like to thank my colleagues in the Chelsea School, University of Brighton and formerly at Roehampton, University of Surrey who have given me support and provided an enjoyable and creative working environment. You know who you are! While there are many who have supported me professionally Alan Tomlinson and Ben Carrington warrant particular thanks for providing ongoing critical feedback in the preparation of this manuscript, and my work more widely. Special thanks also go to my series editors Jennifer Hargreaves and Ian McDonald for their professional guidance, support and for being good friends. They waited extremely patiently and enthusiastically for the manuscript, despite several 'hiccups' along the way, including the birth of my daughter, Poppy. I would also like to acknowledge the assistance from Samantha Grant and her predecessor Simon Whitmore at Routledge, and the ESRC's financial support for my doctoral research on windsurfing (R0042334379). I am of course indebted to all the book's contributors who have been so supportive, patient, and amenable to my changing demands and deadlines.

Personally I'd like to thank Stuart, who probably wishes he'd never introduced me to lifestyle sport, yet throughout my research and writing he has continued to support me, as well as 'taking part' as a 'critical friend.' Special thanks also to my parents; to my dad who even 30 years ago steadfastly refused to believe that 'girl's toys' were interesting, and who instead initiated me into the thrill of 'adventurous leisure'; and to my mum who refuses to slow down, and continues to provide immeasurable emotional support. Lastly to Poppy (now 18 months) who has contributed to this book's tardiness, and to whom it is dedicated.

While most of the material here is published for the first time, Chapter 7 appeared in an earlier incarnation in *Men and Masculinities*.

1 Introduction

Mapping the lifestyle sport-scape

Belinda Wheaton

Prologue: alternative sport comes of age

> Pro skateboarder Tony Hawk is standing aboard a corporate jet on his way to a charity event in Houston. In his hand is a Heineken and on the table in front of him is a platter overflowing with lobster, stone crab, and jumbo shrimp. Doing his best imitation of former Talking Heads singer David Byrne, he stiffens his frame, taps his arm, and says, "And you may ask yourself, Well, how did I get here"?
>
> (Borden 2002: 1)

In May 2002 in a poll conducted by a 'teen' marketing firm in the USA, skateboarding star Tony Hawk was voted the 'coolest big time athlete' ahead of 'mainstream' mega-sport celebrities such as Michael Jordan and Tiger Woods (Layden 2002). If Jordan's status comes even close to Nike's claims (in 1999) that he is 'the most recognized person in the world' (cited in Mcdonald and Andrews 2001: 21), then alternative sport it seems, has come of age. Further evidence of the tremendous growth in alternative and extreme sports comes from participation figures; as Beal and Wilson (this volume) outline, in the USA the growth of skating, based on sales of skateboards, has outpaced the growth of a number of 'big league' traditional sports including baseball. Moreover, it is not just the US market that is seeing such a growth, nor is it just among young teenage men. For example, the snowboarding industry (in 1996) predicted that by 2005, half of all ski-hill patrons will be snowboarders (Humphreys 2003: 407); and in the UK, surfing became one of the fastest growth sports at the turn of the twenty-first century, particularly among women, and men in their thirties and forties (Tyler 2003; Walters 2002; Asthana 2003).

How do we make sense of this popularity in what I have termed lifestyle sport, particularly when one of the central characteristics of these so-called *alternative* sports is that they are *different* to the western traditional activities that constitute 'mainstream' sport?[1] As Rinehart (2000: 506) suggests, alternative sports are activities that 'either ideologically or practically provide alternatives to mainstream sports and to mainstream sport values'. This popularity trend, or process of mainstreaming particularly as manifest in the increased media and market appropriation of alternative sport, has now received a great deal of attention from both academic and non-academic commentators on these activities. As Gliddon (2002: 1) notes:

> Surfing has appeal far beyond the surfers who provide the marketing cool. There's a surf shop in Singapore but the roughest water is the condensation on its windows. A boutique surf store competes with Chanel and Prada for the consumer waves of downtown New York.
>
> (Gliddon cited in Arthur 2003: 162)

This commercial co-option, particularly visible in the burgeoning 'sports style,' is a central debate in the wider literature on lifestyle sports, and a theme running through many of the chapters that make up this collection. However I will start my discussion by explaining what lifestyle sports are, and then outlining a theoretical framework for how we can make sense of their emergence and significance in contemporary Western culture. Lastly I outline the distinctive contribution made by this collection of essays to the emerging literature on these sports and their cultures.

What are lifestyle sports?

There is now a body of academic literature examining the phenomena of what has been variously termed 'extreme', 'alternative', 'lifestyle', 'whiz', 'action-sports'[2], 'panic sport', 'postmodern', 'post-industrial' and 'new' sports. Such labels encompass a wide range of mostly individualised sporting activities, from established practices like surfing and skateboarding, to new emergent activities like B.A.S.E. jumping and kite-surfing. While these labels are used synonymously by some commentators, there are differences which signal distinct emphases or expressions of the activities, characteristics that will become evident in the ensuing discussion.

The academic literature and thus 'labelling' of these sporting activities emerged in the early to mid 1980s with Nancy Midol's analysis of 'new sports', based on what she terms the 'whiz' sports movement in France (Midol 1993). Midol and Broyer (1995) developing Midol's (1993) earlier work, argue that a sporting movement developed around the 'whiz sports' which constitute new sport forms, and new communities based on them:

> This culture is extremely different from the official one promoted by sporting institutions. The whiz sport culture is championed by avant-garde groups that challenge the unconscious defences of the existing order through which French society has defined itself for the last two centuries. These groups have dared to practice transgressive behaviours and create new values.
>
> (Midol and Broyer 1995: 210)

In North America the idea of 'alternative sport' was adopted (Rinehart 1996, 1998a; Humphreys 1997; Beal 1995), although the 'extreme' moniker quickly became prevalent, as an all-embracing label, particularly in popular media discourse, and most significantly in the emergence of ESPN's eXtreme Games, later renamed the X Games (see Kusz this volume).

The meaning of alternative sport has been most systematically considered by Rinehart (Rinehart and Sydor 2003; Rinehart 2000, 1998a, b). It includes an extremely wide range of activities – in fact pretty much anything that doesn't fit under the Western 'achievement sport' (Eichberg 1998) rubric. Rinehart (2000: 505) lists activities ranging from indigenous folk games and ultimate fighting to jet skiing, Scuba diving, beach volleyball, and ultra marathoning, also embracing various media spectacles such as the X Games. A number of commentators have also debated whether these activities are more appropriately (or usefully) conceptualised as forms of play rather than sports (see Stranger 1999; Howe 2003), and have highlighted the importance of their artistic sensibility (Rinehart 1998b; Wheaton 2003; Howe 2003; Humphreys 2003; Booth 2003). However, to understand their *meaning* we need to move beyond simplistic and constraining dichotomies such as traditional versus new,[3] mainstream versus emergent, or other related binaries such as sport versus art. Alternative sport, and so called 'mainstream' sport, can have elements of – to use Raymond Williams's (1977) categorisation – residual, emergent and 'dominant' sport culture[4] (Rinehart 2000: 506). As Rinehart suggests, the difference between, and within, these sport forms is best highlighted by a range of debates, concerning their meanings, values, statuses, identities and forms.

Despite differences in nomenclature, many commentators are agreed in seeing such activities as having presented an 'alternative', and *potential* challenge to traditional ways of 'seeing', 'doing' and understanding sport (Rinehart 1998b; Wheaton 2000a; Midol and Broyer 1995). Historically as Bourdieu (1984) has observed, many 'new sports' originated in North America, particularly in the late 1960s, and were then imported to Europe by American entrepreneurs (what he calls the 'new' and 'petite bourgeoisie'). With their roots in the counter-cultural social movement of the 1960s and 1970s (Midol and Broyer 1995) many have characteristics that are different from the traditional rule-bound, competitive and masculinised dominant sport cultures. Maguire (1999) for example, suggests that the emergence of these sports (he cites snowboarding, hang-gliding and windsurfing) and their challenge to the achievement sport ideology is evidence of the increase in the range and diversity of sport cultures, a 'creolization of sport cultures' (87, 211). Bale (1994), likewise submits that such activities present a challenge to the 'western sport model'.

Lifestyle sport is less all-embracing than the terms alternative or new sport; and although many lifestyle sports are often called extreme sport, the latter tends to be the way the mainstream media and marketers, rather than the participants themselves see them (Sky 2001).[5] As Rinehart (2000: 508) notes:

> Some practitioners – and writers – have disputed the very term 'extreme' as merely a blatant and cynical attempt to capitalize on a wave of oppositional sports forms, and, by doing so, for corporations such as ESPN to appropriate trendy oppositional forms.

This is not to suggest that the media are not central to understanding the experience or cultural significance of lifestyle sports. Rinehart makes a convincing case for the increasing influence of the electronic media in determining the shape of what he calls the 'alternative sportscape' (Rinehart 2000). Lifestyle sports take many shapes, including at the elite level being part of the landscape of 'traditional' sports (witness snowboarding in the Olympic Games), the X-Games (activities include a range of board sports including skating, snowboarding, and sport climbing – see Rinehart, 2000), and increasingly as a marketing tool for advertisers attracting youth audiences. Nevertheless underpinning these forms are lived cultures that are fundamentally about 'doing it', about taking part. Participation takes place in local subcultural spaces, spaces that are often quite 'liminal' (Shields 1992) lacking regulation and control, and the sports are performed in ways that often denounce – or even resist – institutionalisation, regulation and commercialisation.

Moreover, more important than classification is their *meaning* (Rinehart 2000). I use the term *lifestyle sport* as it is an expression adopted by members of the cultures themselves, and one that encapsulates these cultures and their identities, signalling the importance of the socio-historical context in which these activities emerged, took shape and exist. As I will exemplify, 'lifestyle sport' reflects both the characteristics of these activities, and their wider socio-cultural significance.

'It's a lifestyle thang'

In a radio interview in the USA (2002) Jake Burton, a key individual in snowboarding's history,[6] is asked about whether there was any 'agreed-upon definition of 'extreme sport,' or whether, it was 'somewhat in the eye of the beholder'?

> It doesn't have to be an extreme sport at all. There's a lot of people that, you know, snowboard in a fairly conservative manner. But I think what's a better moniker is maybe that it's a *lifestyle sport*, and a lot of the kids and people that are doing it are just completely living it all the time, and that's what distinguishes snowboarding from a lot of other sports. And skateboarding and surfing are the same way. And I'm not sure why that is unique to board sports, but I think the only thing that you can come back to is that they're so much fun.
>
> (Jake Burton 2002, *emphasis added*)

Similarly in my research on windsurfing, and in a range of other activities (Sky 2001), participants described the activity 'as a lifestyle' rather than a sport. It became evident that a particular *style of life* was central to the meaning and experience of windsurfing. Participants sought out a lifestyle that was distinctive, often alternative, and that gave them a particular and exclusive social *identity*. While this is particularly evident in board sports such as skating, surfing, and snowboarding, authors in this collection, and elsewhere, have charted the importance of lifestyle in other new sport activities such as climbing (Lewis this volume; Robinson this volume; Kiewa 2002) adventure racing (Kay and Laberge this volume) and Ultimate Frisbee (Thornton this volume). Like other 'alternative lifestyle' groupings that have emerged from the counter culture these sporting cultures involve locally situated identity politics and lifestyle practices (Hetherington 1988: 3).

In the emergence of these sports and their associated lifestyles, we can see some of the central issues and paradoxes of advanced capitalist or late-modern societies, such as in the changing expression of self-identity, and the individualisation and privatisation of the act of consumption, even in seemingly public spheres (Philips and Tomlinson 1992). Theories about the de-stabilisation of social categories, and the increased fluidity of social relationships have triggered interest in the conception of more 'fragmented identities' (Bradley 1996; Hall and Du Gay 1996). As Kellner (1992) outlines, whereas in traditional society identity was relatively fixed and stable (based on a range of identifiers such as work, gender, ethnicity, religion, age), in late modernity, 'identity becomes more mobile, multiple, personal, self-reflexive, and subject to exchange and innovation' (141). It is argued that with the acceleration of change and increasing cultural complexity, the possibilities of different sources of identification have expanded, in particular the increased significance of consumption practices such as sport and leisure lifestyles in the communication and maintenance of self-identity for growing segments of the population (Chaney 1996; Lury 1996; Bocock 1993). Many of these commentators suggest that the relationship between class and identity has shifted;[7] for some like Bauman (1992) lifestyle has overshadowed 'class' as the social relations of production. Maffesoli (1996) describes the emergence of neo-tribes, collectivities based around new types of identification and interests such as alternative lifestyles, youth 'subcultures' and sporting interests, but that are more fluid in composition than subcultures, and that are not determined by one's class background.[8]

The close relationship between identity and consumption has become a key indicator for examining the changing social terrain in late-modern/postmodern society (Hetherington 1988).[9] Consumer culture presents us with an array of lifestyles to aspire to, manifest in a range of symbols including the leisure and sporting activities we pursue, and signifying self-expression and individuality (Tomlinson 1990). 'Leisure is particularly germane to consumption because it displays so many of the characteristics of consumer culture' (Chaney 1994: 78). These:

> new heroes of consumer culture make lifestyle a life project and display their individuality and sense of style in the particularity of the assemblage of goods, clothes, practices, experiences, appearance and bodily dispositions they design together into a lifestyle.
>
> (Featherstone 1991: 86)

The emphasis is increasingly 'on choice, differentiation, self expression, creativity, fitness, health and the body' (Jacques 1997: 18), characteristics reflected in lifestyle sport's cultures, identities and styles of life. Thus although the lifestyles of the urban middle classes have been the main empirical emphasis and point of illustration of these trends, other types of groupings, such as subcultures based around sporting identification, are also useful exemplars. In the emergence and evolution of lifestyle sport activities what is being sold to the consumer is not merely a sport or leisure activity but a complete style of life, one which is saturated with signs and images that emphasise many of these aspirations of postmodern consumer culture.

Yet, consumption is a socially and culturally constructed act which cannot be understood simply in terms of market dynamics, nor in terms of a 'position which seeks to preserve the field of lifestyles and consumption, or at least as a particular aspect of it (such as sport), as an autonomous playful space beyond determination' (Featherstone 1991: 84). To understand the sociological significance of these activities we need to understand the *context* in which 'free choices' are made; acknowledging that choice is often structured by and contingent on factors such as age, class, gender and ethnicity; and the relation of such activities to other dimensions of lifestyle and the media/consumer industries. As Lash outlines, the audience for postmodernist culture tends to be made up of the members of 'post-industrial middle-classes' (Lash 1990: 252). Likewise, as explored later in this chapter, the consumers of these lifestyle sports tend to be dominated by the privileged white male middle classes.

Postmodern lifestyles, postmodern sports

Some theorists have represented the emergence of these sporting activities, and the subcultures and lifestyles that develop around them, as a new phase in the development of sports, characterised by some as 'postmodern' (Rinehart 1998b; Allison 2001; Wheaton 1997; Rinehart 2000; Stedman 1997).

My own early theorising of the significance of these activities focused on this idea.[10] At that time few commentators were interested in these new sporting activities. Moreover, despite postmodern 'claims' about the dissolution of boundaries, for instance between 'Culture' and 'popular culture' (Rojek 1995; Connor 1989), most commentators on postmodern culture seemed to be (and to an extent still are) oblivious to sport as a central expression of leisure. Postmodern thought – if one can use such an umbrella term to describe the contested, complex and multifaceted intellectual trends that have come together under the banner of postmodernism (Featherstone 1988; Hebdige 1993) – has since had a significant impact on the ways sport is theorised, researched and understood. My conception of lifestyle sport as 'postmodern sport' I came to realise was in many ways a theoretically naïve idea. What I was really interested in was the changes that these (lifestyle) sport and leisure *cultures* and *identities* were undergoing in the theorised shift from modernity to postmodernity, and how the emergence and growth of lifestyle sporting activities were implicated in this alleged socio-cultural shift. Put

another way, what were the elements of lifestyle sports that seemed to reflect this shift towards postmodern culture?

To engage with these debates, and illustrate the ways in which lifestyle sport might be reflective of the core themes in the literature on postmodern culture, requires more than the cursory glance I could give in this chapter. However I have related the emergence of lifestyle sports to wider debates about contemporary postmodern culture, and will make some further observations about characteristics of postmodern leisure and sport. Yet irrespective of the theoretical legitimacy of such claims, their emergence and popularity needs to be considered in relation to these wider issues around changing contemporary Western cultures and identities. Whether one considers that we have entered a 'new' postmodern phase of capitalism – as espoused in Jameson's description of Late Capitalism (1991) – or that these 'changes' represent no more than a shift in perception, new consumer activities and leisure industries play an increasingly prominent and wide-ranging role, with the variety of consumer activities and leisure spending by a large part of the population in Western industrialised nations continually increasing, even in periods of recession (Henley Centre 1993).

Mapping identities in the lifestyle sport-scape

In the twenty-first century lifestyle sports are attracting an ever-increasing number of participants, who encompass a wide range of different experiences and levels of involvement, from increasingly varied global settings. Consider the diverse practices embodied in the description of lifestyle sport consumption offered by these two authors:

> [sports] for the cool by the cool, where fashion and music come head-to-head to produce the sort of off-the-wall action that allows the grazing generation to snack at leisure.
>
> (Roberts 1999: 7)

> When a sociologically circumscribed group has no other aim in life but to live in a world of waves or snow, when an entire life is devoted to one moment of ecstasy, it is time to consider the most intimate ways by which human beings build their own cultural landmarks and make them meaningful.
>
> (Midol 1993: 27)

The first quote evokes a common perception of lifestyle sports as superficial nihilistic, materialistic cultural forms practised by youthful practitioners, such as the Gen-X slackers (Kusz this volume), and experienced in seemingly superficial ways. Represented in this way, these activities appear to display many features of the postmodern landscape, such as a depthless image-based culture, seemingly without substance or meaning, experienced as fragmented and discontinuous (Jameson 1991), replicated in postmodern selves 'allegedly devoid of the expressive energies and individualities characteristic of modernism and the modern self' (Kellner 1995: 236). These media-led perceptions are typified in film representation such as the rebel surfers in *Point Break*, the misogynist skaters in *Kids*, or the dangerous and often irreverent antics typified by *Jackass* (see Kusz 2002).

Nevertheless, such images are part of the lifestyle sport scene, and represent an important set of experiences and identities. As Rinehart (2000) has persuasively argued, the 'alternative sportscape' is increasingly controlled and defined by transnational media corporations like ESPN's X-Games and NBC's Gravity Games, as well an ever-expanding range of international and transnational commercial images and interests. Rinehart cites the increasing popularity of X-Games which in 1998 was beamed via ESPN's different sport channels to 198 countries in 21 languages (Rinehart 2000). Its appeal to the teen or youth market, and their 'counter-culture cachet' (Ostrowski 2000) is what has made a mediated event like the X-Games so commercially successful, despite being initially derided by fans and pundits as 'made-for-TV pseudo-sports created solely to peddle products to the much coveted teen male demographic' (Kusz this volume). This expansion of lifestyle sport programming has also been expansive outside North America. Europe's first extreme sport channel was launched by a British company in May 1999. Underpinning this initiative was the commercial need to tap into the 'soccer centric' British youth. Yet football's televisual costs were escalating and other traditional sport didn't seem to tap into the desires of these teens (Roberts 1999). Described as a 'cross between MTV and sport' the Extreme Sport channel broadcast events that 'were not so much made for TV as made by TV,' a 'territory that lies somewhat between mainstream sport and video games (Roberts 1999: 7). Thus many of these (predominantly young) consumers do not participate in these sports at all, so are labelled by some as 'poseurs.' As a Cornish surfer laments, 'loads of guys come at the weekends with blonde hair and surfboards on camper vans, and don't even go in the water' (O' Connor 2002: 8). Nevertheless, they consume the sports avidly and in increasingly diverse ways ranging from buying the commodities, to watching television, videos, and live performances to playing the video games.[11] These 'participants' seem to display the kind of postmodern grazing that Rojek (1995: 8) proposes is characteristic of the postmodern leisure experiences, in which he suggests individuals are faced with such a 'multitude of differing leisure options and experiences', experiencing a variety of different leisure activities, without ever demonstrating allegiance to any one of them.

However, taking the vision of lifestyle sport represented in the second quote above from Midol's anthropological emphasis, she signals a different emphasis, and one that is reflected in my own research on windsurfing in which I wanted to understand the significance and meanings given to these activities by the sport participants, the subculture members, however marginal their involvement. Those who *do* the sports range from very occasional participants who perhaps sample different lifestyle sports on a summer holiday, through the 'weekend warriors,' to the 'hard core' committed practitioners who are fully familiarised in the lifestyle, argot, fashion and centrally technical skill of their activity. Many of these latter types of participants are extremely *committed* to one (or more complementary) activities, dedicating large amounts of time, money and effort investing in a lifestyle and social identity. For example windsurfers that also surf or snowboard in the winter; snowboarders that skate.

This emphasis on investigating the meaning of, and dynamics within, these leisure subcultures, understanding how these social identities and forms of collective expression are constructed, performed and contested, recognises popular culture's significance as the basis of people's identities. Like the identities constructed in many other forms of popular culture, lifestyle sport identities can represent an engagement with, or site of identity politics, a politics that is expressed around competing and passionate claims about the right to belong, and to be recognised (Street 1997). This approach is shared by many (but not all) of this book's contributors, particularly those who have adopted ethnographic methodologies. Of course, in our postmodern image-saturated culture, the media in all its forms provides many of the resources for identity; how we come to understand ourselves (Kellner 1995). However the 'constant stream of representation in popular culture' (Street 1997: 11) paints only one part of the picture. To understand contemporary sporting practices requires an exploration of what people *do* with this 'barrage of images and identities' (Street 1997: 11), and of 'the complex association between the lived experience and "ways of seeing" – as "embedded in inter-textuality and discourse"' (Wheaton and Beal 2003a: 156).

'Keeping it real': identity and status

> [identity]: it ain't where you'r from, it's where you're at.
>
> (Paul Gilroy quoting Rakim a rap artist)[12]

Previous research on lifestyle sport cultures has suggested that membership, identity and status are influenced by factors including commitment, attitude, style, gender, class, and 'race'.[13] However the 'real' or the 'authentic' tends to be defined around the performance of the activity, around 'doing it' (Wheaton and Beal 2003a). The *meaning* of participation is articulated around personal expression and gratification; the 'thrill of vertigo,' individuals own adrenaline 'rush' (Henio 2000). As Rinehart (2000: 510–511) citing Cook (1995) suggests, the 'pretenders' in lifestyle sports are soon revealed:

> A skater wrote to the editor of *Daily Bread*: 'who fucking cares what people wear when they skate?' Get a life! Any real skater should know that it's not the look it's the attitude. [sic]

Despite the visibility of symbolic markers of the lifestyle sport participant's identity, there are less 'visible' aspects of identity that are often more significant to the insider notions of 'authenticity' (see Kiewa 2002; Wheaton 2000a). These 'symbolic boundaries and behaviours' (Cohen 1985: 71 in Kiewa 2002: 151) include argot, technical skills (sporting prowess and style), 'attitude' and the use of subcultural media and space. For example commentators discuss the significance given to commitment in the participant's lifestyles and identities (Beal and Weidman 2003; Wheaton 2003):

> *Thrasher* [magazine] used to disparage these people who didn't skate every day. I never understood these people. Obviously you should skate everyday. And think about it every minute of every day. I never went anywhere without my skateboard.
>
> (Wilsey 2003: 19)

For many of these subculturalists, particularly the very committed, subcultural statuses and identities were seen to be more important than other spheres of their lives, or identities, including in *some* cases paid work and national, gendered or racialised identities. This does not deny the existence of social inequalities in these subcultures, nor the centrality of gender, class, sexuality and 'race' in structuring identity, difference and forms of exclusion (see on page 16); but recognises that participants did not always concede these facets of their identities in these subcultural contexts. 'Often the most important "I/ we"-identity' (Maguire 1999: 186) of the windsurfer was their subcultural affiliation; that they are 'a windsurfer'. Nevertheless, although class, gender and ethnicity did not stop participants creating new identities and statuses in (some of) these subcultures, other factors such as the expense of the equipment, activity costs, geographical locations, and the time and commitment required to participate were effective in excluding many less-privileged participants (see for example in Wheaton 2003). In these lifestyle sports traditional social demarcations remain significant, but operate in more diverse and complex ways.

Subcultural identities however, are not static, but are contested and re-made over time, and (geographic and metaphorical) space. One way of illustrating the contingent and shifting aspects of these subcultural identities and boundaries, it to examine the relationship *between* lifestyle sport subcultures, particularly those closely interrelated in terms of origin, industry (including technology, consumer and medias) and membership. As already noted, many board sports have their roots in California surf culture in the 1960s (see Wheaton forthcoming). The special relationship between snowboarding, surfing and skateboarding has been described as a 'love triangle' (*White Lines* magazine 1996) due to similarities in motion, attitude and dress. Other derivatives from these board sports have since metamorphosed, such as wake boarding – a hybrid of water skiing, skating and snowboarding – and kite-surfing, a hybrid of power-kiting and water sports like windsurfing and wakeboarding. The chapters by Booth, and Beal and Wilson, discuss changes in the sport and identities of surfing and skating respectively. There are also synergies between different lifestyle sports industries and their media. Corporations make equipment for several lifestyle sports, sometimes under different brand names. Clothing companies like Quiksilver, Roxy and O'Neil sell to a range of lifestyle sport markets including skating, surfing, windsurfing, snowboarding and have been quick to exploit the potential of emergent and rapidly growing activities like kite-surfing.

Thus while each lifestyle sport has its own specificity; its own history, (politics of) identities and development patterns, there are commonalities in their ethos, ideologies as well as the consumer industries that produce the commodities that underpin their cultures. The main defining characteristics of lifestyle sport can be summarised in the following list of nine features. It is not exclusive, nor is it an ideal-type (which might suggest these activities are homogenous, fixed and unchanging), but it illustrates defining features that the subsequent chapters, and wider literature,[14] exemplify in specific sports and contexts.

- Such sports are a historically recent phenomenon. The activities have emerged over the past few decades, involving either the creation of new activities – such as windsurfing, ultimate frisbee and snowboarding (see Humphreys 1997; Wheaton 2000a) – or the adaptation of older 'residual' cultural forms, such as the (re)emergence of surfing culture in California in the 1960s (Wheaton forthcoming 2004; Booth 2001; Finney and Houston 1996), or sport climbing in rock climbing (Morgan 1994; Kiewa 2002; Lewis this volume; Donnelly 2003).
- The emphasis is on 'grass roots' participation. Unlike some alternative extreme sports, lifestyle sports are fundamentally about participation, not spectating, either in live or in mediated settings (such as watching the X-Games, or other media festivals). Nevertheless, practitioners are self-consciously aware of 'being seen', and presentation of self to others – whether in lived settings or mediated forms – seems to be a part of the experience (Rinehart 2000). Similarly Allison regards these 'postmodern sports' as representing a revival of Amateurism (2001: 44).
- The sports are based around the consumption of new objects (boards, bikes, discs, etc.), often involving new technologies (see studies by Allison 1986; Booth 1999; Lewis this volume; Midol 1993; Bourdieu 1984; Donnelly 1993; Midol and Broyer 1995), yet embracing change and innovation. Improvements to technologies have resulted in rapid developments in many lifestyle sports, such as the fragmentation and diversification of the culture, and its forms of identity. This fragmentation can produce new scenes, or even the creation of new activities (see Lewis this volume). For example Booth (this volume) describes the revival of long-boards in surfing, and concurrently the invention of tow-in-surfing.
- Commitment in time, and/or money and a style of life and forms of collective expression, attitudes and social identity that develops in and around the activity (Stamm and Lamprecht 1997; Midol and Broyer 1995). See for example, in skating (Beal 1995; Beal and Weidman 2003; Beal and Wilson this volume; Borden 2001); in surfing (Pearson 1979; Lanagan 2003; Stedman 1997; Stranger 1999; Booth 2001); snowboarding (Humphreys 1997; Humphreys 2003; Henio 2000), windsurfing (Wheaton 2000a, 2003) and climbing (Kiewa 2002; Donnelly 2003; Lewis this volume).
- A participatory ideology that promotes fun, hedonism, involvement, self actualisation, 'flow,' (Csikzentminalyi 1990) living for the moment, 'adrenalin

rushes' and other intrinsic rewards. They often denounce – and in some even resist – institutionalisation, regulation and commercialisation, and tend to have an ambiguous relationship with forms of traditional competition.[15] Most lifestyle sports emphasise the creative, aesthetic and performative expressions of their activities (cf. Wheaton 1997; Howe 2003; Humphreys 2003; Booth 2003). Rinehart (1998b) has termed these activities 'expressive sport' (rather than the reward driven 'spectacle' sports), they are rarely conducted for spectators or competitive practice, emphasising the aesthetic realm in which one blends with one's environment. Some practitioners refer to their activities as art.

- A predominantly middle class, white, Western participant composition. However despite being associated with 'youth' many activities have wider-based age ranges, and in some cases are less gender differentiated than 'traditional' sports (see discussion in Part 2 of this book).
- Predominantly, but not exclusively, individualistic in form and/or attitude. Ultimate frisbee and adventure racing are two interesting exceptions that are examined in this book. Rinehart (2000) discusses how ESPN and other media transnationals have attempted to promote 'team based' versions of alternative sport, such as Border-X in which several snowboarders compete alongside each other.
- They are non-aggressive activities (see for example Thornton, this volume on ultimate frisbee)[16] that do not involve bodily contact (Bourdieu 1984), yet they embrace and even fetishise notions of risk and danger (Fiske 1989; Midol and Broyer 1995; Le Breton 2000; Stranger 1999; Lewis this volume; Palmer this volume).
- The spaces of consumption are new or appropriated outdoor 'liminal' zones (Shields 1992: 7), mostly without fixed or created boundaries (see Borden 2001). Many occur in non-urban environments, and are 'cultural spaces in which one 'blends with' or 'becomes one with the' sea / mountain' (Midol and Broyer, 1995). Many non-urban lifestyle sports express a nostalgia for an imaginary past rural life, and a sense of nature as 'something mysterious and spiritual' (Hetherington 1998: 338) to be revered, protected and nurtured (see Lewis this volume; Midol and Broyer 1995; Wheaton and Beal 2003a). Urban-based activities like skating or B.A.S.E. jumping off buildings, adapt and redefine urban city spaces (Borden 2001).

The scope and organisation of the book

It is not the purpose of this book to chart the histories or characteristics of different lifestyle sports. The chapters are more critical essays that address either particular trends within a specific lifestyle sports culture (namely skating, climbing, surfing, adventure racing and ultimate frisbee) or explore discourses around lifestyle sports (such as risk, travel, masculinity and whiteness). The overarching theme is how to understand the social significance of this sporting movement, particularly as related to its consumption, and the expression and politics of identity and difference. The authors do not necessarily embrace my classification of lifestyle sport, so use terms such as extreme and alternative. Nor do they all acknowledge or adopt the cultural meanings and social significance of these sport that I have outlined in this introductory chapter. Their methodologies are also different, ranging from 'insider' ethnographic accounts in which the authors are also participants (see Thornton; Wheaton; Lewis; Kay) – and in some cases also journalists documenting the activity (Kay; Palmer) – to those embracing historical accounts (Booth), and analysis of the inter-textual and conjectural texts that frame the discourses in and around lifestyle sport (Kusz; Palmer). While methodology is not the focus of these chapters, some do contribute to wider debates about the politics of representation and the nature of the ethnographic enterprise. Nevertheless, these different engagements with the cultural phenomenon of lifestyle sports, drawing on varied theoretical perspectives, collectively demonstrate its complex and contradictory character both in the lived culture and across popular media discourses.

The book is divided into two sections; Part 1 Commercialisation: culture, identity and change and Part 2 Ambivalent masculinities: identity and difference. These are interrelated, with some essays addressing themes central to both sections. In the remainder of this introductory chapter I will give an overview of these two areas, indicating the contributions made by each chapter. I conclude by highlighting key omissions, and direction for further research.

Commercialisation: culture, identity and change

Part 1 Commercialisation: culture, identity and change examines the increasingly evident influence of commercial forces in lifestyle sports development, sporting practices and identities.[17] As Humphries observes, 'Debates over selling-out pervade' – and consume – this 'new leisure movement particularly in its professional wing' (Humphreys 2003: 417). The expansion of consumer capitalism is particularly evident in the ever-expanding array of commodities linked to these activities such as equipment, clothing, videos and magazines. In 1999, surf clothing giant Quiksilver's sales of surf-related products had rocketed to over US$450 million (Abell 2001); by 2002 the global surf industry was reported to be worth around AU$7.4 billion (over 2 billion dollars) (Gliddon 2002 in Arthur 2003: 154). Distributors or importers of the multinationals like Quiksilver and Oakley exist in many countries, helping to produce standardised products and promotional materials. This market's ability to diversify and grow is reflected in the speed in which 'surf style' for women expanded during the 1990s, the catalyst being initially the success of the ladies' board shorts (see Booth this volume). Nevertheless, research in different 'local' subcultural settings has highlighted the complex and contradictory influence of the market on lifestyle sports cultures, particularly in the ways identities are constructed, and commodities are consumed in various lived contexts (Wheaton forthcoming, 2000a; Humphreys 2003). Commercialisation is not solely a co-opting force; lifestyle sports cultures – like many youth cultures – also adapt and change, contesting subcultural meanings, spaces and identities:

> Despite the 'resilient belief' that 'grassroots' or 'authentic' culture resists and struggles with a 'colonizing mass-mediated corporate world,' (Thornton 1995: 116) the media and consumer industries' roles are more complex, contradictory and fluid than simply incorporation and co-option; these subculturalists are not simply 'victims' of commercialism, but shape and 're-shape' the images and meanings circulated in and by global consumer culture.
>
> (Wheaton forthcoming)

Recent sociological research that has moved towards a more sophisticated understanding of the complex dynamics between subculture, the mass media, and global commercial culture (Thornton 1995; Bennett 2000; Muggleton 2000), and ways in which 'resistance' is expressed (see also Atkinson and Wilson 2002), is better able to explore these dynamics.

Furthermore, global consumer capitalism penetrates these lifestyle sports in increasingly multifarious ways. 'Selling-out' debates are not just about commodities, but relate to the (commercial) appropriation of lifestyle sports' ethos and ideologies – such as attitudes to 'risk', 'freedom', anti-competitiveness and anti regulation – re-packing and selling their values and lifestyles for mass consumption. The institutionalisation process, especially as expressed through attitudes to competition and regulation, provides an interesting aspect in understanding the commercialisation of these activities (see Booth this volume). In sports like surfing, skateboarding, snowboarding and windsurfing, there have been (ideological and 'real') battles over their inclusion in traditional 'mainstream' forms of sporting competition such as the Olympic Games (Wheaton forthcoming; Humphreys 2003), and media-driven competitions such as the X-Games (see Rinehart 2000, 1998a).

Becky Beal and Charlene Wilson (Chapter 2) explore the contested and contradictory ways in which skaters' identities have been transformed in the context of rapid and widespread commercialisation of the US skating culture in the twenty-first century. Their discussion is wide-ranging, considering the impact of the X-Games, the importance and influence of the subcultural and mainstream medias, skateboarders' relationship with the skating industry, and the effect of these processes on *different* and increasingly fragmented expressions of subcultural identities. They reveal evidence of changing attitudes to commercialisation, demonstrating that skaters are less critical of sponsorship and professionalism, seeing the benefits they bring to the skating community. Nevertheless, they continue to resist changes that will lead to increased regulation or a change in the ethos of skating, such as in creative/artistic sensibility, self-expression and an individualistic attitude. Beal and Wilson also explore how commercialisation processes are constitutive of new, or shifting identities and status hierarchies within skating, exposing how these are intertwined with distinctions based on gender, class, age and 'race'. For example, distinctions between vert, ramp and street skating styles, in which the latter – which is more risky, less regulated and controlled – is considered the most 'hard core', are also reflective of, and give cultural power to, 'hard' working-class masculinities.

The discourse around risk is a theme running through many of the chapters in the book. Climbers, surfers and B.A.S.E. jumpers literally 'play with death' ; they are sports that are often 'free' from the restrictions based on safety (Midol and Broyer 1995; Callinicos 1989). Danger and excitement are often fetishised in the – masculine defined (see Kay and Laberge and Robinson, this volume) – 'go for it attitude' that characterises these activities. Catherine Palmer (Chapter 3) explores the 'selling of risk' in and around lifestyle sport, and its industry. Her chapter illustrates how these attitudes to risk and hedonism have been appropriated to sell mainstream products (see also Beal and Wilson); how 'risk taking has gone mainstream'. Palmer explores two revealing and concerning examples of this process in the adventure tourism industry; the widely publicised Everest expedition of 1996, and the Interlaken tragedy in 1999. These examples illuminate the potentially disastrous consequences of this trend to sell extremity to inexperienced participants.

Neil Lewis (Chapter 4) also explores attitudes to danger in his phenomenological examination of British climbers' embodiment, illustrating that 'doubt, contingency and risk' are central to the leisure experiences of adventure climbers. Drawing on Simmel, Heidegger and other 'critique of modernity' philosophers, he examines how philosophies about the 'sacred' spaces of nature (Heidegger), and the ambivalent character of modern technology, are reflected in different expressions of climbing. Technological development, he suggests, has facilitated both adventurous mountain leisure (risky with low levels of routinisation) and more commoditised touristic leisure with high levels of routinisation.[18] However the *traditional* climbers that are his ethnographic focus, let '*nature* dictate the route or the path' (Lewis, this volume, p81, emphasis added); they see 'authentic' dwelling as the 'proper' use of nature, which translates into the 'natural preservation of this cliff environment. These climbers resist these processes of commercialisation and rationalisation by deliberately seeking to maintain high levels of risk and uncertainty; British adventure climbers, he claims are 'prepared to die for their leisure experiences'(p81). Employing Lefebvre's (1979) suggestions that leisure spaces are not just an 'escape' from everyday life, but a place for critiquing it, Lewis argues that these climbers' embodied adventure practices highlight the 'continuing possibilities to engage critically with everyday life' (p89).

Douglas Booth (Chapter 5) charts the history and changing expression of the surfing identity and lifestyle in Australia. The surfing lifestyle in the 1960s emerged in the counter culture as an irreverent culture situated in opposition to 'mainstream' and institutionalised sport; however codification and professionalisation soon took hold, transforming the surfing culture and its anti-competition identity. Yet despite the widespread professionalisation of surfing, these 'anti-competition' and 'anti-popularity' debates and attitudes prevail. Booth charts how competition for prestige and physical capital among surfers is often centred on big-wave surfing. He explores a controversy in the surf community that was sparked by the emergence of tow-in-surfing, an assisted way of surfing bigger waves considered to be 'phoney' by many surfers. As explored in the next section of this introduction, this pursuit of prestige through risk taking and physical prowess is often associated with masculinity. Booth thus explores surfing as a 'fratriarchial' culture that excludes women, highlighting contradictions for the identity of female surfers, and particularly their sexist commoditised representations in the surfing media. Booth concludes that despite the recent increase in female participation, the culture in Australia does little to challenge the gender order.

Ambivalent masculinities: identity and difference

Continuing with this theme of gender identity, Part 2 explores whether lifestyle sports challenge the gender roles, identities and power relationship in 'traditional' sports.

It has been widely demonstrated that traditional institutionalised sport has been, and still remains, central in creating, maintaining and reproducing notions of male dominance, and difference from women, and 'other' (for example, homosexual) men in many Western cultures (Whannel 2002; McKay *et al.* 2000; Connell 1995). Many high-level competitive and professional sport cultures promote and celebrate a masculinity that is marked by combative competition, aggression, courage and toughness, that can be sexist, endorse violence, often promoting homophobic and racist tendencies (see Carrington and McDonald 2001). However sport is not a 'monolithic structure; gender is re-created, performed and resisted differently in the 'many activities considered sport':

> The masculinities of the runner, football player, and rock-climber are qualitatively different; each sport combined various symbolic discourses to create a masculinity particular to the sport.
>
> (Anderson 1999: 56)[19]

It is therefore misleading to view 'sporting masculinity' either in its media representations or lived identities (as player or increasingly as fans and spectators) as essentialised and fixed. Like other masculinities it varies over time and cultural spaces, between men of different, backgrounds, particularly based on social class, age, ethnicity and sexual orientation, and is subject to a continual process of contestation, reinterpretation and revision (cf. Cornwall and Lindisfarne 1994; Connell 1995).

Therefore, the central question lifestyle sport researchers have sought to answer is whether these newer non-traditional sports offer *different* and potentially more *transformatory* scripts for male and female physicality, than the hegemonic masculinities and femininities characteristic of traditional sports cultures and identities. As Thornton (this volume) asks 'do these new identities express or exhibit changes in existing gender, race, class, and body dominance'? How do these new sporting practices become gendered? (Anderson 1999: 57); how are these gender performances regulated and monitored (Butler 1990, 1993), and how is the marking of 'difference' or otherness related to exclusion processes and claims to subcultural authenticity and 'in authenticity'? Research has examined how gender (and in some cases how class, age and racial) identities are related to membership status and associated exclusion process across different lifestyle sporting contexts, including: skateboarding in the US (Beal 1996; Beal and Wilson this volume) and UK (Borden 2001); windsurfing in the UK (Woodward 1995; Wheaton this volume, 2000b; Wheaton and Tomlinson 1998); snowboarding in the USA (Anderson 1999) and Norway (Sisjord 1997); climbing in the UK (Robinson 2002); surfing in Australasia (Booth this volume; Lewis 2003; Booth 2001; Stedman 1997; Henderson 2001); adventure racing (Kay and Laberge this volume) and ultimate frisbee (Thornton this volume). Chapters in the book make a significant contribution to this growing body of work, exploring new sporting sites, and adopting diverse theoretical influences and insights.

The chapters by Victoria Robinson (Chapter 6) and Belinda Wheaton (Chapter 7) explore whether the boundaries of sporting masculinities are broadened in the UK context. Wheaton's research in the windsurfing culture (Chapter 7) illustrates that the prevailing (but un-named) lived masculine subjectivity – 'ambivalent masculinity' – was less excluding of women and 'other men' than many institutionalised sport cultures, or middle-class work cultures in which they were embedded. 'Laddishness' particularly as played out through competitiveness over status, and masculine identification based on the subordination and commodification of women as passive, sexual objects, was largely confined to younger, elite men. Participants of both genders emphasised the supportiveness and camaraderie among men and between men and women in the culture. The younger men tended to be the most competitive over their subcultural status; their need to *demonstrate* their masculine identities in this context was greater than for older men who drew on a range of masculine identifies such as work and fatherhood.

Robinson's study of climbing masculinities (Chapter 6) also adopts Connell's (1995) hegemonic masculinity framework, which she uses to explore and map the diverse, fluid and at times contradictory masculine identities of the climbers. She explores their attitudes to competition, risk, intimacy, their bodies and female climbers. Robinson offers the idea of 'mundane extremities' to problematise commentators' focus on the spectacular, arguing for a theorisation of the study of sport into wider conceptions of 'everyday' culture and experiences.

Wheaton's, and (to a lesser extent) Robinson's chapters suggest that these lifestyle sporting cultures represent both a re-inscription of traditional masculinities – most notably in relation to 'compulsory heterosexuality' as well as the *potential* for more progressive sporting identities. Robinson however warns that the more transgressive aspects of climbers' masculine identities may not transfer outside of the climbing cultural sphere. Moreover, other studies, particularly where the participants are teenage males, and dominated by the less middle class, such as in surfing (see Booth this volume; Stedman 1997; Henderson 2001) and skateboarding (Beal and Wilson this volume) – point to the enduring nature of traditional 'hegemonic' masculinities.

It is not just the individualistic, non-competitive lifestyle sports that have the potential to '*do* gender' differently. Thornton (Chapter 9) and Kay and Laberge (Chapter 8) make important contributions to this debate, exploring the team and gender-inclusive sports of adventure racing and ultimate frisbee respectively.

Joanne Kay and Susanne Laberge (Chapter 8) explore gender relations in the ultra-tough and endurance-based adventure racing (AR) activity. Adopting Bourdieu's concepts (of symbolic power, field, and his social theory of practice) they explore how AR discourse vaunts the (traditionally male associated) values of *physical toughness* and *risk taking* for participation in the sport, while simultaneously privileging the alternative values of *teaming* and *risk management* (seen to be feminine attributes) as a measure of AR achievement. AR therefore appears to subvert and transform the gender regime of sport. However, the practices – as expressed by the participants' voices – contradict these wider representations of AR. Their analysis seeks to unpack this 'difference' between discourse and practice. They explore women's heterogeneous experiences and 'gendered form of capital' in this 'field of practice,' investigating women's different experiences, strategies and struggles for valued capital. Despite the potential for transgression, the authors conclude that AR is a symbolic site that 'naturalises women's weakness and thus legitimates male domination'.

Gender equality has also been an important issue in ultimate frisbee (Ultimate), seen as a symbol of its anti-establishment 'alternative' character. Andrew Thornton (Chapter 9) explores how gender, class and 'race' differences are part of Ultimate players' identities and sporting embodiment. Drawing on Judith Butler's (1990) ideas about performativity, and post-structuralist conceptions of identity structured in ambivalence, Thornton offers an analysis of the ways Ultimate players 'play around' with their sporting identities, *claiming* to be developing and living different modes of (gender) embodiment and identification. He concludes – similarly to Kay and Laberge – that 'Ultimate frisbee represents an interesting, if unrealised, potential for the subversion of dominant sporting identities'. Ultimate, he suggests 'fails to produce practices and identities that are beyond' those that are dominant in 'existing sports'.

Thornton's analysis also alludes to the ways in which Ultimate identities produce 'a general but unnamed reference group' based on normative heterosexuality and an 'unmarked, apparently autonomous white/Western self' (Frankenberg 1993: 17). As Frankenberg claims, 'the white Western self as a racial being has for the most part remained unexamined and unnamed' (17). Kusz's chapter (Chapter 10), informed by this race theory that has turned its critical gaze towards whiteness (cf. Dyer 1997; Frankenberg 1993; Pfeil 1995; Bonnett 2000), highlights that media representations of extreme sport have become important contemporary sites of whiteness. Kusz's conjunctural analysis of media discourses of extreme sports in North America at the end of the 1990s, shows how mainstream press articles have celebrated extreme sports as the 'symbol of a new American zeitgeist,' understood as the revival of traditional and specifically American values such as 'individualism, self-reliance, risk taking, and progress'. Kusz examines how these discourses give a specifically masculinised and patriotic representation of extreme sports that re-articulates and naturalises the link between whiteness and America. This, he suggests, 'can be read as a symptom and imagined solution to North America's perceived 'crisis of white masculinity'. He interprets the construction of this particular white sporting masculinity as part of a broader conservative cultural politics that seeks to re-secure the dominant cultural positioning of white masculinity in the American Imagination .[20]

To summarise, these chapters suggest that lifestyle sports present opportunities for more transgressive embodied social identities that differ from masculinities in traditional sports. There are some departures, suggesting in some cases a 'broadening of boundaries'; yet femininities continue to be framed by discourses and practices that perpetuate stereotypes of white heterosexual attractiveness, and masculinities based on normative heterosexuality and whiteness, skill and risk, working within, rather than subverting traditional patterns of gendered and bodily domination in sport (Wheaton and Tomlinson 1998: 270).

Omissions and future directions

This volume cannot claim to give a comprehensive coverage to this complex, expanding phenomena, and the picture these chapters paint is one that is partial and incomplete. There are important omissions; gaps that reflect research on sport more widely. The focus here has been on masculinities, and so (reflecting the lived cultures) the voices of female participants are largely absent or marginalised in this collection. Most chapters have foregrounded gender as the basis on which to explore social identity and difference, which in some cases has resulted in the exclusion or marginalisation of other central aspects of participants' social identities, and particularly normative heterosexuality and whiteness.

Research on lifestyle sport more widely has – largely – failed to explore these multiple axes of difference. We need to consider the ways in which *white* masculinities and *white* femininities are articulated, and maintain and reproduce their privileged position (cf. Frankenberg 1993; Long and Hylton 2002; Scraton 2001). Do lifestyle sport cultures provide less 'racially' differentiated spaces than more traditional sports; and how do participants with different ethnic identities experience and perform their sporting identities?[21] Borden offers an optimistic view of exclusion processes in skateboarding suggesting that it 'has values that can transcend barriers of race, gender, class, and so tends to marginalize their importance and significance' (Borden 2001: 140). His evidence for this claim is that skaters in the 1990s come from different class and ethnic backgrounds and they declare this to be the case in skate magazine articles:

> There aren't the biases that exist in other areas of life. It's like we are our own race.
>
> (Billy Miller interviewed in *Heckler*, cited in (Borden 2001: 141)

Beal (Wheaton and Beal 2003b; Beal and Wilson this volume) however suggests that in the US skaters' attitudes to 'racial issues were often contradictory', and underpinned by racial stereotypes evident in other sporting spheres.

Furthermore, what are the experiences and identities of non-Western participants, such as Polynesian and Brazilian surfers? Surfing is practised in many non-Western countries. Lewis (1998: 66) suggests that 'capitalist colonisation' and 'continuing cultural imperialism'[22] is evident in many of the 'classic' surf films, in which surfers voyage to uncrowded waves in the previously colonised world.

Expressions of authenticity and identity in – and between – these subcultures also need further exploration. What, for example, is the relationship between the commodities and consumers in the context of increasing commercialisation; what is the part played by the different subcultural micro media; and how are these shifting notions of identity and authenticity played out across different 'local' and trans-local subcultural spaces? The temporal changes documented in Beal and Wilson's chapter remind us that lifestyle sport subcultures are not fixed in time or geographical space. Empirical research needs to map the subculture's dynamic relationship with the parent culture that it has emerged from, and the way that values, meanings and ideologies are contested, and change temporally and spatially (Donnelly 1993). People, commodities, information, technology and ideas flow across subcultural systems, a process which has been intensified by globalisation processes (Maguire 1999).The impact and influence of these global flows, particularly the flow of media, tourism and migration and their relationship to 'local' and trans-local lifestyle sport cultures, have as yet eluded sustained academic study (Wheaton forthcoming 2004). However as those who have studied the effects of globalisation on (sub)cultures in other contexts have illustrated, 'local' cultures interpret and respond to these global cultural flows of commodities, medias and images in complex and nuanced ways (Bennett 2000; Appadurai 1996; Lull 1995; Carrington and Wilson 2002).

Issues raised in this book also have important implications for policy makers interested in understanding, for example, *why* young people choose sports that exist outside of the 'mainstream' policy provision, or why any attempt to promote or institutionalise lifestyle sports is likely to be met with resistance. Furthermore, those who are interested in the use and regulation of open space may find research on lifestyle sports informing in understanding the motivations of these hedonistic yet reflective consumers of the countryside.

In summary, the chapters in this collection suggest that although these activities *do* differ in their meaning, consumption and identities from many traditional pre-modern and modern sporting cultures, there is only limited evidence of transgressive sporting cultural practices and identities (cf. Midol and Boyer 1995). There are however clear differences between activities, geographical location, and importantly differences depending on the degree of popularity and co-option of their activity in the cultures in which they are embedded. Nevertheless, as Wheaton and Beal (2003a) have argued, despite evident mainstreaming and co-option, explaining the *meanings* of lifestyle sports solely in relation to 'market incorporation' and 'resistance' to the market, ignores the centrality of consumer capitalism and the media industries in their very inception and meanings of the sports practices. In these subcultural spaces, participants do not resist materiality, but contest the discourses about commercialisation, regulation and control, and importantly about who has power to define and shape those discourses (Wheaton and Beal 2003a).

Conclusion

Within these highly individualised cultural spaces of late modernity and among their predominantly middle-class male and white participants, a number of tensions and paradoxes in their consumption exists, such as between conspicuous consumerism and resistance to consumption; competitiveness and participation; personalised consumption and group conformity; body discipline and pleasure; freedom and control. As Kay and Laberge contend:

> Performance is paradoxical – imbued with individualism and collectivism, the ludic and the prosaic, aesthetics and kitch. What emerges are tenets that contradict and co-exist; participation and competition, amateurism and professionalism. Urban play and wilderness adventure, the authentic and the constructed, the youthful and the nostalgic, the self-determined and the regulated, the resistant and the compliant.
>
> (2003: 381)

Although lifestyle sports provide the possibility of re-negotiated identities, traditional structures of social and cultural power and inequalities continue to be reproduced within them. The emergently progressive elements in the sport cultures are constrained by, and co-exist with, the dominant and residual elements. That these possibilities of re-negotiation in contemporary society exist is progressive, but the 'ways in which they work within, rather than subvert, traditional patterns of gendered (racial and class) domination in sport, illustrates how cultural change can be contingent, gradual, partial, a matter of negotiation of and within existing social relations' (Wheaton and Tomlinson 1998: 270). Thus against the backdrop of debates about globalisation and fragmentation of culture, the perceived break-down of established cultural identities, the 'pluralisation of styles', and the ephemeral, spectacular aspects of contemporary culture (Hall *et al.* 1992) the studies in this book suggest that even among the white, affluent Western middle-classes, there are clear limits to the extent to which identities are free floating, and self-selected. Yet in contemporary culture, identity *is* 'subject to new determinations and new forces' (Kellner 1992: 174), and lifestyle sport practices and cultures provide one of these manifestations.

Notes

1 This of course raises important and interesting theoretical questions about how – if at all – we characterise the mainstream, a debate that has characterised much of the recent literature on youth subcultures and postmodern culture more widely. See for example Muggleton (2000) and Thornton (1995). Such work raises important theoretical questions, that bears directly on the ways we understand the 'alternative' status of increasingly commoditised lifestyle sport cultures; for example, how we understand, and assess, 'resistance' in a post-authentic, postmodern world characterised by ambiguity and ambivalence. See also Palmer, and Beal and Wilson, this volume.
2 Action-sport is a North American industry-defined term.
3 On this point see also Robinson, this volume.
4 Echoing Kellner in his investigation of contemporary media culture and identity, where he usefully advocates that 'rather than taking postmodernity as a new cultural totality, I would thus argue that it makes more sense to interpret the many forces of the postmodern as an emergent cultural trend in opposition to residual traditional and modern values and practices' (Kellner 1992: 171). Kellner outlines that it is precisely this coexistence of traditional, modern and postmodern cultural forms, which describes the 'postmodern' (1992: 171). The coexistence of emergent cultural practices with traditional and residual practices and forms is – following Kellner – what constitutes a postmodern sport culture.
5 In the recently published (at the time of going to press) collection on extreme sport by Rinehart and Sydor (2003) many chapters could also be considered to fit under the rubric of lifestyle sports.
6 Burton himself was one of the early innovators of the snowboard, and his company remains one of the largest brands of equipment (producing snowboards, boots, bindings, as well as a range of clothing and accessories).
7 Nevertheless as Lash submits, a distinction needs to be made between the decentring of individual and collective identities, particularly in relation to the outcome of different 'social class' identities. For example, he posits that postmodernism can either further the 'hegemonic project of the new middle-classes' or foster different types of collective identities among class groups such as around lifestyles (Lash 1990: 37).
8 Elsewhere I consider – at length – whether lifestyle sport cultures constitute clearly defined, and easily identifiable collectivities such as 'subcultures' or more fluid social groupings that can usefully be thought of as neo tribes.
9 While consumption is the focus here, clearly there are other arenas in which expressions of identity have been examined as important cultural and political issues; notably questions of cultural hybridity 'ethnicity' and racism, gendered identities, nationalism as well as new social movements.
10 My initial interest in lifestyle sports was sparked during the early 1990s, when I was introduced to theorists of postmodernity and postmodern culture during master's study. When I embarked on my PhD research I set out looking at the three sports of windsurfing, surfing and mountain-biking to see if these activities might be a new phase in sport that could be termed postmodern. Central to my initial ideas was the question of periodisation that these activities had emerged in or around the 1960s, the (albeit contested) point at with the alleged historical break between modernity and postmodernity occurred. The 'perspective' I adopted was based on Jameson's discussion of postmodernity as an intensification of capitalism; postmodernism, he claims is a new socio-economic stage, an extreme form of capitalism (1991:4). He argues the concept of 'late capitalism' suggests a continuity with the past, rather than the break or rupture with modernity suggested by the 'post-industrial' society concept (Jameson 1991: 11) Furthermore, Jameson (1984: 4) does not regard all cultural production as postmodern, rather he relates this 'cultural moment' to Raymond Williams' (1977) notion of dominant, emergent and residual culture. Postmodernism for Jameson is the 'cultural dominant' or hegemonic norm of production and consumption of late/multinational

capitalism (Jameson 1991: 4). The transition from one cultural moment, such as modernity, to the next (postmodernity) does not result in the complete collapse of the cultural and economic features of the previous era; many modernist elements will remain, however the postmodern cultural mode becomes the dominant (in Western capitalist societies), but not the only cultural mode. Jameson thus provides an approach for examining the specificities of the development and emergence of 'lifestyle sport in relation to the broader postmodern culture'. From this perspective, it becomes possible to explore the extent to which lifestyle sport are emergent postmodern cultural practices, formed in opposition to the dominant (modernist) sport culture.

11 I am mindful that such claims that 'real' participation is not mediated, evoke problematic binaries in which 'real' or authentic sport is not made-for-TV or commercialised sport (see Rinehart 1998).

12 Cited in Borden (2001)

13 See for example chapters in Rinehart and Sydor (2003); also Wheaton (2003, 2000a); Wheaton and Beal (2003a); Henio (2000); Anderson (1999); Rinehart (2000); Farmer (1992); Lanagan (2003).

14 Most significantly the exciting and long awaited arrival of Rinehart and Sydor (2003) just as this book was in its final stages. I have therefore attempted to make some connection with this text – a luxury not afforded to all this book's contributors.

15 Interested readers can find these characteristics documented in the studies referenced in the previous bullet point.

16 Although the use of aggressive means in turf wars have been well documented in skating and surfing. (See for example; Goodwood 1995; Abell 2001; Booth 2001; Borden 2001.)

17 I explore the issues raised in this section in greater depth in Wheaton (forthcoming).

18 Although his risk assessment in commoditised mountainous leisure contradicts Palmer's chapter.

19 Miller (2001: 10) is critical of the hegemonic masculinity thesis. He suggests that the gender politics of (mainstream) sport has become increasingly complex, particularly in terms of sexuality. He contends that in contemporary capitalism Gay men have become an increasingly lucrative niche market; that the commoditised sporting male body has become an object of male desire (Miller 2001). Yet one aspect of masculine identity that seems to be shared among lifestyle sports is the construction of masculinity through asserting their heterosexuality and subordinating homosexuality.

20 The themes Kusz highlights around the nostalgic representation of the white North American frontier man, are also echoed in Kay and Laberge's (2003) analysis of Warren Miller's extreme skiing films, and Thornton's analysis of masculinity (this volume).

21 An exception is Anderson who attempts to explore how 'race' is related to other aspects of identity and exclusion in snowboarding in the USA (Anderson 1999). See also Gottdiener's (1995) observation on surfing youth.

22 See also Kay and Laberge's (2003) discussion of American cultural imperialism in ski videos.

References

Abell, J. (2001) Values in a sporting sub-culture: An analysis of the issues of competitiveness and aggression in surfing. Master thesis, University of Warwick.

Allison, L. (1986) *The Politics of Sport*, Manchester: Manchester University Press.

Allison, L. (2001) *Amateurism in Sport: An Analysis and a Defence*, London: Frank Cass.

Anderson, K. (1999) Snowboarding: the construction of gender in an emerging sport. *Journal of Sport and Social Issues*, 23,1: 55–79.

Appadurai, A. (1996) *Modernity at Large: Cultural Dimensions of Globalization*, Minneapolis: University of Minnesota Press.

Arthur, D. (2003) Corporate sponsorship of sport: its impact on surfing and surf culture in *Some Like it Hot: The Beach as a Cultural Dimension* (eds, Skinner, J., Gilbert, K. and Edwards, A.) Oxford: Meyer and Meyer Sport.

Asthana, A. (2003) Girls just want to have fun too. *Observer*: 20

Atkinson, M. and Wilson, B. (2002) Bodies, subcultures and sport in *Theory, Sport and Society* (eds, Maguire, J. and Young, K.) Oxford: JAI.

Bale, J. (1994) *Landscapes of Modern Sport*, Leicester: Leicester University Press.

Bauman, Z. (1992) *Intimations of Postmodernity*, London: Routledge.

Beal, B. (1995) Disqualifying the official: An exploration of social resistance through the subculture of skateboarding. *Sociology of Sport Journal*, 12,3: 252–67.

Beal, B. (1996) Alternative masculinity and its effect on gender relations in the subculture of skateboarding. *Journal of Sports Behaviour*, 19,3: 204–20.

Beal, B. and Weidman, L. (2003) Authenticity in the skateboarding world in *To the Extreme: Alternative Sports Inside and Out* (eds, Rinehart, R. and Sydnor, S.) Albany: SUNY Press.

Bennett, A. (2000) *Popular Music and Youth Culture: Music, Identity and Place*, Basingstoke: Macmillan Press Ltd.

Bocock, R. (1993) *Consumption*, London and New York: Routledge.

Bonnett, A. (2000) *White Identities: Historical and International Perspectives*, London: Prentice Hall.

Booth, D. (1999) Surfing: The cultural and technological determinants of a dance. *Culture, Sport, Society*, 2,1: 36–55.

Booth, D. (2001) *Australian Beach Cultures: The History of Sun, Sand and Surf*, London: Frank Cass Publishers.

Booth, D. (2003) Expression sessions; surfing, style and prestige in *To the Extreme: Alternative Sports, Inside and Out* (eds, Rinehart, R. and Sydor, S.) Albany: State University of New York Press.

Borden, I. (2001) *Skateboarding, Space and the City: Architecture and the Body*, Oxford: Berg.

Borden, M. (2002), X-Treme Profits: The economy stinks. Tech's a mess. Not exactly fun and games out there – unless, like Activision, you're making videogames. InfoTrac Web: Expanded Academic ASAP electronic collection A 38095949Vol. 2002 Fortune, March 4th 2002.

Bourdieu, P. (1984) *Distinction: A Social Critique of the Judgement of Taste*, London and NY: Routledge & Kegan Paul Ltd.

Bradley, H. (1996) *Fractured Identities: Changing Patterns of Inequality*, Cambridge: Polity Press.

Burton, J. (2002) Analysis: Popularity of snow boarding and extreme sports, *Talk of the Nation*, broadcast Feb. 13 2002.

Butler, J. (1990) *Gender Trouble: Feminism and the Subversion of Identity*, London: Routledge.

Butler, J. (1993) *Bodies that Matter: On the Discursive Limits of 'Sex'*, London: Routledge.

Callinicos, A. (1989) *Against Postmodernism: A Marxist Critique*, Oxford: Polity Press.

Carrington, B. and McDonald, I. (eds) (2001) *'Race' Sport and British Society*, London: Routledge.

Carrington, B. and Wilson, B. (2002) Global clubcultures: Cultural flows and late modern dance music culture in *Young People in Risk Society: The Restructuring of Youth Identities in Late Modernity* (eds, Cieslik, M. and Pollock, G.) Aldershot: Arena.

Chaney, D. (1994) *The Cultural Turn: Scene-setting Essays on Contemporary Cultural History*, London and NY: Routledge.

Chaney, D. (1996) *Lifestyles*, London and NY: Routledge.

Cohen, A. P. (1985) *The Symbolic Construction of Community*, London: Elis Horwood.

Connell, R. (1995) *Masculinities*, Cambridge: Polity Press.

Connor, S. (1989) Postmodernism and popular culture in *Postmodernist Culture: An Introduction to Theories of the Contemporary*, Oxford: Basil Blackwell.

Cook, J. (1995) Sk8 by shootings. *Daily Bread*, 10.

Cornwall, A. and Lindisfarne, N. (1994) *Dislocating Masculinity: Comparative Ethnographies*, London and NY: Routledge.

Csikzentminalyi, M. (1990) *Flow: The Psychology of Optimal Experience*, New York: Harper and Row.

Donnelly, P. (1993) Subcultures in sport: Resilience and transformation in *Sport in Social Development: Traditions, Transitions and Transformations* (eds, Ingham, G. and Loy, J.) Champaign, IL: Human Kinetics Publishers.

Donnelly, P. (2003) The great divide: Sport climbing vs. adventure climbing in *To The Extreme: Alternative Sports, Inside and Out* (eds, Rinehart, R. and Sydor, S.) Albany: State University of New York Press.

Dyer (1997) *White*, London: Routledge.

Eichberg, H. (1998) *Body Cultures: Essays on Sport, Space and Identity*, London: Routledge.

Farmer, R. (1992) Surfing: motivations, values and culture. *Journal of Sports Behaviour*, 15,3: 241–57.

Featherstone, M. (1988) In pursuit of the postmodern: An introduction. *Theory Culture and Society*, 5,2–3: 195–215.

Featherstone, M. (1991) *Consumer Culture and Postmodernism*, London, Newbury Park, New Delhi: Sage Publications.

Finney, B. and Houston, J. (1996) *Surfing. A History of the Ancient Hawaiian Sport*, San Francisco: Pomegranate Artbooks.

Fiske, J. (1989) Reading the beach in *Reading the Popular*, London: Unwin Hyman.

Frankenberg, R. (1993) *White Women, Race Matters: The Social Construction of Whiteness*, London: Routledge.

Glidden, J. (2002) Mad Wax. The bulletin. Last accessed October 2002. Online at http://bulletin.ninemsn.com.au/bulletin/EdDesk.nsf/printing/E42861F710bE80BACA256C07002381BF

Goodwood, C. (1995) California surf gangs go to war over their favourite waves. *Sunday Times*, 22.

Gottdiener, M. (1995) *Postmodern Semiotics: Material Culture and the Forms of Postmodern Life*, Oxford, UK and Cambridge, USA: Blackwell.

Hall, S. and Du Gay, P. (1996) *Questions of Cultural Identity*, London: Sage.

Hall, S., Held, D. and McGrew, T. (1992) *Modernity and its Futures*, Cambridge: Polity Press with the Open University.

Hebdige, D. (1993) A report on the Western Front: postmodernism and the 'politics' of style in *Cultural Reproduction* (ed. Jenks, C.) London: Routledge.

Henderson, M. (2001) A shifting line up: men, women and Tracks surfing magazine. *Continuum: Journal of Media and Cultural Studies*, 15,3: 319–32.

Henio, R. (2000) What is so punk about snowboarding? *Journal of Sport and Social Issues*, 24,2: 176–91.

Henley Centre (1993) Leisure Fixtures.

Hetherington, K. (1988) *Expressions of Identity: Space, Performance, Politics*, London: Sage.

Hetherington, K. (1998) Vanloads of uproarious humanity: New age travellers and the utopics of the countryside in *Cool Places: Geographies of Youth Cultures* (eds, Valentine, G., Skelton, T. and Chamber, D.) London: Routledge.

Howe, J. (2003) Drawing lines: A report from the extreme world [sic] in *To the Extreme: Alternative Sports, Inside and Out* (eds, Rinehart, R. and Sydor, S.) Albany: State University of New York Press.

Humphreys, D. (1997) 'Skinheads go mainstream?' Snowboarding and alternative youth. *International Review for Sociology of Sport*, 32,2: 147–60.

Humphreys, D. (2003) Selling out snowboarding: The alternative response to commercial co-optation in *To the Extreme: Alternative Sports, Inside and Out* (eds, Rinehart, R. and Sydor, S.) Albany: State University of New York Press.

Jacques, M. (1997) Worshipping the body at altar of sport. *Observer*: 18–19

Jameson, F. (1984) Postmodernism, or the cultural logic of Late Capitalism. *New Left Review*, 146, 53–92.

Jameson, F. (1991) Culture: The cultural logic of Late Capitalism in *Postmodernism or the Cultural Logic of Late Capitalism*, London, New York: Verso.

Kay, J. and Laberge, S. (2003) Oh say can you ski? Imperialistic constructions of freedom in Warren Miller's *Freeriders* in *To the Extreme: Alternative Sports, Inside and Out* (eds, Rinehart, R. and Sydor, S.) Albany: State University of New York Press.

Kellner, D. (1992) Popular culture and the construction of postmodern identities in *Modernity and Identity* (eds, Lash, S. and Friedman, J.) Oxford, Uk and Cambridge, USA: Blackwell.

Kellner, D. (1995) *Media Cultures: Cultural Studies, Identity and Politics Between the Modern and the Postmodern*, London and NY: Routledge.

Kiewa, J. (2002) Traditional climbing: metaphor of resistance or metanarrative of oppression? *Leisure Studies*, 21 145–61.

Kusz, K. (2002) Fight Club and the Art/politics of white male victimization and reflective sadomasochism. *International Review for Sociology of Sport*, 37,3–4: 465–470.

Lanagan, D. (2003) Dropping in: Surfing, identity, community and commodity in *Some Like it Hot: The Beach as a Cultural Dimension* (eds, Skinner, J., Gilbert, K. and Edwards, A.) Oxford: Meyer and Meyer Sport.

Lash, S. (1990) *Sociology of Postmodernism*, London and NY: Routledge.

Layden, T. (2002) What is this 34-year-old man doing on a skateboard? Making millions. *Sports Illustrated*: 82–96: 24: cited in electronic collection A86849699

Le Breton, D. (2000) Playing symbolically with death in extreme sports. *Body and Society*, 6,1, March: 1–12.

Lefebvre, H. (1979) Work and leisure in daily life in *Communication and Class Struggle: Capitalism, Imperialism*, (eds, Mattelart, A. and Siegelaub, S.) New York: International General.

Lewis, J. (1998) Between the lines: surf texts, prosthetics, and everyday theory. *Social Semiotics*, 8,1: 55–70.

Lewis, J. (2003) In search of the postmodern surfer: Territory, terror and masculinity in *Some Like it Hot: The Beach as a Cultural Dimension* (eds, Skinner, J., Gilbert, K. and Edwards, A.) Oxford: Meyer and Meyer Sport.

Long, J. and Hylton, K. (2002) Shades of white: an examination of whiteness in sport. *Leisure Studies*, 21,2: 87–104.

Lull, J. (1995) *Media, Communication, Culture: A Global Approach*, Cambridge: Polity Press.

Lury, C. (1996) *Consumer Culture*, Cambridge: Polity Press.

Maffesoli, M. (1996) *The Time of the Tribes: The Decline of Individualism in Mass Society*, London: Sage.

Maguire, J. (1999) *Global Sport: Identities, Societies, Civilizations*, Cambridge: Polity Press.

McDonald, M. and Andrews, D. (2001) Michael Jordan: Corporate sport and postmodern celebrityhood in *Sport Stars: The Cultural Politics of Sporting Celebrity* (eds, Andrew, D. and Jackson, S.) London: Routledge.

McKay, J., Messner, M. and Sabo, D. (eds) (2000) *Masculinities, Gender Relations, and Sport*, Thousand Oaks: Sage.

Midol, N. (1993) Cultural dissents and technical innovations in the 'whiz' sports. *International Review for Sociology of Sport*, 28,1: 23–32.

Midol, N. and Broyer, G. (1995) Towards an anthropological analysis of new sport cultures: The case of whiz sports in France. *Sociology of Sport Journal*, 12 204–12.

Miller, T. (2001) *Sportsex*, Philadelphia: Temple University Press.

Morgan, D. (1994) It Began with the piton: The challenge to British rock climbing in a post-modernist framework in *Leisure, Modernism, Postmodernism and Lifestyles* (ed, Henry, I.) Eastbourne: LSA publications.

Muggleton, D. (2000) *Inside Subculture: The Postmodern Meaning of Style*, Oxford: Berg.

O'Connor, J. (2002) Surfin' UK, the easy way. *Observer*: 8–9

Ostrowski, J. (2000) Corporate America cozies up to the tattooed extreme world. *Street and Smith's SportsBuisness Journal*: Special Report Extreme Sport: 24;

Pearson, K. (1979) *Surfing Subcultures of Australia and New Zealand*, St Lucia, Queensland: University of Queensland Press.

Pfeil, F. (1995) *White Guys: Studies in Postmodern Domination and Difference*, London and NY: Verso.

Philips, D. and Tomlinson, A. (1992) Come on down? Popular media culture in post-War Britain in *Homeward Bound: Leisure, Popular Culture and Consumer Capitalism* (eds, Strinati, D. and Wagg, S.) London: Routledge.

Rinehart, R. (1996) Dropping hierarchies: Towards the study of a contemporary sporting avant-garde. *Sociology of Sport Journal*, 13,2: 159–176.

Rinehart, R. (1998a) Inside of the outside: Pecking orders with in alternative sport as ESPN's 1995 'The eXtreme Games'. *Journal of Sport and Social Issues*, 22,4: 398–414.

Rinehart, R. (1998b) *Players All: Performances in Contemporary Sport*, Bloomington and Indianapolis: Indiana University Press.

Rinehart, R. (2000) Emerging arriving sport: Alternatives to formal sport in *Handbook of Sport Studies* (eds, Coakley, J. and Dunning, E.) London: Sage.

Rinehart, R. and Sydor, S.(eds) (2003) *To the Extreme: Alternative Sports, Inside and Out*, Albany: State University of New York Press.

Roberts, K. (1999) TV sport goes to extremes for teens. *Observer*: 7

Robinson, V. (2002) Men, masculinities and rock climbing in *Everyday Culture Working Paper*, Vol. 5 The Open University.

Rojek, C. (1995) *Decentring Leisure: Rethinking Leisure Theory*, London: Sage.

Scraton, S. (2001) Reconceptualizing race, gender and sport: The contribution of black feminism in *'Race' Sport and British Society* (eds, Carrington, B. and McDonald, I.) London: Routledge.

Shields, R. (1992) *Lifestyle Shopping*, London: Routledge.

Sisjord, M. (1997). Snowboard as youth culture. Paper presented at at the ISSA Seminar, Oslo, June 28–2 July

Sky, M. (2001) The influence of media marketing in the intrinsic culture of 'extreme' sport. B Sc. Hons thesis, University of Surrey Roehampton.

Stamm, H. and Lamprecht (1997). From exclusive life-style to mass leisure: An analysis of the development patterns of new sports. Paper presented at the ISSA Seminar, Oslo, June 28–2 July,

Stedman, L. (1997) From gidget to gonad man: surfers, feminists and postmodernisation. *Australian and New Zealand Journal of Sociology*, 33,1: 75–90.

Stranger, M. (1999) The aesthetics of risk: A study of surfing. *International Review for the Sociology of Sport*, 34,3: 265–276.

Street, J. (1997) *Politics and Popular Culture*, Cambridge: Polity Press.

Thornton, S. (1995) *Club Cultures: Music, Media and Subcultural Capital*, Cambridge: Polity Press.

Tomlinson, A. (1990) *Consumption, Identity and Style: Marketing, Meanings and the Packaging of Pleasure*, London: Routledge.

Tyler, A. (2003) Bed and board for beach babes. *Observer*: 6–7

Walters, J. (2002) Cornwall's artificial reef to cash in on surf boom. *Observer*: 8

Whannel, G. (2002) *Media Sport Stars: Masculinities and Moralities*, London: Routledge.

Wheaton, B. (1997) Consumption, lifestyle and gendered identities in post-modern sports: the case of windsurfing. PhD thesis, University of Brighton.

Wheaton, B. (2000a) Just Do it: Consumption, commitment and identity in the windsurfing subculture. *Sociology of Sport Journal*, 17,3: 254–274.

Wheaton, B. (2000b) 'New Lads?' Masculinities and the New Sport participant. *Men and Masculinities*, 2,4: 436–458.

Wheaton, B. (2003) Windsurfing: A subculture of commitment in *To the Extreme: Alternative Sports, Inside and Out* (eds, Rinehart, R. and Sydor, S.) Albany: State University of New York Press.

Wheaton, B. (forthcoming) Selling out? The globalization and commercialisation of lifestyle sports (ed, Allison, L.) *The Global Politics of Sport*. London: Routledge.

Wheaton, B. and Beal, B. (2003a) 'Keeping it real': Subcultural media and the discourses of authenticity in alternative sport. *International Review for the Sociology of Sport*, 38,2: 155–176.

Wheaton, B. and Beal, B. (2003b) Surf divas and skate betties: consuming images of the 'other' in lifestyle sports in *New Leisure Environments: Media, Technology and Sport*, Vol. LSA Publication No. 79 (eds, Fleming, S. and Jones, I.) Eastbourne: Leisure Studies Association.

Wheaton, B. and Tomlinson, A. (1998) The changing gender order in sport? The case of windsurfing. *Journal of Sport and Social Issues*, 22 252–274.

Williams, R. (1977) *Marxism and Literature*. Oxford: Oxford University Press

Wilsey, S. (2003) Using so little. *London Review of Books*: 19 June: 18–21;

Woodward, V. (1995) Windsurfing women and change. Masters thesis, University of Strathclyde.

Part I

Commercialisation

Culture, identity and change

2 'Chicks dig scars'

Commercialisation and the transformations of skateboarders' identities

Becky Beal and Charlene Wilson[1]

Prologue

In September of 2000, I visited San Diego to continue my research on skateboarding. I attended the All-Girls-Skate-Jam, an interesting and revealing venue for investigating my ongoing interest in how gender was being constructed and contested in the skating culture and its industry. Because southern California is the Mecca of the 'action sports'[2] industry, it wasn't surprising to discover that another event, the Action Sports Convention, was taking place close by. Many of the industry representatives from the Action Sports Convention found their way to the Skate-Jam, a skate competition for female skateboarders. I talked with two industry representatives who said they were looking for women to sponsor. Their goal was to expand their lines explicitly to target a female market which is part of an emerging trend in skateboarding. The venue was littered with stickers, posters and merchandise, and with the marketing hype came the promotional t-shirts. One proclaimed that 'Chicks dig scars'. The shirt was worn by a male in the crowd who was there to watch the women skate. Although the event was designed to celebrate the accomplishments of women in a male dominated sport, the t-shirt illustrated how much skateboarding was still being held to masculine standards. The statement reminded me that the industry still positions women as being interested in the risk-taking, daring man who gets hurt and lives to tell about it. The women are not being rewarded for their athleticism, but still remain the trophies for the men. This is just one of the contradictions I encounter as I continue to investigate the production of skateboarding identities. In this chapter I (re)examine skating in the twenty-first century, exploring the continuities and shifts in the ways in which skaters construct their identities, particularly in the context of increasing popularity and extensive commercialisation.

Skateboarding in the twenty-first century: continuity and change

Since I did my original research in the early 1990s, skateboarding has undergone tremendous commercial and global expansion. The X-Games, Gravity Games, and several smaller competitions, such as the All-Girls-Skate-Jam, have made these activities commonplace, and a select few participants, such as Tony Hawk, are now household names.[3] In the United States the growth in skateboarding can be seen in the number of sales over ten years, outpacing more traditional sports such as baseball (Ruibal 2001; see also Wheaton, this volume). In addition, the 'extreme' moniker has taken on broader social significance as can be noted by its use to sell everything from trucks and antiperspirant, to religious faith.[4]

In my initial investigation of skateboarding (Beal 1995, 1996, 1998) I was interested in examining their sub culture and associated identities. I framed my research within a hegemonic perspective (a broadly cultural studies perspective), drawing especially on previous insights of the subcultural theory emanating from the CCCS (Birmingham Centre for Contemporary Cultural Studies) examining the ways in which this youth subculture resisted the 'mainstream' (cf. Hall and Jefferson 1976; Willis 1977). Therefore, my assumption was that subcultural identities were being constructed in opposition to conventional sport identities. I spent two years doing ethnographic work with a group of skaters who lived in Colorado, and found that the participants valued an 'outsider' position. They were consciously rejecting some of the meanings and forms of mainstream sport. For example, skaters often contrasted their style with 'jocks', who were usually identified as football players, claiming that they were more intellectual, creative, and independent. Skaters revelled in an informal physical activity in which they could express themselves in risk–taking and 'artistic' ways. On a regular basis they challenged adult authority and expressed disdain for extrinsic rewards and standards. For example, they often mocked those who wanted to become 'professional' skaters. On the other hand, their actions did not challenge other forms of normative culture. In particular, their gendering of skateboarding reinforced masculinity not only by the emphasis of risk-taking, but in how females were situated in the subculture. Female skaters were either marked as a 'skate betty,' a groupie, or as the exception to the rule of female sporting inferiority (cf. Birrell and Cole 1994; Connell 1995; McKay *et al.* 2000).

The more involved I become in the subculture the more I realise the variation and fluidity in identities and the contradictions within skaters' own proclaimed ideals. Skateboarders try to distinguish themselves from 'mainstream' sport (in a sense, they resist it) but simultaneously their claims to distinctiveness obscure their mainstream forms, including social inequity. Skaters will claim that their activity is open to all (a sense of challenging elitism), yet simultaneously the informal male networks tend to restrict and control female participation (Young 2003). In this way, gender bias is often defused by the skaters' beliefs that females are not skilled or interested enough to 'earn' legitimate status. Another form of contradiction is expressed in their attitudes around commercialisation. They claim 'authenticity' to be based on an attitude that is intrinsic; one's motivations should be oriented to the act of skating and not solely for money. But they do not discredit commercial processes that they rely on for equipment, communication, and for making a living. Skaters distinguish themselves from what *they* consider the mainstream, being motivated by money, but they do so through the mainstream avenues.

These internal contradictions are more common than a clear-cut sense of social resistance. I can no longer assume that skateboarders' identities are created in a separate 'marginal' space and, therefore are a uniform response created in opposition to the mainstream. Instead (as Wheaton and Beal, 2003, discuss in some depth), it has become apparent that identities are partially constituted through mainstream commercial processes which provide some of the raw materials as well as the discourses from which skaters can draw. And, with respect to the blurring of 'subculture' and 'mainstream,' skaters themselves are part of the marketing of these discourses and products. More recent ethnographies of youth cultures acknowledge and theorise the complexities in the processes of identity formation where the binary distinctions between 'grassroots' subcultures and mainstream cultural industries themselves have rightly been challenged (Best 1998, LeBlanc 1999; Muggleton 2000; Thornton 1996)[5]. Best (1998) has discussed how the commercial industries are always involved in the development of youth cultures, but not only as an 'outsider' that simply co-opts. Instead, identity is always contingent upon the negotiation among 'youth cultural expression, the cultural industry and mass media representation' (Best 1998: 23). Thornton (1996) describes how the media and cultural industries are central to the process of subcultural formation. For example, youth rely on the production of mediated symbols, but use them in a variety of ways. In this sense, commercialism permeates their social worlds but the symbols circulated may take on various meanings.

Commercialisation is not only a controlling or co-opting force (although it certainly is because the industry and media play a powerful role in actively framing the discourse), but a means to distribute symbols whose use and meanings may vary in specific spaces of consumption. Storey (1999) states that consumption practices are the moments of articulation, the moments in which meaning and identities are (re)created. Muggleton (2000) argues that in order to understand the dynamic changes within youth cultures one must take into account these individual moments of articulation. These researchers persuasively argue that the relationship between subcultural members and the cultural industries can not be assumed (such as being dichotomous, as resistance, or as co-optation), and must be empirically examined in order to explain accurately the construction of subcultural identities. They argue for a reconceptualisation of traditional CCCS explanations of subcultural formations by addressing the agency and fluidity of subcultural participants. However, they do not ignore the power dynamics within the society at large as well as within each subculture.

Chapter outline

This chapter provides empirical evidence to examine the skaters' interpretation and use of industry products in creating their identities and resultant status hierarchies. It is organised in two main sections. First, skateboarders' use of specialist and mass media in their identity construction will be considered. Second, the variability in how skaters' position their identity in relation to the 'mainstream' will be explored, paying particular attention to the ways in which gender power is reproduced.

The qualitative empirical research the chapter draws on included observation and semi-structured interviews conducted from 2000–2003. I did not attempt to create a 'realist' description, but to assess the participants' uses of mediated discourses and brand symbols in their construction of individual identities as well as subcultural practices more widely. As Storey (1998: 163) notes, 'Cultural studies ethnography is not a means to verify the "true" meaning of a text; rather, it is a means to discover the meanings people make; the meanings which circulate and become embodied in the lived cultures of people's everyday lives.'

The 33 participants represented in this study were primarily residents of northern California. Their skill levels varied from beginners to advanced, and included those who were sponsored[6]; several of the participants were industry insiders as well as being skaters. The range in age was 16–28 years old. Of the 33 interviewed, 25 were men of whom 18 were white, three were Asian-American, two were multi-raced, one was African-American, and one was Hispanic.[7] Six of the eight females were white, one was Hispanic, and one was Asian-American.

Media consumption and construction of skaters' identities

This section will describe the various media skaters consume, and the meanings they attribute to that consumption. Although this study is sensitive to developments in cultural studies that foregrounds the fluidity of meanings and identities, it also recognises the enduring importance of power structures generated through the media, and in the media's interpretation and use. Therefore, a critical examination of the discourses and images circulated in and through the media will also be presented.

Those who have done similar research with youth subcultures have identified that the subculturalists themselves tend to make distinctions between 'core' or 'authentic' members and 'posers' or 'outsiders' (e.g. Thornton 1996; Muggleton 2000; Wheaton 2000). In particular, Thornton (1996) described the different roles that specialist and mainstream media had for the participants' claims to authenticity. She found that specialist media is used to define the more central features, while mainstream media is used to identify what is *not* valued. Youth subcultures tend to define themselves as different from the mainstream and, therefore, the mass media depictions of their activity are often distrusted.

There are a variety of national and international magazines dedicated solely to skateboarding.[8] Each of these has a unique tone. For example, *Big Brother*, was owned by Larry Flint publications, and included 'gross' teenage humour that uses explicit sexual imagery. In the United States it is sold in plastic wrapping due to its 'adult' content, and several skateboard shop owners interviewed would not sell it in their stores. The most popular magazine, *Transworld Skateboarding*, is owned by Time Inc. Skaters describe this as the most generic of all, a catalogue of products and skaters. In addition, skaters create their own 'zines' at the local level. Mirroring the print media is the video market. Videos generally are dedicated to showing skateboarders in action. Different skateboarding companies display their new products, using their sponsored riders, in these videos, and interviewees acknowledged that skaters' reputations are often made in these videos.

Mainstream media coverage of skaters occurs on television, sport magazines, and occasionally in newspapers. Disney-owned cable network ESPN has created the 'Olympics' of action sports, the X-Games. NBC has also programmed a multi-sport competition similar to the X-Games called the Gravity Games. ESPN also covers a variety of different skate competitions as well as 'reality,' pseudo-documentaries, that includes skateboarding.[9] The Fox Broadcasting Networks are also featuring action sports, many of which highlight skateboarding. Skateboarding has received coverage in magazines such as *Sports Illustrated* and *Outside*, however when skateboarding gets discussed in United States' newspapers, it is usually not in the sports section, but covered as an 'interest item' such as a rally to procure legal places to skateboard.

Wheaton and Beal (2003) found participants' consumption of specialist magazines served to provide information about equipment, techniques, argot, places to skate, and the values of the skater community. An 18-year-old participant described the role of skate magazines, as 'Not an identity of a skateboarder because they can be whatever, this is just a reference guide.' His statement acknowledges the interplay between the magazines' framing of important information and images and his ability to use that information resourcefully to construct his identity. Wheaton and Beal also recognised that magazines were not simply a source of attaining information, but were also used as an avenue to *display* insider knowledge. For example skaters demonstrated their insider status by their ability to critique appropriately the magazine content or products displayed. Skaters would identify certain products and their advertisements as less legitimate. Finally, it became apparent that those who were attaining subcultural status were more reliant on them for constructing and displaying their skater identity than those skaters who were well established.

The participants clearly identified videos as a crucial part of the skate culture. In fact, industry videos were given more merit than specialist magazines because they were said to represent the broader culture of skateboarding. Many said that magazines provided information but not the 'brotherhood' of skateboarding. One female who had been skating for 13 years claimed that only local videos can provide the sense of bonding that goes on in an informal skate practice, also known as a session. One skater claimed 'I try to watch videos whenever I can.' When I asked him if he'd watch a video before picking up a magazine, he replied: 'For sure, a video totally gives you a stoke.[10] In addition, these industry videos are one way that skaters compete with each other, both in artistry and in the tricks they are performing. On the local level, skaters mimic this by creating their own video on a hand-held camcorder where they get to demonstrate their style (Borden 2001). Occasionally, skaters will use their homemade videos to sell their skills to companies in an attempt to get sponsorship.

Not surprisingly, skaters use and explicitly reference these industry videos to explain 'true' skater identity. This tactic reflects the merging of commercial processes with the creation of 'authentic' identities. This mixing of skater and commercial worlds is represented by apparent contradictions in the claims to authenticity. The skateboarder identity is centred on the notion of being committed to the activity for its own sake, as an avenue of self-expression, and not primarily for money (cf. Beal 1995). Yet skaters are using mass mediated commodities to express an anti-materialist and individualistic stance. For example, John refers to a fictional media created character – derived from a video made in 1987 'The Search for Animal Chin[11]' – to describe how intrinsic motivation is a core skateboarding value:

B: How do you think working for a corporation affects skating? Does it matter?
J: No, the best skater in the world might not even be sponsored. No one knows him. Maybe he is skating in the back woods of Louisiana on a platform. Maybe he has his own skate park in his own yard but doesn't want to be known. His name is Animal Chin.

Joe, a 20-year-old, who works in a skate shop, expressed another example of this blurring between 'outside' commercial processes and 'insider' identity. Joe was discussing how his view of skateboarding differed from the younger generation, especially pre-teens, that he sees in the shop. Although he didn't explicitly demean them, he did express concern over their increasing desire to skate for external rewards. Interestingly, he relied on a quote from a video to exemplify his attitude:

> [there's a] Good quote [in a video], 'Skateboarding is like high school, there are different cliques, there are guys who pose, and those who go after it, but you got to do what you want and keep it real.' That was a good line. His attitude, got to do your own thing, is like my attitude.

These examples illustrate how commercial products in the forms of industry videos were invoked to help construct an authentic identity. This is contrasted to how the *mass media* were implicated in distributing erroneous knowledge. In the following examples skaters identified the representation on television as ill-informed. Andy, for example, criticised people who only got their knowledge of skateboarding through the X-Games:

> You think of skateboarding, you think of Tony Hawk. Because he is on TV… they [the posers] don't buy skater videos or read skater magazines, they go by what is on TV, and he has won all the X-Games.

Laura, who has been skating for 13 years, commented on how television is 'pushing it mainstream'. She recalled a story about visiting her friend's grandfather who, when he found out that she skated, started discussing Tony Hawk's 900 with her.[12] This surprised her, and she went on to lament how most mainstream media were distorting skateboarding's core values by highlighting records and formal competitions.

The mainstream media, however, are aware of this positioning and if they want to be seen as 'legitimate' that they must be careful about how they frame skateboarding. Goldman and Papson (1996: 147) discuss the continued pressure on brands to have signs that represent legitimacy: 'They [advertisers] cannot avoid addressing the relationship between authenticity and the consumption of commodity signs.' Sometimes media and advertisers attempt to use 'insider' conventions to portray this attitude. Certain brands were considered more core or authentic primarily because of their long-standing commitment to skateboarding and especially to the 'core' attitudes. Companies are aware of this, and explicitly try to portray this attitude. For example they create a 'feedback loop' by sponsoring skaters where they ask for insights and comments on their products. This knowledge is used to develop themes of their products and videos. Displaying the core values marks those companies as insiders and, thus, legitimate. These videos, in turn, impact the broader audience's view of skating while simultaneously increasing brand loyalty. Another strategy used by the media is to provide an anti-mainstream message. For example, *Stance*, a magazine geared toward young males that are interested in alternative sport, boasts the by-line 'lifestyles of the young and dangerous'. It tries to capture the skater perspective in a column, (ironically) called Media Watch. The column derides the use of skateboarding images to sell other (non-skating) mainstream products. Alongside pictures of the offending product is commentary poking fun at the motivation behind its use:

> I can just picture the think tank that came up with this ad – a room full of 40-year-old marketing execs saying things about how they need to tap into this X-games/extreme sports market.
>
> (*Stance* 2002: 40)

Yet, this 'irony' has another level; *Stance* was owned by Transworld Publications, which in turn is owned by the multinational media corporation Time Inc. (Fine 2001). So, this anti-mainstream strategy may have been created by a think tank of 40-year-olds.

To summarise, these examples provide an overview of some of the ways in which skaters have used the media in identity construction. Specialist media was often given more authority by the skaters than the mainstream. In addition, mainstream media and advertising are aware of this dynamic and strive to capture 'authenticity'. Identity construction is also underpinned by issues of power; the voice and images that are disseminated and affirmed simultaneously work to marginalise others. Therefore, exploring *who* controls the production and circulation of symbols is critical. Certain groups of people have more influence in choosing the signs that are circulated, affirming those signs 'authenticity', and framing the discourse of legitimacy.

Insider status, power and gender

One important aspect of this power dynamic is that those who control the specialist media also control access to insider status. One woman, who has tried to promote female skateboarders, discussed her struggle with specialist magazines. She tried to get the editors to accept photos and stories of top females, but without success. She decided to go to the mainstream press where she found editors glad to print her stories and photos. Thus, female skateboarders have found some avenues for publicity, but this strategy of using the mainstream press reinforces their marginalised status in the skateboarding world. This is especially true with little or no representation in specialist magazines. The one specialist magazine that features females is called *Wahine*, a magazine that is produced by women and its focus is on female participation in a variety of board sports (see also Booth, this volume). Although an important site for representations of active and committed females, the inclusion in this magazine doesn't directly challenge the masculinist hegemony of the other specialist magazines.

Thus insider status and legitimate knowledge has a gendered component. Research on the content of specialist magazines (Rinehart 1999; Treas 2000) clearly demonstrated sexist assumptions and depictions. Females are rarely represented and when they are, tend to be sexually objectified. When asked about whether skate magazines portray their experiences, a female skateboarder responded negatively:

> Um, not really. [...] They have all of those girls in bikinis. They are barenaked but holding a skateboard. It isn't for girls' skating it is for guys.
>
> (Abby)

'There aren't a lot of girls skate magazines out there. Boys skate magazines, they make, I don't know, it's not good for girls.' (Michelle) [I asked Michelle to explain] 'It puts all guys doing tricks and no support for women. If they mention women it's not in support of skateboarding. It's just kind of a guy's magazine.' [...] 'I don't think it (*Big Brother*) helps. I mean the more and more women that come out to represent themselves rather than having the magazines do it [the better].'

Research has confirmed the female skaters' concerns that the content of these magazines has a masculine bias. For example, advertisements have been identified as representing 'outlaw' culture and heroic masculine values, especially risk-taking behaviour (Rinehart 1999; Treas 2000). One current example is the ad campaign for a video series called 'Guilty.' The ads depicted the skaters posing for their 'mug shots' in a police station connoting that they have been arrested. Several magazines have columns admiring the pain and severity of athletes' injuries, not on their prevention. For example, *Thrasher* has 'Hall of meat' and *Skateboarder* has 'Skate Anatomy'. As Mike put it 'Yeah, sometimes I read the articles about people getting busted or getting hurt, and that is familiar.' As noted earlier, and as explored in previous work (Beal and Weidman 2003), the advertisers in these magazines were conscious of displaying an 'insider' mentality, one which highlighted core values including risk-taking, individualism, and traditional masculinity.

Wheaton and Beal (2003) also found that subcultural status was based in normative assumptions of maleness *and* whiteness. Those interviewed were hesitant explicitly to identify gender or race as integral in their sport culture. Instead, skaters wanted to talk about 'generic' characteristics that any individual needed to achieve. These characteristics were not neutral, but reflected heroic masculine adventure, complicating full inclusion for female participants. As noted previously (Beal 1996) male skateboarders tend not to see females as desiring heroic adventure, and explaining those that do, as 'the exceptions to the rule'. Female skateboarders, on the other hand, were quite aware that their acceptance was contingent upon maintaining the delicate balance of proving their skills on masculine-based standards without forfeiting their feminine or heterosexual identity. This is a similar predicament to other sport cultures that are controlled by male networks and embrace normative masculinity. Dworkin and Messner (2002: 24) describe the inequity in the standards of 'acceptable' athletic females: 'Heterosexualized, flirtatious, moderately muscled female athletes who are accomplished and competitive but expected to be submissive to the control of men coaches and managers'.

Nonetheless, there were some skaters who were aware of these struggles over gender appropriate embodiment. Sean, a 21-year-old who had skated for seven years, discussed the different standards for attaining acceptance:

> It is all about respect, and I think there is a higher standard that women have to meet to gain respect. I have no idea why, it just seems that way… I think that's why you see a lot of black skaters who are good. A lot of black kids that I skate with were good, and they had to be good, because if they weren't they would get no respect at all. So, it's definitely a minority thing.

Similarly, John's discussion about the changes he had seen in skateboarding pointed to different standards for non-white participants:

> It was easier for white trash kids to ride a skateboard than other trash kids. I don't know why. It turned into a white trash thing for awhile.[13]

As these skaters have articulated, whiteness and maleness provided immediate access to legitimacy, while others had to perform at a higher level to gain the same insider status. However it is interesting to note that skateboarding magazines tend to represent a racial mix of skaters, and skaters pointed to that representation to show that skateboarding is not racially biased. Yet, it was apparent that most tended to skate with their friendship groups which were often (but not always) segregated or showed disproportional representation by one race.

Commercialisation and its relationship to skaters' identity

This next section explores the skaters' identity in relation to the mainstream. Their subcultural positioning is examined through their own assessment of the commercialisation process. I will demonstrate that skaters are not uniformly against the commercial process, but show concerns about how their activity is portrayed and the resultant impact that may have; the skaters' assessment of commercialisation is represented by some ambiguity and contradiction. Even in this contested environment, the media and commercial processes are used to create a variety of subcultural identities and positions which helps to illustrate the mutually constitutive processes in the construction of skateboarding identities.

As noted above, crucial components of skating include the non-mainstream aspects of creative/artistic sensibility, a commitment to the actual process and an individualistic attitude. Skateboarding is primarily performed 'for oneself'. Thus, the 'resistance' that skaters live and talk about is the distinguishing of their activity from adult run sport organisations; skateboarding is an act of self-direction. Skaters struggle to maintain these core values while enjoying the legitimacy that comes from professionalisation. From the interviews it became apparent that there are competing interpretations which in effect represent the complex ways the skaters negotiate the increasing popularity of their sport. The analysis, which explores some of these different interpretations, is organised into three main categories (although these are meant as organising constructs, and are not mutually exclusive). First, how commercialisation has undermined skating's core values; second, how commercialisation has promoted the sport, and lastly how commercialisation of skateboarding has impacted the mainstream itself. The significance of these interpretations, or subcultural discourses, is that they are used in creating different subcultural positions and identities.

Commercialisation challenging the 'core skater' values

One of the most influential subcultural positions is that of anti-authoritarianism. This position is what most skaters refer to as the 'core' attitude. The discursive strategy employed in this position argues that the intrusion of commercial values is undermining skateboarding. The concerns addressed most often were co-optation and loss of intrinsic motivation to skate. Steve's comment reflects this:

> The typical attitude of a skater, I suppose, would be fuck the commodisation [sic] of skateboarding, or they obviously don't like the popularity of it.

To highlight this position, skaters try to distinguish their sport from the mainstream by suggesting that skateboarding loses its value when people participate in the activity to gain social status or to be 'cool.' It's not that these skaters oppose their style of physical activity being legitimated, but they tend to conflate legitimacy with uncritically adopting mainstream forms and values. Skaters were concerned that the flexibility of skateboarding was at risk as it became more popular. Bonnie, for example, did not want to see it become an Olympic sport because it would be too regulated and too competitive; whereas '[the] whole point of skating is opposite of becoming a sport.' Tom distinguished skating from mainstream forms and values of competition:

> everybody's extreme now, I think it's stupid, I don't refer to it as an extreme sport. [B: What do you call it?] I call it a hobby. I don't really see it as a sport, when I think of sport, I think of competition, and I guess there are skate competitions but they are not that big of a thing. I would never do a competition; I mean that's not why I skateboard to be better than everybody else and to prove that I am better. I skate to have fun, so I don't think of it as a sport.

The desire for skateboarding to remain different from competition and external validation is echoed in this 19-year-old's discussion of what behaviours earn respect:

> You don't want to go out there looking to "beat" someone. Someone could be like "oh I can do this and that", good for you then. Don't tell me about it though. Who are you doing those tricks for? I hope its not me 'cause I don't care. See what I'm saying? The best skate sessions are when you skate with someone, not against them.

Emilio's comment nicely summarises the concern that commercial success undermines 'core' values:

Like a lot of people are not committed, they just skate around 'cause it looks cool… It's to the point where it's becoming trendy.

Commercialisation as promoting the sport

Another position articulated was the assumption that commercialisation does not pose an inherent threat to the core values of skaters. In particular, those skaters who started their careers after the creation of the X-Games (1995) asserted that core values can be expressed within a commercial context. The long-time skaters frequently identified this younger generation as having a more 'professional' approach to skating. The discursive strategy employed in this position was to offset any negative connotations of commercial success by displaying 'core' values.

Informing examples of this negotiation was articulated in their response to whether they would support and participate in highly commercial venues such as the X-Games. Commonly, skaters responded with ambiguity to the mega-events, but said they'd participate if given the chance. Raul commented:

> I don't know, I don't think skateboarding is Olympic material, the attitude for it, if it happened people would think they are sell outs [B: how do you judge that?] snowboarding is legal, skateboarding is illegal, a person who does it just to get money. You can get sponsored [in skateboarding], but you got to have fun, can't just do it for the money.

In this case, Raul was clearly identifying that he sees snowboarding as a legitimate mainstream sport, whereas skateboarding is not. Sponsorship would only be accepted in skateboarding by displaying the right attitude, intrinsic motivation, and that would override issues of being perceived as a sell-out. Andy's reply to the question concerning his future goals illustrated this fine distinction between being a professional and selling out:

> If it turns out that I am [a professional], sweet, I skate and I get money, but if I don't that's fine, that's not the reason, it's not that I want to be sponsored and I want to become famous, it's because it's fun, it's a hobby, sort of addictive.

Not all skaters, however, were so concerned about being considered a 'sell-out'. As Joe explained;

> The X-Games are alright, I mean, I'm okay with it. Some people are totally against it, people competing for money. Everyone is in it for the money now, it's good if you can make money off it, you should do it.

His only qualification was that not enough people were given the opportunity to compete for money: '[you] see the same people [in the media] all the time.' Moreover, most young skaters who started their career after the advent of the X-Games were supportive of increased popularity, as exemplified by Tom:

> As far as the X-Games I think that's pretty cool, 'cause gets more people to see it, get interested, get started. Good publicity for skateboarders even though I don't like vert [ramp skating, which is premiered in that event], I like it.

Limited support: from generation X to generation Y

One of the significant trends from this research is the difference in subcultural positions of older and younger generations with the younger skaters embracing commercialisation more. As one of the executives of a major skateboarding company recently stated, that generation X is 'disgruntled' with the increased commercialisation whereas generation Y is willing to be 'hooked up' with the products.[14] The structure and content of the most recent commercial venues, I contend, is one source of this difference. In particular, many people are making money through the promotion of skateboarding as a 'legitimate' sport. Van's[15] has sponsored eleven 'mega-skate parks' in the United States often associated with shopping centres (Ruibal 2002). Independent skate parks or groups often sponsor lessons. This official 'coaching' is antithetical to 'core' values, but parents often feel more comfortable supporting their children in supervised settings. I observed many parent-children interactions at skate parks. Parents often stayed on the outskirts while their young children were skating. At one YMCA[16] skate park, I watched a father inquire about skate lessons for his six-year-old son. As he asked the supervisors if there were skating classes available, the child did not seem particularly interested in the conversation (which was about him) nor did he seem interested in the skaters around him. During the same day, I watched as children were dropped off and picked up from the facility. My assumptions were confirmed by the site supervisor: the average age of most skaters that day was less than 10 years. To participate, one needed to pay a fee and to wear protective equipment, which also costs money. Add in the cost of 'authentic,' branded skate clothing (which they all wore) and the ride to the park. The parents were very involved in the activity in which their children participated, a far cry from the stereotypical image of anti-authoritarianism.

Most long-term skaters identified and discussed this influx of young children to the sport. They were unenthusiastic about these newcomers because they saw them as products of adult-run events (such as described above or the X-Games) where the activities are supervised and physical risk is limited which, fundamentally, challenged the forms and values of their skating world. They also commented that the younger participants were much better than they ever were at their age. Older skaters carefully traversed these new grounds, the increased skill with the change in their culture.

One of the interviews was with a female who had started skating before the advent of the X-Games. Bonnie articulated the key tension that long-time skaters commonly expressed, the relationship between increased acceptance and loss of distinction. This is illustrated in her discussion of a variety of contradictions within the skateboarding world. For example, she was happy that the sport has become more established because there are now more places to skate, but didn't like the trendiness. As a result, she was concerned that people were doing it because it was popular, as opposed to developing a lifestyle. She is delighted that skateboarding is no longer seen as a 'loser thing' and that kids can look up to skaters. She qualified this by suggesting that it is not as underground anymore because skateboarding is now a way for companies to make money and for kids to fit in. Another internal tension she discussed was the loss of control that came with this increased recognition and concurrent commercialisation. She described friends who were sponsored and were struggling with their companies because they were being told what to wear and when to perform: a direct challenge to long-held values of individualism and self-expression.[17]

Sean, also a long-time skateboarder, recognised this struggle and suggested that there will always be a core of skaters who maintain and live the central values, and others who will be 'weekend warriors.' He responded to the question of whether skateboarding has fundamentally changed.

> I don't think so, I think like if you enjoy skating that's what it's all about, it's all about you wanting to skate ... there's just going to be a lot more people that are latching on to it and trying to make money off of it. I'm trying to think of another sport where that's happened where there's a serious group of people and then a not so serious group of people, and they're completely different.

Sean, like many seasoned skateboarders, is able to recognise the corporate advertising strategies of targeting a variety of groups to sell their products (Wheaton and Beal 2003). Embedded in their reading is a judgment by long-term skaters who continue to make distinctions of legitimacy or 'seriousness' within their social world.

Skateboarding influencing the mainstream

The final positioning of skateboarders was the least common and was held primarily by long-term skaters. It involved turning my questions upside down. Instead of framing how commercialisation has impacted skateboarding culture, a few skaters discussed how the ethos and images of skateboarding have permeated mainstream culture. For example, Noree commented on the use of skateboarding symbols to sell other products:

> Yeah, cell phones, cars... I don't pay much attention to it... for a long time skaters were looked down upon, now they want to use us or skaters to promote stuff, which is kinda funny.

Although Noree held a flippant attitude, other skaters argued that the core culture was influencing mainstream media and entertainment, and that the relationship of skateboarding and media was not simply one of assimilation. This positioning of skateboarding 'core' culture as a trendsetter was the least developed of the discursive strategies. Generally, it took the form of an argument where key components and people who were now accepted in mainstream media were identified. For example, one skater provided two specific examples. First is a comedy series called *Jackass* that is shown on MTV. This is a program that features human pranks that have serious physical risk. The show was created by many of the people associated with the magazine *Big Brother*. He also named Spike Jonze, the director of the movie *Being John Malcovich* and *Adaptation*, as starting his career directing many of the skate industry videos. He saw the skateboard humour and style as influencing mainstream media and style. Another interviewee who worked as a videographer noted that skate-video style has made its way into mass media. Mainstream adverts are given more legitimacy when they resemble the style of skate videos. This style is exemplified in the technique of displaying clips with a fisheye lens as the camera angles are parallel to the performer. Understandably, some skaters see this trend and their participation in it as very empowering.

Cultural critics such as Kyle Kusz would caution such an interpretation, by suggesting that a larger political context explains the newfound acceptance of this skate style. Kusz (2001) claims that the 1990s popular media shifted the presentation of the white middle class male, from privileged to not privileged. Kusz argued that this increased media representation was a counter to the feminist claims that white males are socially advantaged. Although punk/grunge skate style may be gaining acceptance within mainstream, one could interpret this 'penetration' as a politically expedient way for white males to be represented. Therefore, this may be empowering for some groups, but not for all.

The different interpretations skateboarders have about commercialisation demonstrate the social positions they take within their subculture. The discursive strategies associated with each position helps illuminate the identities these skaters are constructing. One of the main trends found was the rift between longtime skaters and relative newcomers about the goals and attitudes of skaters in relation to the mainstream. As noted earlier, this social positioning is always done in context, so not only does length of career matter, but so does the commercial context itself. The next section will examine other positions articulated within skateboarding and the role of media has in developing various identities of skaters.

Transformations of skaters' identities: commercialisation and the generation of new distinctions

In many subcultures, participants describe themselves by identifying what they were not (see Rinehart 2000; Henio 2000; Wheaton 2004). Skaters referred to 'outside' groups such as in-line skaters or football players, but interestingly the 'other' was also identified *within* the ranks of skateboarding. The following discussion identifies some of these distinctions identified by skaters, exploring how different styles of skateboarding earn different levels of respect, which are related to age, gender and class. This chapter will finish by examining the ways in which media and commercialisation processes are constitutive of these new types of distinctions and fragmented subcultural identities.

'Posers'

The concept of 'poser' is crucial in identifying what constitutes legitimate membership status. One of the interesting changes that has occurred in this social world is the diffusion of the concept of 'poser'. In the early 1990s, posers were universally seen as those who dressed the part but didn't skate. However my recent interviews suggest that skaters back away from the concept of poser. I attribute this mainly to the popularity of skater fashion; that today people who don't even make a claim to be skaters, wear skater clothes. One skater who worked at a shop, talked incredulously about how older adults would buy the shoes for their looks only. Although it is disturbing on some level for a core participant to have posers buying the products that create the image of a skateboarder, those who are now making a living selling those products are willing to make exceptions. It still baffles some skateboarders, even ones that work in the stores, that one would buy a particular uniform for an activity that they do not participate in. However, many of those interviewed in the skating industry did not see a 'problem' making money from those who were not directly connected to skateboarding, or who are less serious about the central values. In fact, one owner of shop said that he 'probably stays in business because of posers'.

The increased commercial appeal of skateboard apparel has impacted definitions and indications of legitimacy. Although current skaters are aware of the concept of poser, they rarely connect it with how one dresses; instead it is primarily linked to demonstration of commitment and an attitude of 'live and let live'. Commitment could be inferred through the signs of equipment use. Mike's comments on determining a poser was reflective of many interviewees:

> [his] Shoes aren't worn down. [you] Look at the side of their shoes. [Look for] scratches. See if they can ollie.

Another very interesting trend was that the 'proper' attitude was often linked with age. Skaters frequently attributed the 'wrong' attitude to young kids. For example, Steve claimed:

> I don't choose to use the term poser, a funny old term. I don't address it. I don't really care. I just go to skate and like have a good time. I don't care who is there. But they can be bothersome, the kids that don't do anything. They just kinda hang out and like talk shit and make fun of people and be really annoying. I guess that would be my modern day poser type of person.

As the old definitions of poser are diffused, new forms of distinction have emerged that distinguish more strongly the types of 'alternative' sport and the styles of skateboarding.

I have argued that skaters – like other lifestyle sport participants (see Wheaton, this volume) rely on risk and difficulty to determine status (Beal and Wilson 2002). Steve listed the sports he respected most, which were those perceived to be most risky and difficult:

> I have a list. It goes: surfing, skating, snowboarding. [...] I would say skating is definitely competing with surfing right now because of the cold ass water and the time it takes to get to the beach and wearing a wetsuit, and surfing really scares me. The ocean scares me. That is something I have to work out with myself... It [surfing] is the best aesthetic feeling, but skating is right up there. Snowboarding is kind of weak because you are all stuffed in and you can't really do as many tricks on a snowboard. It's not as much fun for me. I picked it up really easily. So I don't' think there is an amount of respect that I didn't have because of that. The reason I stopped rollerblading because it was easy to do something that was relatively hard.

The following sections will describe how the status hierarchies and distinctions created around risk get linked to gender, class, and age.

Ongoing distinctions: risk and gender

Younger male skaters often explained the lack of female participation in the same fashion as they did in the early 1990s, saying 'girls don't like to get hurt'. Many older male skaters were more thoughtful about their explanations, which included an understanding of gender norms. Jim, for example discussed trying to convince a female friend not to quit skating, recognising how for teenage girls 'the feminine thing and image' is important; 'plus they don't like the style, like baggy jeans and shirt' preferring dresses and tight pants'.

The interpretation of skateboarding as a masculine space was also articulated by the females with whom we talked. Bonnie, claimed that she was a 'guy girl' and not a 'girly girl,' because she identified her risk-taking as distinguishing herself from other females. She later qualified the self-imposed label of 'guy girl' by asserting her heterosexuality. Other females we talked with used this masculine activity to distinguish themselves from mainstream femininity. Carly talked about changing herself from being a cheerleader, a 'sheep', in high school to being more of an individual after high school. Part of her attraction to skateboarding was that it challenged traditional notions of femininity. She explained that she liked *Big Brother* because 'girls aren't supposed to read it… it's full of gross boys stuff.'

Skaters often inscribed gender and sexuality onto various sports as a means of conferring status. Heterosexual masculinity was the standard of legitimacy which meant that the participants distinguished skateboarding from that which is deemed feminine. In his explanation of why females have high levels of participation in in-line skating, Steve points to extrinsic motivation and lack of difficulty, things which are antithetical to skateboarding:

> I am not sure but I think that it derived from a fitness technique and an obvious hunger to be thin probably made women get into that a lot more. Not that guys don't care about their weight or whatever but I think that might be one of the underlying reasons why there's more girl rollerbladers. It is much easier if you ask me. I think a lot of typical skaters would probably say that rollerblading is for girls or whatever. That comes from difficulty and style, I think. It is not hard to do like a big trick on roller blades.

The lack of respect most skateboarders had for in-line skating is frequently equated with femininity and homosexuality. One skater said that she and her friends called in-line skates, 'gay boots'. I have often heard in-line skaters referred to as 'roller fags'. One participant said he was bi-sexual because he rode a skateboard as well as in-line skated. This attitude is perpetuated by media. *Big Brother* sells t-shirts that have an outline of an in-line skate that is filled in with the rainbow flag.[18] David even claimed that one reason he didn't like in-line skating is that it couldn't differentiate girls from boys because there is no skill level difference. This statement exemplifies the need to distinguish oneself as masculine. David goes on to talk about why he respected BMX and motocross because there is a lack of protective equipment and structure; ultimately they are 'not afraid to get hurt'. For him, and the majority of those we interviewed, activities become legitimate if they are associated with risk and pain, indicators of heterosexual masculinity (Dworkin and Messner 2002).

Emerging distinctions: risk, space and class

Risk is not only associated with masculinity, but by the type of skateboarding one practises. Skateboarding is a multifarious practice which is often categorised based on style and location. There are three main categories: Street, ramp and vert skating. In turn, these styles use different spaces. For example, ramp and vert skating require specially made obstacles (e.g. the ramps) used in a dedicated place. It usually occurs in someone's private residence, a backyard or driveway. If it is public it is often city or corporate sponsored and adult supervised. Street skating, on the other hand, takes place in the everyday urban setting. Skaters find and use obstacles such as curbs, handrails, and parking blocks that weren't made on purpose for skateboarding (e.g. Borden 2001).

Ramp skating necessitates access to resources which implies one's class location. As noted above, ramp skating is done in a yard or driveway and buying and building ramps costs money and often requires the assistance of a carpenter. Vert skating requires a bowl or half pipe, both of which are very large structures that cost a great deal of money, and takes place in designated 'official' parks. Access and control of skating becomes limited because organisations build these structures and run the parks. These parks charge fees and force participants to wear expensive padding. Therefore ramp and vert skating has been discussed as less risky both physically and legally. These types of skating are also criticised for the use of controlled space that is monitored and regulated by adults. In this way, ramp and vert skating are associated with the middle classes and has the connotation of being 'protected'.

Festivals and competitions are held at skate parks, barring the 2002 X-Games in Philadelphia, which were televised from the steps of city hall. Such events are indirectly promoting those who are more privileged because the participants have regular access to ramps or skate parks. However 'access' is linked to money and one's social class background. Televised skateboarding has primarily focused on ramp and vert, whereas skate videos focus on street skating. Skaters interviewed would comment that vert and ramp skating is more spectacular for those who do not skate, whereas one would have to be a seasoned skateboarder to appreciate the intricacies of street style. Street skating requires an urban setting with public spaces that are not supervised. In fact risk-taking behaviour is exemplified by street skating because tax-paying citizens post signs against skating and police officers enforce anti-skating laws. Street skating maintains its status as more 'core' because it most strongly reinforces the ethos of the activities which values physical and legal risk-taking as well as being equally open to all who want to participate.

Street skaters carry an anti-social image that becomes translated as a positive attribute among other skaters. Randall and Mike, who work at a skate park and are vert and ramp skaters themselves, had the following comments about the distinctions among the different types of skating. Randall:

> There are different kinds of skating. Vert and street. A lot of people skate ramp, half pipe, bowl, vert…it's kind of clean-cut skaters. The street skaters are always the punks 'cause they are the ones that are out on the street.

Mike adds, 'They have an attitude with everyone. The street skaters never want to wear the pads.' When asked why he skated street instead of vert a 12-year-old had this to say:

> 'Cause it's crazy. With vert, when you fall you have a thousand pads. The first thing you would break is a toenail.

Emerging distinctions: age and attitude

As noted throughout this chapter, distinctions associated with age were apparent. Many of the long-term skaters view the next generation of skaters as possessing the wrong attitude about skating; the outcome has become more important than the process. David thinks that younger kids are getting better faster because they are turning it into work and are not having as much fun. In relation to this trend, older skaters believe that the newer skaters are more concerned with the competitive and commercialised scene, such as who are the top professional skaters, what products and clothes are the coolest, and within their friendship groups who is the better skater. For example, Joe talks about how competition is more prominent among younger skaters than as reported in Beal's (1995) research. He provides examples of youth who come to the shop at which he works. They ask Joe about the newest up and coming professional skaters. In addition, Joe distinguishes his friends from the younger skaters by the concern given to competition:

> we are at the same level, so there is no real competition, we're cool about things, but we want to one up each other. The new kids who we do skate with, try to show us up, to show us they're better, doesn't get us mad, we just acknowledge they are good, but don't try to beat them or anything.

As Steve claims, 'little kids talk shit'. This competition tends to undermine the camaraderie that long-time skaters value. Instead of an activity of enjoyment, recreation and friendship, it is about achieving proficiency and recognition quickly. How skaters use space illustrates this point. A common observation from the established skaters was that new skaters are oblivious to the etiquette of sharing space, a norm that acknowledges the public and supportive environment that nurtures skateboarders. According to the older skaters, the younger generation is pursuing extrinsic rewards at the expense of community.[19]

Conclusion: shifting notions of style and power

As skateboarding becomes more commercialised there are institutional pressures to create a product that will be received by a mass market as opposed to solely the core participants. Rinehart (2003) has shown how the mainstream media, in particular, frames the production of alternative sporting events in mainstream ways in order to reach a broader audience. From the evidence presented in this chapter, it appears that most skaters have an ambivalent attitude toward commercialisation of their activity. They do not like the fact that it is moving toward the mainstream, but they do take pleasure in the legitimacy they gain from its increasing popularity. Skateboarders negotiate this mainstreaming in several ways. Importantly, one of their main strategies is to continually distinguish themselves from the mainstream. Simultaneously, the industry accelerates these distinctions for they see the opportunity to develop niche markets by selling distinct products and styles to different groups.

Therefore, commercialisation is implicated in the continual dividing of skateboarding into a variety of styles. As noted previously, there is an on-going negotiation between the industry and the consumers. The skaters make judgements about the legitimacy of these styles and products which, in turn, impacts future decisions of the industry. This process is explained well by Thornton:

> In a post-industrial world where consumers are incited to individualize themselves and where operations of power seem to favour classification and segregation, it is hard to regard difference as necessarily progressive. The flexibility of new modes of commodity production and the expansion of multiple media support micro-communities and fragmented niche cultures.
>
> (1996: 166)

The distinctions that have emerged in skating suggest that the younger skaters are more professionally oriented, and that there is a growing separation among street, vert and ramp skaters.

A critical assessment of these new distinctions must take into account how these styles and values impact the skaters' worlds and identities. The standards that long-time skaters used are centred on risk. This gets transposed in two main ways. To begin with the willingness to risk is equated with heterosexual masculinity. Female skaters are marginalised because of the assumption that they are unwilling to take risks. Risk is also associated with social class. Skaters deride those who are protected by their social class standing. Those who can afford to skate ramp and vert are seen sitting somewhere lower on the skating hierarchy. Not only does this represent elitism, but more fundamentally, this privilege is also seen as protection from risk. Vert and ramp skaters frequently wear protective equipment in an adult supervised space.

As the image of skateboarding has gained cultural power, one may question whether that has translated to power for skaters. There are two levels of analysis. First, this increased commercialisation has given skaters more material to utilise, both symbolically and materially. This, and previous research (see Wheaton and Beal 2003) suggests that skateboarders are savvy consumers, and they are keenly aware of companies trying to cash in on youth style. Their ability to create individualised meanings of mass produced products or reject what is 'mainstream' is one avenue of expressing power.

The second level of analysis attends to examining the symbolic significance of core values of skateboarding to see if these are contesting the mainstream. This chapter argues that their willingness to risk and display rugged individualism is central. I contend that these values which may empower males do so in traditional ways and therefore, are restricted. As noted above, skateboarding is rarely a site for females' empowerment. I believe the media reinforces these mainstream masculine attributes primarily because it speaks (sells) to a broader and wealthier audience. For skaters in the industry, 'Chicks (still) dig scars'. The standards of masculinity have not changed with the evolution of skating. Woman are still referred to as 'chicks' and held in a category different from 'real' skateboarders. Scars are the merit badges of the real skater, and an enticement to the 'other'. Although commercialisation has increased the types of skateboarding and choices associated with it, the core value of traditional masculinity and its resultant power relations has not significantly changed.

Notes

1 Becky Beal is an associate professor of sport sciences at the University of the Pacific. Charlene Wilson is the program director of a YMCA. Beal has been researching skateboarding since 1989, and in 2001 Wilson came 'on board'. This chapter represents a joint project, but is presented in a singular voice for rhetorical purposes only.

2 Researchers have used various labels for 'alternative' sports including whiz sports, lifestyle sports, and extreme sports. These are often individual sports that do not rely on formal organisation and place risk taking as a central to the ethos. Generally, these sports include skateboarding, snowboarding, surfing, bmx biking, motocross, and freestyle skiing. The industry developing around the production and marketing of these events has labeled them 'action sports'.

3 A poll conducted by a teen marketing firm, Alloy, in May of 2002 found that Hawk was voted the 'coolest big time athlete' ahead of Tiger Woods and Michael Jordan (Layden 2002).

4 Beal and Wilson have two papers directly related to the use of skateboarding images to brand the action teenage lifestyle (2002, 2003). The Promise Keepers slogan for 2001 was a call for 'extreme' faith in which they made an explicit connection to the alternative sport movement. See the Program Overview, Promise Keepers Conferences, Promise Keepers Official Home Page. Retrieved 1 July 2001 from the World Wide Web: http://www.promisekeepers.org/conf/conf10.htm

5 The critique of CCCS (Birmingham Centre for Contemporary Cultural Studies) has been fully discussed by Muggleton (2000).

6 The sponsors were usually clothing companies or local skateboarding stores.

7 The skaters were asked to self-identify their race or ethnicity.

8 *Heckler*, *Slap*, *Thrasher*, and *Transworld Skateboarding* are such examples.

9 In particular, they have 'Tony Hawk's gigantic skateboard park tour'.
10 A 'stoke' is slang for getting energized, or excited in a positive manner.
11 'The Search for Animal Chin' was made in 1987 by Powell Peralta. It described the spirit of skateboarding as an intrinsic desire to have fun, cautioning the audience of emerging professional emphasis on the extrinsic.
12 The 900 is an aerial trick where the skater does two and a half spins in the air and then lands it. Hawk was the first one to accomplish this in a competition.
13 'White trash' is a derogatory term used in the United States to describe socially disadvantaged whites, especially those who lack cultural capital.
14 Charlene Wilson heard Jay Wilson, an executive for Vans, state this at the 2002 Actions Sports Conference.
15 Van's, a shoe and apparel company founded in 1966, is a leading endemic brand among the skating industry.
16 Young Men's Christian Association (YMCA) organisations frequently sponsor sporting activities as part of their outreach and service to the community.
17 Alon Kleinman (2003) found similar patterns with the 7 professional male skaters he interviewed for his master's thesis, 'Post X-Games Skateboarding: An Exploration of Changes in the Skateboarding Subculture'.
18 Rainbow flag is a sign for gay rights.
19 Again, Kleinman's research confirms these findings.

References

Beal, B. (1995) 'Disqualifying the official: An exploration of social resistance through the subculture of skateboarding', *Sociology of Sport Journal*, 12: 252–67.

Beal, B. (1996) 'Alternative Masculinity and Its Effects on Gender Relations in the Subculture of Skateboarding', *Journal of Sport Behavior*, 19: 204–20.

Beal, B. (1998) 'Symbolic Inversion in the subculture of skateboarding', in M.C. Duncan, G. Chick, and A. Aycock (eds) *Play and Culture Studies*, Volume 1, Greenwich, CT: Ablex Publishing.

Beal, B., and Weidman, L. (2003) 'Authenticity in the skateboarding world', in R. Rinehart and. S. Sydnor (eds) *To the Extreme: Alternative Sports Inside and Out* Albany: SUNY Press.

Beal, B. and Wilson, C. (2002) 'The shifting landscape of an alternative sport: Commercialization and the transformations in the meanings of skateboarding', paper presented at the conference, Sport and the all consuming cultures of (p)leisure, University of Surrey, Roehampton, England. July 27, 2002.

Beal, B. and Wilson, C. (2003) 'All aboard: Skateboarding and the branding of the "action lifestyle"', paper presented at the annual meeting of the North American Society for the Sociology of Sport, Oct 29–Nov 1, Montreal, Canada.

Best, B. (1998) 'Over-the-counter-culture: Retheorizing resistance in popular culture', in S. Redhead (ed.) *The Clubcultures Reader*, Oxford: Blackwell.

Birrell, S. and Cole, C. L. (eds) (1994) *Women, Sport, and Culture*, Champaign, IL: Human Kinetics Press.

Borden, I. (2001) *Skateboarding, Space, and the City: Architecture and the Body*, Oxford: Berg.

Connell, R. W. (1995) *Masculinities*, Berkeley: University of California Press.

Dworkin, S. and Messner, M. (2002) 'Just do…what? Sport, bodies, gender', in S. Scraton and A. Flintoff (eds) *Gender and Sport: A Reader*, London: Routledge.

Fine, J. (April 23, 2001) 'Magazines see 6.8% drop in ads for the first quarter; Biz titles take hit; skateboard pub posts big gains', *Advertising Age* 72: 16.

Goldman, R. and Papson, S. (1996) *Sign Wars: The Cluttered Landscape of Advertising*, New York: The Guilford Press.

Hall, S. and Jefferson, T. (eds) (1976) *Resistance through Rituals: Youth Subcultures in Post-war Britain*, London: Hutchinson.

Henio, R., (2000) 'What is so punk about snowboarding?', *Journal of Sport and Social Issues*, 24: 176–191.

Kleinman, A. (2003) Post X-Games skateboarding: An exploration of changes in the skateboarding subculture. Unpublished Master's thesis, Temple University, Philadelphia

Kusz, K. (2001) '"I want to be a minority": The politics of youthful white masculinities in sport and popular culture in 1990's America', *Journal of Sport and Social Issues*, 25: 390–416.

Layden, T. (June 2002) 'What is this 34-year-old man doing on a skateboard? Making millions', *Sports Illustrated*. p. 80–93.

LeBlanc, L. (1999) *Pretty in Punk: Girls' Gender Resistance in a Boys' Subculture*, New Brunswick, NJ: Rutgers Press.

McKay, J., Messner, M. and Sabo, D. (eds) (2000) *Masculinities, Gender Relations, and Sport*, Thousand Oaks: Sage Publications.

Muggleton, D. (2000) *Inside Subculture: The Postmodern Meaning of Style*. Oxford: Berg.

Rinehart, R. '"Babes," boards, & balance: Women as co-opted sports model in extreme sports', Paper presented at the North American Sociology of Sport Association, Cleveland, November 1999.

Rinehart, R. (2000) 'Emerging arriving sport: Alternatives to formal sport', in J. Coakley and E. Dunning (eds) *Handbook of Sport Studies*, London: Sage.

Rinehart, R. and Sydnor, S. (eds) (2003) *To the Extreme: Alternative Sports, Inside and Out*, Albany: State University of New York Press.

Rinehart, R. (2003) 'Dropping into sight: Commodification and co-optation of in-line skating', in Rinehart, R. & Sydnor, S. (eds) *To the Extreme: Alternative Sports, Inside and Out*, Albany: State University of New York Press.

Ruibal, S. (August 17, 2001) 'X Games roll from the edge to the burbs', *USA Today*, pp. 1a, 6a.

Ruibal, S. (March 14, 2002) 'Boards, circuses hit road', *USA Today*, p. 16c.

Stance (January 2002) volume 11, issue 1.

Storey, J. (1999) *Cultural Consumption and Everyday Life*, London: Arnold.

Thornton, S. (1996) *Clubcultures: Music, Media and Subcultural Capital*, Hanover, NH: University Press of New England.

Treas, S. 'Sports, Space, and in-your-face masculinity in skateboarding magazines', Paper presented at the Pacific Sociological conference, San Diego, CA, 2000.

Wheaton, B. (2000) '"Just do it": Consumption, commitment, and identity in the windsurfing subculture', *Sociology of Sport Journal*, 17: 254–74

Wheaton, B. (2004) 'Selling out? The globalization and commercialisation of lifestyle sports', in L. Allison (ed.) *The Global Politics of Sport*, London: Frank Cass.

Wheaton, B. and Beal, B. (2003). '"Keeping it real"': Subcultural media and the discourses of authenticity in alternative sport', *International Review for the Sociology of Sport*, 38: 155–76

Willis, P. (1977) *Learning to Labour: How Working Class Kids Get Working Class Jobs*, New York: Columbia University Press.

Young, A. (2003) 'Being the "alternative" in an alternative subculture: Gender differences in the experiences of young women and men in skateboarding and snowboarding', paper presented at the annual meeting of the North American Society for the Sociology of Sport, Oct 29–Nov 1, Montreal, Canada.

3 Death, danger and the selling of risk in adventure sports[1]

Catherine Palmer

> Danger, for its own sake, seems to me to be no better than drug taking as a social activity. Danger can be powerfully addictive, and those of us with no taste for it at all consider it as appalling as a taste for crack. It would be better not to glamorise danger, not to prize foolhardiness.
>
> (Polly Toynbee, cited in Rose and Douglas 1999: 273)

Introduction

Contemporary sports culture has seen the emergence of a new class of adventure sports that provide their practitioners with a substantial chance of injury or even death. Through activities such as rock climbing, mountaineering, canyonning, bungy jumping and snowboarding, the sports domain now includes a circle of athletes who actively seek out risk and danger. The postmodern turn has brought with it a new breed of adventure seekers for whom risk taking is routinely – and seemingly unquestioningly – appropriated into a particular set of lifestyle experiences. To elaborate this argument ethnographically, this chapter examines some of the narrative shifts that have accompanied the cultural construction of risk taking within a contemporary sporting context. It traces some of the shifts in definitions and experiences of risk taking that have emerged from the increasing commodification of those activities labelled in popular discourse as extreme sports, lifestyle sports, adventure sports or alternative sports. To interrogate the shifting subjectivity of risk that the commercialisation of these sports has brought about, this chapter explores two inter-related dimensions of the ever-expanding extreme/adventure sports market. First, it examines the incorporation of an iconography of risk-taking behaviour into a whole range of popular cultural products. In the Australian media particularly, but by no means exclusively, sports such as mountaineering, canyonning, bouldering, free-style motorcross, tow-in surfing, snow boarding and street luge, amongst others, now appear in feature movies and music film clips, and in television commercials for soft drinks, sandshoes and sunglasses. As is explored in the first part of this chapter, these once marginalised sports now occupy key places in the public domain. That is, these once alternative sports are now fully incorporated as part and parcel of popular culture, and it is the particular consequences that this has for the packaging and presentation of risk taking that this chapter is concerned initially to explore.

In the second part, this chapter examines the construction of a very particular kind of 'extreme athlete' within the adventure tourism market. Attracting a market with little skill or experience in sports like canyonning or mountaineering, a variety of commercial operators now offer sporting neophytes the chance to take part in a range of frontier challenge activities that are billed as 'high thrill, low risk'. In doing so, these activities are sold to an inexperienced tourist market in such a way that the ever-present possibility of death and danger is rationalised away from the experience. To elaborate this argument, this chapter draws on the much publicised, ill-fated ascent of Mount Everest in 1996, and the Interlaken canyonning disaster of 1999, as illustration of this popularisation of risk taking. In both of these instances of 'selling extremity', the subjective experience of the risks involved in participating in these sorts of sports has been diluted. By appealing to inexperienced practitioners, the very real prospect of death and injury in extreme sports has been stripped from the activities themselves.

A risky business: the commercialisation of extreme sports

As is well documented in the sociological and anthropological literature, extreme sports are attracting an ever-increasing body of participants (see, for example Midol 1993; Midol and Broyer 1995; Beal 1995; Humphreys 1997; Rinehart 1998a, b; Palmer 1999). Ranging from 'weekend warriors' who do no training, have little skill and are content to subject themselves infrequently to the waves, the single tracks or col faces, through to hard core practitioners who are fully assimilated into the argot, fashion and technical skills of their preferred discipline, the extreme sports market is indeed a hotchpotch of interests and expertise.

In response to this growing market, an ever-burgeoning industry has inevitably flourished. Given the centrality of specialised equipment and associated paraphernalia to extreme sports, it is not surprising that a sizeable media industry now promotes a tantalising range of state of the art sporting exotica. Gloves, sunglasses, helmets, T-shirts, sandshoes, protective padding, bikes and surf wax, among other things, are all on sale for the discerning extreme buyer. Even so-called 'alternative' youth cannot escape this commercial involvement in their sport. Beal, writing about social resistance in the subculture of skateboarding, for example, notes that 'those involved in corporate bureaucratic skating are termed "rats"; individuals who brought the commercially produced paraphernalia and plastered all their belongings with corporate logos' (1995: 255).[2] Thus, the landscape of contemporary sport is now pockmarked by the increasing presence of a range of commercial images and interests, and an examination of aspects of this media provides an ideal touchstone to some of the values and attitudes of those who engage in these frontier challenge activities.

Irrespective of whether one B.A.S.E jumps, mountain bikes or snowboards, the specialised media of each sport promotes it in language that reflects the risky nature of the activity. Even the names of the publications themselves reflect the discourse of extremity that they actively promote. The leading British mountain climbing magazine is called *On the Edge*, the names of skateboarding magazines include *Thrasher* and *Slam*, surfers read *Carve* and *Rip Tide*, while snow-skiing magazines go by the names of *Powder Hound* and *Ballistic*. Other forms of media incorporate into their discursive presentation the thrills, the rush, the excitement and exhilaration that is offered by these activities. An article in a mountain climbing magazine, for example, begins with a quote from Renton, of *Trainspotting* (the movie) fame: 'take the best orgasm you've ever had, multiply it by a thousand, and you're still not even close'[3] (*Climb Australia and New Zealand*, Autumn, 1997: 48). In most media, these extreme sports are presented in almost cataclysmic terms. A recently released rock climbing video – *Coming at Ya Hyper* – is billed as 'hi-octane, in ya face entertainment'. Employing technical styles and modes of production more common to a rock music video – fast cuts, images coming in and out of focus and constant movement between locations – the footage of these men and women dicing with death is unquestionably dramatic. Accompanied by a 'pumping' soundtrack, *Coming at Ya Hyper* is a relentless introduction to the ways in which a very particular discourse of extremity is promoted and packaged for its own audience.[4]

Indeed, the intensity of belonging to a culture of extremity is repeatedly amplified through the media. Trading on the notion that extreme athletes are amongst a sporting elite, advertisements for the Hydra Fuel range of sports drink, for example, claim 'we didn't make them for the masses. We didn't make them for the average jock. We didn't make them for athletes who settle for second best', while those for Exceed sports nutrition products feature the slogan 'Don't tell me I can't,' suggesting that these are products for people for whom nothing is impossible. In other words, the discourse that surrounds these sports plays with the notion that they offer more than sports as they are customarily imagined; lifestyle sports take their adherents faster, higher and further than all others, and it is from the considerable media resources that accompany adventure sports that the extreme athlete emerges as a fearless figure, supremely brave and ever adventurous as he or she negotiates a series of hair-raising episodes. As detailed here, these qualities are transmitted through detailed media attention, and it is out of this that a discourse of extremity is principally constituted.

What is important to note about this discourse of extremity however, is that it now enjoys a wide social circulation. No longer simply an index of attitudes and values internal to particular sporting subcultures, the non-specialised media have recognised the rise in popularity of these sports, and employ many of the insider themes and images to sell their products and paraphernalia. Previously 'on the edge' behaviour now features in a whole range of media to sell a whole range of mainstream commodities such as sunglasses, soft drinks, watches, alcoholic beverages and clothing. On Australian television, for example, a spate of commercials selling Bacardi Rum incorporated the iconography of risk taking into its fairly ubiquitous publicity. In keeping with the stylistic presentation of living on the edge, these advertisements employed modes of technical production more common to a rock music video. With the backing sound track belting out 'My Generation' (The Who), various shots in the Bacardi commercial featured helmet-less business men fearlessly riding scooters, crowd surfing in nightclubs, and engaging in reckless sexual behaviour. While not exactly 'sport', such scenes nonetheless promote an image – a lifestyle – in which dangerous behaviour has a high 'cool factor'. Here, risk taking goes mainstream; sport and commoditisation no longer remain separate entities (Rinehart 1998a: 2; see Rojek 1995 or Lewis, this volume, for a discussion of some of the broader theoretical perspectives on the commercialisation or 'Disneyfication' of leisure).

It is this conceptual collapse between risk and mainstream that is of crucial concern for this chapter, in that it creates the impression that *anyone* can take part in these kinds of activities. The fact that inexperienced actors can leap from a plane or bungy jump creates the allusion that no expertise is needed to engage in extreme sports. In other words, these made-for-media versions of extreme sports are short-lived *imitations* of risk, rather than serious sporting initiations into activities in which physical fitness and technical nous are of paramount importance. As is made clear in the following section, this mediated normalisation of risk taking is particularly problematic in that it gives the impression that nothing goes wrong in extreme sports. In the popular packaging of these 'panic sports' (Kroker *et al.* 1989), those activities for which there is a sizeable tourist market are presented as being entirely without risk or danger.

A closer examination of several of the more recent disasters in adventure sports however, reveals that this is not the case at all. The selling of risk is a careful exercise in discursive manipulation (by adventure tourism operators and advertisers keen on attracting a young, usually male and usually affluent market), and the following section examines the particularly tragic consequences that have accompanied this selling of risk as it is played out in the adventure tourist market.

Selling adventure

As part of the world-wide adventure holiday market, a variety of commercial operators now offer backpacking sporting neophytes the chance to take part in mountaineering, canyonning and other adventures. In spite of the relatively high levels of skill, athleticism and technical nous that are needed to master these activities, such past times are nonetheless constructed in very particular ways, so as to attract an amateur, tourist based clientele, with little or no experience in the activity they are undertaking. The particular kind of selling of risk that the commercial proponents of adventure travel engage in has fundamentally altered people's perceptions of risk, trust and danger, and it is this shift in the subjective experiences of sporting practice that this chapter is now interested to detail.

The domain of adventure travel is an extraordinary phenomenon indeed.[5] Steering away from traditionally safe destinations such as the capital cities of Western Europe, a new breed of travellers gravitate instead to 'adventure tourism centres'; places like the Himalayas, the south island of New Zealand, or to

Switzerland, in areas around Interlaken, the self-proclaimed 'adventure capital of the world'. In such locations, predominantly young tourists pay commercial operators (with names like 'High n' Wild Mountain Adventures' or 'Extreme River Canyonning Adventures') large sums of money to experience activities such as single-track mountain biking, para-gliding, bungy jumping, white-water rafting and, of course, canyonning, a peculiar activity that mixes abseilling, hiking and white-water river running. In other words, local industry in these wilderness areas has discovered that tourists are a lucrative source of income. As the Australian journalist Andrew Bain, writing in relation to these kinds of activities in New Zealand points out: 'adventure is a poker game of spiralling stakes. Create an adventure and there is an immediate scramble to up the ante' (Bain 2000: 11).

The most problematic application of adventure tourism, however, is illustrated in the package tour market. Each year, operators such as Contiki[6] take busloads of 18- to 35-year-olds on the 'adventure of a lifetime'. In addition to the usual museums, galleries and scenic wonders visited by more conventional tourists, Contiki also offers its young travellers a series of packages described in their promotional literature as being 'adventure options'. White water rafting in Austria or paragliding in the Greek Islands are included in these adventure options, while in Switzerland, the options include a 200 metre bungy jump from a cable car, or, as will be discussed shortly, a hair-raising ride down a river canyon. The contemporary travel experience is thus peppered with sites or locations at which the captive market of adventure travellers can live 'on the edge', seemingly without ever meeting with misfortune. More importantly, in this packaging of adventure, sport and thrill are condensed into a delimited time frame: the 'adventure of a lifetime' takes just 21 days.

It is within this domain of adventure travel, where we find an extraordinary range of sporting *novices* taking part in activities that depend upon a marked degree of technical and sporting competence. Sports such as canyonning or white water rafting require a keen understanding of weather patterns, river currents, and so forth, while activities such as mountaineering or rock climbing require a certain level of technical skill to perform them safely, as well as an awareness of local weather conditions. Despite their dependence, however, on technical expertise, local weather knowledge, and substantial levels of strength and fitness, it is exactly these kinds of sports that an increasing number of backpackers, with little or no experience, are adding to their travel itinerary. While Contiki sells their adventure options as part of an overall package tour, even independent travellers are incorporating what are unequivocally high-risk activities into their travel plans. On safari in Africa – climb Mt Kilimanjaro or take in a spot of micro flighting. In Nepal – grab a sherpa and hike through the Himalayas, or in New Zealand – take an adrenaline filled jet boat ride on Lake Wakatipu. Within the backpacking scene, in other words, we find a dangerous number of thrill seekers whose appetite for adventure often exceeds their skills and competence.[7]

However, in the context of lifestyle sports, the emergence of this new breed of traveller seeking self-gratifying and expensive pursuits is entirely appropriate and expected. Such activities are more than just a particular consumer choice; they are very much about marking and validating entry into a particular experiential world, whereby taking part in dicey or death-defying activities are hallmarks of subcultural legitimacy. That is, for the new breed of affluent youth travellers, you really haven't travelled unless you've experienced some sort of danger – and have the photographs, journal entries or 'pub tales' to prove it.

Importantly, the ephemerality of the experience – 30 seconds on the end of a bungy rope – fits with the postmodern maxim that 'culture is no longer built to last' (Baudrillard 1990: 9). The experiences that 'make meaningful' these particular forms of leisure activities are, by definition, fleeting, sensory and commodity driven. Equally, such activities capture the postmodern tension between individualism and collective consumption. While such sports are 'sold' as unique and individual, whereby each backpacker can test their own limits and endurance, there is still a commonality to the experience, as queues of similarly aged and similarly experienced fellow travellers line up to take part in their own adventure of a life time.

Despite, or because of the relative inexperience of the tourists taking part in these kinds of activities, the commercial operators of mountaineering, canyonning and other expeditions routinely package the adventure sports on offer as being entirely without risk. Indeed, publicity brochures and other pamphleteering which accompanies the adventure holiday market work hard to reassure the safety of the sporting novice. Publicity for AJ Hackett Bungy – a company operating out of Queenstown in New Zealand – beckons with the slogan 'Safe? We invented safe'. Adventure Sports – a UK-based adventure travel company – offers holidays for the 'adult market' that are 'fun and safe. No previous experience is necessary, and singles and groups are welcome', while the promotional literature for Adventure World – the company at the centre of the Interlaken canyonning tragedy – claimed that, since 1993, it has led more than 36,000 canyonneers, with no mishap more serious than a broken leg.[8]

In spite of the rhetoric that suggests these activities are sports without hazards or danger, things can and *do* go wrong. In 1996, a British tourist was killed when he was sucked into a whirlpool on a French canyonning adventure. In 1997, five skydivers on a tourist flight from Auckland jumped from a plane, hoping to free-fall to Antarctica. Three of the five plummeted at more than 200 km/h into the packed ice, their chutes failing to open. In the same year, eleven hikers also died during a canyonning adventure in Arizona. In 1999, a jet boat accident near Queenstown in New Zealand killed one Japanese tourist, while in June 2000, two abseillers were killed in the Blue Mountains, Australia, and a British tourist on a canyonning trip near Katoomba (also in the Blue Mountains) was also killed, when her body was dragged underwater.

Given such statistics, the fact that relative novices are *enticed* to take part in sports that are obviously risky, death-defying and down-right dangerous remains of central concern. With this in mind, in this chapter attention is given to two case studies: the ill-fated ascent of Mt Everest in 1996, and the more recent Interlaken canyonning disaster in 1999.

Interlaken 1999

The picturesque Swiss village of Interlaken is a regular stop on the Contiki travel circuit, and in August 1999, 45 young backpackers set off on a 'canyonning adventure of a lifetime'. With varying degrees of outdoor experience and, according to various reports, no special instruction from Adventure World – the operator in whose hands these young lives were placed – the tourists paid the equivalent of A$75 for a ninety minute excursion through the white water of the Saxtenbach Gorge. As the weather closed in, and the gorge filled with water, eighteen of the tourists and three of the eight guides were swept to their death by a flash flood.

In the aftermath of the tragedy, however, a host of objective or commonsense reasons emerged which would have more than suggested that to participate in this particular canyonning trip would certainly have been tempting fate. Indeed, it is when reconstructing the various hazards encountered by these tourists that the contradictions inherent within the discursive presentation of such activities become maximally apparent.

Given the intense media coverage that this incident attracted, reconstructing the unfolding events in the Saxtenbach Gorge is a relatively straightforward exercise. Like most other extreme disasters, a large part of the Interlaken tragedy can be attributed to the topography of the region. The Saxtenbach Gorge is steep and narrow, and any flash storm would have been – and was – a disaster. On the day of the accident, rain had set in, yet according to media and eyewitness accounts, Adventure World still led its 45 clients into the narrow gorge. The sheer cliffs of the gorge meant that scrambling to safety should the river suddenly surge was not an option. From the bottom of the canyon, participants had a limited view of the weather conditions overhead, or of any activity in the river upstream.

Further to these precarious weather patterns, the technical competence of the travellers involved was, again, according to eyewitness accounts, not checked, yet canyonning is an activity that demands a pronounced degree of technical skill. Simply entering a gorge requires that canyoneers 'drop in' by abseilling towards the river below. For the frightened or the inexperienced, inching your way down a steep cliff is painstaking at the best of times. In wet weather however, the presence of rain on the rocks makes an easy abseil both laborious and treacherous, well beyond the competence of the average Contiki tourist. Once in the canyon, participants then need to surf the currents of the river, negotiating the rocks and rapids on their back. A simple life jacket provides buoyancy, and a wet suit protects against the chill of an alpine river, however the actual technical manoeuvres required to descend through the gorge are once more surely beyond the competence of the average tourist. To quote one Australian backpacker, who took the canyonning option on an earlier Contiki tour of Europe: 'you go completely underwater many times. At other times you go headfirst over waterfalls. Just about everybody came out with bumps and bruises. There's a place called "the washing machine" – you get pushed under a waterfall, and it drives you round and round in circles' (personal communication). Not surprisingly, canyonning is described by habitués of the sport as being 'white water rafting without the raft' (personal communication).

Given this presentation of events, it seems surprising that an inexperienced, untrained backpacker would embark on this sort of adventure, in which skill, knowledge and competency is of paramount importance. But, to return once more to the issue of discursive presentation, such activities are rarely described or detailed in a way that documents the very real risks and dangers involved. According to the father of a young Australian student killed at Interlaken, his daughter would have never gone canyonning if she had known the risks. Yet the risks *are* undeniable, and in light of the hazards and dangers presented above, it remains curious that young backpackers continue to risk their lives in these kinds of ways. Given the precarious balance between a successful trip and an unmitigated tragedy, it seems naïve that people externalise risk in the belief that 'it will never happen to me'.

Yet, this externalisation of risk is made possible through the kind of discursive management and manipulation undertaken by commercial operators such as Adventure World. Given that they have little experience in the activity they are undertaking, travellers are thus totally and utterly dependent on the guiding companies, who construct themselves as very particular kinds of *experts*. As the promotional literature for Adventure World beckons 'our veteran guides will ensure your safety, as you have the time of your life'. Here, the veteran tour operator is constructed as a wily, infallible professional, with years of experience under his belt. In related examples, the UK-based Adventure Sports company claims that 'our staff are talented athletes with a level of expertise that ensures you are in good hands', while Extreme River Canyonning Adventures, who also operate out of Switzerland, maintains that 'our activities are run by qualified and extremely experienced outdoor pursuit instructors, not business men'. Such personal affirmations, however, cease to matter when the people who take part in the activities are *not* athletes – and therein lies the problem. In the construction of these adventure sports experts, we find a blurring between expert athlete and sporting neophyte; between the need for experts and the construction of the activities as being risk-free and therefore capable of being undertaken by just about anybody. On the one hand, the tour guides are presented as being very particular kinds of experts, fearless adventurers, capable of meeting any challenge, yet, on the other hand, the same discourse of extremity runs the line that *anyone* can do it.

The analytical point to emphasise from such accounts is two fold. First, the construction of the adventure sports expert raises questions for the ways in which power is deployed, negotiated, expressed and transformed, as the neophyte and the expert confront one another within the context of adventure travel. In such scenarios, the differentials of power and knowledge shape even the most well meaning encounter between traveller and commercial operator. Here, power is loaded with Foucaudian notions of the 'right' to behave in particular ways, as the experts exert their control and authority over the situation, thereby 'effecting' their power through the presentation of privileged knowledge (Foucault 1980). Equally, those without knowledge (about the activity, the weather and so forth) must consent to a form of submission that 'it will be all right on the day', precisely because they lack the power to contest the authority of the experts, as constructed by the experts. In this particular presentation of expertise, notions of trust, as well as of risk, have all but collapsed. As 'experts' the outfitters of these operations take care of all the details, to the point that the tourist just has to turn up on the day. Equipment is supplied, weather patterns are checked and the canyon is chosen – by the experts. In embarking on these high-risk adventures, therefore, the sporting novice has to take *no* responsibility for their limits or their abilities. And, in this particular presentation of expertise, there is no sense of the experts having to *earn* trust, of having to prove their credentials. Their expertise is taken as a given. In every possible way, the knowledge and qualifications of the guides – embodied in dress and demeanour – is established in such a way that downplays the highly risky nature of the sports that they lead the tourists through. Thus, the conundrum as to why people would want to put their lives in the hands of people that they've never met is answered, when knowledge and power are managed in such ways so as to strip the ever-present possibility of death and danger from the experience.

Such tragedies however, appear to have no learning curve in which future adventurers learn from the mistakes of the past. Less than two years before, a sporting tragedy of unparalleled proportions had unfolded on the high slopes of Mount Everest, surely suggesting the need for caution where inexperienced athletes engage in adventure sports.

Everest 1996

In many ways, the Everest disaster bears certain similarities to the Interlaken tragedy. Like canyonning, high altitude mountaineering is an extremely risky business, with a remarkably high incidence of injury and death. Various figures are bandied about, with the ratio being somewhere between 1 in 5 to 1 in 10 deaths for every success.[9] Equally, climbing the world's most feared and famous mountain is now a key commercial venture for the adventure tourism industry (see Lewis, this volume, for a discussion of the collapse of adventure and tourist leisure experiences in relation to climbing). As the writer and mountaineer, Joe Simpson, points out: 'a Himalayan holiday, including an ascent of a couple of twenty thousand foot mountains is no longer a pipe dream, but one of the staples advertised in almost every trekking brochure you open. Everest is simply another holiday destination, just more expensive than the others' (1997: 61).

However, while canyonning and mountaineering adventures are both sold in very particular ways, in the case of Everest, the 'extreme experience' is sold to a very different kind of tourist than the backpackers of Interlaken. Climbing Mt Everest is increasingly attracting a breed known as 'executive adventurers', predominantly white collar professional men, who spend their weekends and holidays mountaineering. While their substantial amount of disposable income enables these executive adventurers to engage in challenges such as climbing Everest, it also creates its own set of tensions that were played out, with tragic consequences, on the high slopes of Everest in 1996. In May of that year, eight people lost their lives when bad weather set in, trapping them high above help. In a grim twist, one of the expedition leaders – a New Zealand climber named Rob Hall – managed to patch a final radio call through to his heavily pregnant wife, adding an element of pathos to an already very public drama.

To a far more marked degree than we saw in Interlaken, serious economic imperatives triggered the events that transpired in May of 1996. A lucrative industry had developed in the Kathamandu Valley, with several guiding companies competing for the executive adventure market. With these weekend climbers paying in the order of US$60–70,000 to climb Everest, competition was fierce between companies. Indeed, on the day of the disaster, no fewer than five parties were attempting the climb, and given that future business is generated from every successful summit, there were strong pressures for these companies to get their clients to the top. Thus, the two companies at the centre of the tragedy – Adventure Consultants and Mountain Madness – were locked into a rivalry to get their clients to the summit. Once again, we see inexperienced athletes, whose appetite for adventure far exceeds their skills and competence. Several members of the Mountain Madness party had never climbed at high altitude, with one member, a New York socialite named Sandy Pittman, who was covering the climb for *Vogue*, taking gourmet food, as well as a tv and video player, so that she could watch movies in her tent – a fair indication that Pittman was not expecting the trip to be much more than an exotic camping adventure, rather than the serious test of technical skills and competence that it was.

More critically however, for the events that unfolded, in the rival Adventure Consultants camp, three clients were suffering fatigue *before* they even embarked on the climb to the summit, and this had dangerous repercussions for the events that took place on the higher slopes. To climb Everest, mountaineers must work within a very tight and strictly enforced time frame. On Everest, safety effectively hinges on speed. If an ascent takes longer than expected, it increases the chance that climbers will run out of oxygen or be overtaken by darkness on their descent. On the day of the disaster, however, the three climbers with Adventure Consultants, addled by fatigue and altitude sickness, slowed the rate at which the entire party could climb, yet the ascent went ahead regardless.

The fact that these executive adventurers had paid a serious amount of money to climb Everest successfully created a series of tensions between the experienced guides, the local sherpas and the Western climbers being pack hauled to the top. Whereas the Interlaken tragedy can be attributed to a collapse in perceptions of risk and trust, the Everest disaster pivoted around money, and the *rights* that paying extraordinary large sums of money can supposedly buy an executive adventurer. Economic imperatives, in other words created an expectation of completion. Despite their physical limitations, lack of climbing experience, and the very real dangers posed by the inclement weather, the fact that these weekend mountaineers had paid extraordinary sums of money seemingly bought them the right to risk not only their own lives, but those of their Western and sherpa guides too.

Indeed, the commercialisation of Everest is well documented by a range of sources, who all agree that the selfless ethics that once characterised mountaineering have been eroded or displaced by the kind of corporate colonisation of Everest described here.[10] On the anthropological front, Sherry Ortner (1999) has recently detailed the changing relationships between sherpa guides and their Western clients, based on more than thirty years of fieldwork in the Kathmandu Valley. In other genres, writers such as Joe Simpson (1997) or Jon Krakauer (1997) describe a situation in which a fixed rope – virtually a handrail – has been installed along the climb, allowing these executive adventurers to 'bag the big one'. In Simpson's book, *Dark Shadows Falling*, he reports one instance in which as many as forty people reached the summit in a single day. In *Into Thin Air*, the American journalist, Jon Krakauer, recounts final comments of a now dead American executive, who mortgaged his house to the hilt to make the ascent, were that the 'experience is over-rated. I'm telling you. They've built a yellow brick road to the summit'. As such accounts make clear, money mediates or mitigates risk, in doing so producing a dubious kind of expert: if you have sufficient money, then that qualification is enough to get you to the top of Everest.

As was the case with the adventure tourism market, the emergence of these executive adventurers seeking self-gratifying and expensive pursuits is entirely appropriate and expected. Attracting, in many ways, a similar demographic of affluent, educated males, climbing Everest represents a critical means by which to distinguish yourself from the crowd; to have a very different kind of leisure experience to the 'average' holiday maker. The money and time commitment involved helps to separate these executive adventurers as a unique class apart for whom pursuing a certain lifestyle has no limits – provided you can afford it. Indeed, such activities present a situation in which the individual can dramatically, if sometimes fatally, distinguish himself from the crowd.

Gendering extremity

The use of the male pronoun above was deliberate: the discourse of extremity is highly gendered, which makes it culturally unacceptable for women to dramatically, if fatally distinguish themselves from the crowd. As the 1998 death of the Scottish climber, Alison Hargreaves, and the 1996 media pillorying of the aforementioned Sandy Pittman make clear, where women are involved in dangerous pursuits, all sorts of cultural definitions and limitations are placed upon their behaviour. In other words, there are quite clear cultural boundaries placed on being an extreme athlete. Whereas lone men barrelling down single tracks or tackling insurmountable cols fit comfortably within the category of the supremely brave and ever adventurous 'hero', female adventurers are perceived as being 'driven', or 'egocentric'; selfish qualities that are not only ill at ease with the cultural definition of hero, but are also unbecoming for a lady to boot!

To cite the experiences of Sandy Pittman, who was criticised for leaving her wealthy husband and child to risk the Everest climb, Pittman writes that many of her Manhattan friends considered her ambitions misguided: 'Aren't you afraid that your husband will take up with someone else while you're away,' she reports they asked her. 'How can you be a good mother when you're gone for so long?' (Rose and Douglas 1999: 28). Equally, Alison Hargreaves fell foul of the morality of risk taking. Reaching the summit of Switzerland's Mount Eiger in 1988, Hargreaves created a stir when it was discovered that she was five months pregnant at the time. She was attacked by the British journalist and now domestic goddess Nigella Lawson, as personifying 'me-first mountaineering', with Lawson describing Hargreaves' climbing as a 'neurosis that shows a reality-denying self-centeredness'. 'I was pregnant, not sick,' Hargreaves responded. 'What kind of mother would I be if I sacrificed climbing for my children? It makes me me, and is what makes me the good mother that I am.' Hargreaves went on to become, in 1995, the second person, male or female, to climb Mount Everest solo without using oxygen (Rose and Douglas 1999: 29).

Three years later, she was killed descending from another successful summit of Everest in 1998. It was here that we saw the morality of risk taking go into overdrive. As a mother of two, Hargreaves had effectively abandoned her children by taking such extraordinary risks. The particular cultural definitions and limitations imposed upon Hargreaves ensured she would never dramatically, if fatally distinguish herself from the crowd as a *climber*, but rather as an errant, unthinking mother. As a group of British women journalists noted, every news report about her accomplishments started with the words 'mother of two'. By contrast, when a male climber either summited or died in the attempt, the headlines never read 'father of one killed on Everest' (Rose and Douglas 1999: 26). Indeed, in May 2000, a South Australian climber, Mark Auricht, was killed, having turned back less than 1000 metres from the summit. In a whole sweep of media descriptions, Auricht was a man who 'died doing what he loved' or 'who embraced a challenge'. He was a driven man who knew no limits; a man who could fatally distinguish himself from the crowd. Forty-eight hours later no fewer than 90 climbers had conquered Everest, including the oldest climber, and the first blind climber, which brings into question the authenticity of the individual noble quest, when such accomplishments are now 'a dime a dozen'.

Conclusion

This chapter has been concerned to tease out some of the discursive complexities that have emerged from the increasing commercialisation of adventure or lifestyle sports. In particular, it has been interested to examine the ways in which commercial operators sell their services so as to make them attractive to relative, if not total, sporting novices, such as those found around Interlarken or at the base camp of Mount Everest.

The material presented here raises one central issue for contemporary sporting culture and practice: what is it about such activities that encourages inexperienced backpackers or executive adventurers to take part in activities that are so clearly beyond their skill set, to put their lives in the hands of people that they've never met, when the risks are so patently apparent?

One of the principal arguments developed in this chapter is that, in such activities, the odds of meeting with misfortune are stripped away from the activity itself through a complex process of discursive manipulation by which such activities are packaged and presented to a key market of young, affluent adventurers. These are not sports in which anything will go wrong, and participation in such activities seeks to legitimate their adherents' status as authentic members of a particular subculture of travellers and adventurers, whereby close calls and near misses are part of their lived experience. Packaged and presented as such, these activities are part and parcel of the contemporary travel experience. They are no longer 'sport' as more broadly conceived and understood. Instead, they are lifestyle markers; further 'proof' of ones' ability to cut it in a dangerous and uncertain world.

There is, however, another level to such activities that, in many ways, goes over the head of the sporting novice who engages in such activities as part of their adventure holiday. One of the principal reasons that true *aficionados* of activities like mountaineering or canyonning give as their motivation for continually dicing with death in activities that they *know* to be risky is that that the activities are undertaken, not so much for fun or relaxation; not so much as a holiday experience, but rather, because they provide a means of penetrating to realities not encountered in daily life. It is these personally inflected motivations that are often overlooked in the increasing commercialisation of risk taking. In the selling of adventure, the emotional and symbolic import of mountaineering, canyonning and other forms of 'deep play' (Geertz 1973; MacAloon and Csikszentmihalyi 1983), are often lost on those outside of the sport.

Acknowledgments

I am indebted to Paul Smith for conversations that have greatly helped in assembling parts of this chapter.

Notes

1 An earlier version of this chapter was presented at the Australian Anthropological Society Conference, in Perth, Australia, October, 2000.

2 Gray (1992) makes a similar point with regard to mountain biking.

3 Here Renton is, of course, explicitly referring to his experiences with heroin. As indicated by the prefacing quote from Toynbee, allusions to drugs are a common way of configuring the rush of adventure sports.

4 The almost stratospheric commercial success of the eXtreme Games provides perhaps the finest example of the way in which so called 'alternative' sports, which are meant to buck the system, are increasingly attracting big money and big sponsors (see Rinehart 1998a, 1998b). While worthy of detailed consideration in themselves, the structural and symbolic content of the eXtreme Games are beyond the scope of this chapter.

5 In perhaps the most extreme form of adventure travel, a particular band of tourists actively seek to spend their time in war-zones, areas of civil unrest, or in locations where the chance of some kind of natural disaster occurring are disproportionately high. To cater for this particular breed of adventure travellers, a leading publisher has released a guidebook to the world's most dangerous places. As is the case with the activities pursued while visiting an adventure tourism centre, travel to the world's most dangerous places presumably takes place without risk or danger, the intrepid traveller returning with little more than a couple of great stories to tell of how he or she dodged the bullet or diced with death in any number of the world's trouble spots.
6 Contiki is a travel company specialising in the 18- to 35-year-old market.
7 The risks of terrorism have, of course, added a new dimension to risk taking on holidays, with the tragic bombing in Kuta Beach, Bali targeting precisely the affluent traveller market at whom adventure tourism is aimed. While outside the scope of this current chapter, it would be interesting to see whether these global risks have affected the adventure tourism market in any way; to see whether the target market is still feeling bullet proof about the kinds of decisions they make when on holidays.
8 By way of something of an ethnographic footnote, in May 2000, Adventure World suspended all activities in and around Interlaken, after another tourist was killed in a bungy jumping accident.
9 As Ortner notes 'the most frequent kind of death is sudden and shocking – a slip or a drop off a sheer face, or a fall into a crevice, the biggest killer in terms of numbers – burial in an avalanche, or a slow death from altitude sickness. Here an inadequate supply of oxygen reaching the bloodstream produces strokes, cerebral and pulmonary oedema and other bodily breakdowns' (1999: 6).
10 Georg Simmel (1997) writes more broadly on the decline in pedagogic value that the wholesale 'opening up' of the European Alps has brought about.

References

Bain, A. (2000) 'Summer high' in *The Age*, November 2000.

Baudrillard, J. (1990) *Revenge of the Crystal*, Leichardt: Pluto Press.

Beal, B. (1995) 'Disqualifying the official: an exploration of social resistance through the subculture of skateboarding' *Sociology of Sport Journal* 12: 202–67.

Foucault, M. (1980) *Power/Knowledge* Brighton: Harvester.

Geertz, C. (1973) 'Deep play: Notes on the Balinese cockfight' in *The Interpretation of Cultures*, New York: Basic Books.

Gray, J. (1992) 'Mountain biking as counter culture' Paper presented at the North American Society for the Sociology of Sport Conference, Toledo, OH.

Humphreys, D. (1997) 'Shredheads go mainstream? Snow boarding and alternative youth' *International Review for the Sociology of Sport*, 32/2:300–14.

Krakauer, J. (1997) *Into Thin Air: A Personal Account of the Everest Disaster*, London: Macmillan.

Kroker, A., Kroker, M. and Cook, D. (1989) *Panic Encyclopaedia: the Definitive Guide to the Postmodern Scene*, New York: St Martin's Press.

MacAloon, J. and Csikszentmihalyi, E. (1983) 'Deep play and the flow of experience in rock climbing' in J.C Harris and R.J. Park (eds) *Play, Games and Sports in Cultural Contexts*, Champaign, Il. Human Kinetics.

Midol, N. (1993) 'Cultural dissents and technical innovations in the whiz sports' *International Review for the Sociology of Sport*, 28: 23–33.

Midol, N. and Broyer, G. (1995) 'Towards an anthropological analysis of new sport cultures: the case of whiz sports in France' in *Sociology of Sport Journal*, 12: 204–12.

Ortner, S. (1999) *Life and Death on Mt Everest: Sherpas and Himalayan Mountaineering*, Princeton, NJ, Princeton University Press.

Palmer, C. (1999) 'Smells like extreme spirit: punk music, skate culture and the packaging of extreme sports' in G. Bloustien (ed.) *Musical Visions, Selected Conference Proceedings from 6th National Australian/ New Zealand IASPM and Inaugural Arnhem Land Performance Conference*, Adelaide: Wakefield Press.

Rinehart, R. (1998a) *Players All: Performance in Contemporary Sport*, Indiana University Press: Bloomington.

Rinehart, R. (1998b) 'Inside of the outside: pecking orders within alternative sport at ESPN's 1995 'the eXtreme Games' *Journal of Sport and Social Issues*, Vol 22, 4: 398–415.

Rojek, C. (1995) *Decentering Leisure: Rethinking Leisure Theory*, London: Sage.

Rose, D. and Douglas, E. (1999) *Regions of the Heart: the Triumph and Tragedy of Alison Hargreaves*, Michael Joseph: London.

Simmel, G. (1997 [1991]) 'The Alpine journey' in D. Frisby and Featherstone, M. (eds) *Simmel on Culture*, London: Sage.

Simpson, J. (1997) *Dark Shadows Falling*, London, Random House.

4 Sustainable adventure

Embodied experiences and ecological practices within British climbing

Neil Lewis

> Gregory Bateson, the anthropologist, who was no believer, once pointed out how the erosion of the concept of divine immanence in nature led men to see the world around them as mindless, and therefore not entitled to moral, aesthetic, or ethical consideration. This led them to see themselves as wholly set apart from nature; when this loss of a sense of organic unity was combined with an advanced technology Bateson argued, 'your likelihood of survival will be that of a snowball in hell'.
>
> (Fuller 1985: 282–283)

Leisure practices within contemporary cultural formations offer valuable scripts when attempting to narrate modern lifeworld experiences, often revealing aspects of social life that might otherwise remain hidden or be less immediately apparent when observing more mundane everyday social and cultural phenomena (Urry 1990: 2; Buzard 1993: 6). As a distinctively embodied cultural practice historically embedded in the modern period, and with strong antecedents with the 'birth' of tourism,[1] mountain recreations such as rock climbing are ideally suited to the task of informing us of broader social, cultural and technological transformations both within the travel and leisure industry and society as a whole. As part of their embodied reconstruction of modernity, Mellor and Shilling (1997) have emphasised the need for investigating 'the *forms of embodiment* which underpin thought, belief and human interaction' so that we may better 'understand the chief characteristics of how modern persons come to act upon the world around them' (1997: 4). In taking up this behest and physicalising our relationship with modernity so that we might perceive the embodied character of human–lifeworld interaction, I explore modern leisure practices as instances of a 'choreographed history' (Foster 1995), embodying within a microcosm, the changes and continuities expressive, more generally, of the modern period.

In this chapter I will consider the impact certain technological innovations have had upon the embodied experience of rock climbing in the British Isles (see Lewis 2000 for more on the senses of the climbing body; see Robinson, this volume on climbing and masculinity). By contrasting the cultural practices of traditional British climbing with those found in continental Europe, the chapter explores the different motivations and practices expressed by these two climbing traditions via their respective incorporation of technological developments in climbing protection. Alongside this ethnographic data I draw parallels with the theoretical formulations of 'critique of modernity' theorists such as Ritzer, Simmel, and Heidegger, in order to position climbing discourses regarding human relationships with nature and technology within a broader sociological framework. In particular, I follow Heidegger and work within a substantive understanding of technology: that is, I regard technology as embodying specific values that are revealed more clearly during our modernity than at any time previously. In short, our epoch reveals the rational essence of technology, enabling the possibility for a culture of universal control; a rational global culture of efficient precision that incarcerates human beings and their environments within a nexus of infinite mastery. The example of sport climbing will illustrate this understanding of technology. Moreover, Heidegger's phenomenology (along with others such as Merleau-Ponty 1962) presents this culture as exerting itself primarily upon the human body, transforming and challenging our very capability to do things. Yet, as embodied creatures, how we do things constitute significantly who and what we are.[2] And so, for Heidegger, the way we choreograph and perform our fleshy lives, be it at work, at rest, or at play, reveal to us the choices we make of technology as we extend ourselves into the world. Thus, in contrast to the gloomy and overly deterministic view of Ritzer (1993), Heidegger asserts that we can say both 'yes' and 'no' to technology; that we can choose to invite technology into our lives or choose to keep it outside (1966: 54). For Heidegger, then, the question concerning technology is, therefore, primarily about *technological practice* (Young 2002: 38). The example of adventure climbing will illustrate this understanding of technology. And so, if postmodern leisure is, as Rojek (1995: 7) argues, primarily concerned with 'existence without commitment', and composed of a 'depthlessness and transparency' of action, then adventure (or traditional British) climbing, as we will see, fails abysmally to meet such criteria.[3] Indeed, the powerful cultural residual of 'tradition', 'ethics' and 'morality of practice' that inflects many aspects of British adventure climbing, highlights the extent to which 'retro-culture' (or retro technology) and perceived 'authenticity' (Rojek 1995: 8-9) serve to delineate the developmental boundaries of adventure climbing.

The space of modern leisure: a critique

While leisure and recreation are often discussed as a flight or escape from the routines of everyday life (Cohen and Taylor 1992), Lefebvre (1979) perceptively notes that leisure might also provide a place for criticising daily life. Through leisure encounters, he argued, we conjure up opposing images and practices of the lives we might yet live. Lefebvre held that leisure experiences often compensated, or made up, for those perceived deficiencies felt to be emblematic of the mundane and everyday. Leisure could provide a critical and alternative rubric for contemporary living, whereby people increasingly 'find' in leisure that which is missing from the work and family environment. Leisure studies then, can tell us a great deal about our fears and aspirations of the sort of leisure-activist we would like to be; even the sort of person we would like to be, and the kind of world we would like to live in. Consequently, Lefebvre argues that the world of leisure could not develop 'without constant reference to everyday life and the changing contrasts implied by it' (1979: 137).

Many contemporary writers, however, have questioned the radical space leisure might inhabit, and point towards the seemingly irresistible urge for leisure and recreational activities to be subsumed within the same processes of rationalisation and commodification emblematic of everyday life (see Palmer, this volume; Jary 1999; Heywood 1994; Johnston and Edwards 1994; Donnelly 1993, 1996). For George Ritzer (1993), the contemporary rationalisation and bureaucratisation of recreation transforms the space of leisure and tourism into an efficiently produced, predictable, and controlled environment. Ritzer's theory of massification – the 'McDonaldisation of society' – was introduced primarily as a paradigm to sum up the tendency towards rationalisation of the modern lifeworld. For Ritzer (1993), a key tenet of rationalised consumption practices is the guarantee of getting exactly what one expects: calculation, control, efficiency and predictability, all enable the sameness of the Big Mac to be a hermetically sealed and knowable culinary experience the world over (or your money back). There is no uncertainty or risk at a McDonald's, be it a Beijing or a Bolton outlet as the 'human robots' merely heat up the 'preformed, precut, presliced, and preprepared' food before handing it over to the customer (1993: 105). With human error kept to a minimum, for there is very little human input at McDonald's, the Big Mac represents the quintessential known and safe product of the rationalisation project that manifests our modernity.

Similarly Ritzer describes the package holiday or tour as being as 'oriented to predictability as it is to efficiency. That is, a person who signs up for a package tour is looking for a trip that offers no surprises. [...] Each day has a firm, often quite tight schedule, so that there is little time available for spontaneous and unpredictable activities' (Ritzer 1993: 90). Such a scenario is a far cry from viewing leisure time as the 'escape attempt' from the repetitions and restraints of everyday life. More recently, and following Bryman's (1995) sympathetic study into the world of Disney, Ritzer and Liska (1997), now focusing more specifically on tourism, have coined a fresh neologism – 'McDisneyisation' – to account for the endemic rationalising and consumer-packaging impetus of the tourist industry, and also, the increasing control and constraint the McDisney-style theme park exudes upon the individual.

Similar criticisms have been voiced regarding the sanctity of mountain tourism in evading the iron-cage or 'golden arches' of McDonald-esque rationality (Palmer, this volume, discusses the commodification of mountain tourism). As long ago as 1895, the German social commentator, Georg Simmel (1997 [1991]) wrote of the 'wholesale opening-up and enjoyment' of the European Alps. 'Destinations that were previously only accessible by remote walks can now be reached by railways, which are appearing at an ever-increasing rate' (1997 [1991]: 219). Even difficult and strenuous peaks, such as the Eiger, could now be ascended via the comfort of a railway carriage. Simmel was therefore keen to point out that the nature of the Alpine environment had already been significantly altered or levelled by late nineteenth-century metropolitan culture (Frisby 1997). Consequently, any form of mountain leisure would, by default, be of a similarly enframed and prepared package as that of an urban amusement. Thus Simmel ultimately regards the climber who is willing to risk death to be delusional through a romantic excitation with climbing having no ethical viewpoint; that is, it fails to actualise the critical space Lefebvre insists that leisure can inhabit.[4] For Simmel, climbing had become nothing but an aesthetic masquerade, an extension of metropolitan modernity into the mountains. Yet, prior to their 'opening-up', Simmel writes:

> Alpine journeys had a pedagogic value in that they were a pleasure that could only be had by a self-reliance that was both external and internal to oneself. Now there is the lure of the ease of an open road, and the concentration and convergence of the masses – colourful but therefore as a whole colourless – suggesting to us an average sensibility…
>
> All in all I accept that the advantages of this socialistic wholesale opening up of the Alps outweigh the reliance on the efforts of the individual. Countless people who previously were barred because of their lack of strength and means are now able to enjoy nature.
>
> (1997 [1991]: 219)

Lurching heavily between contrasting perspectives, Simmel both recognises the egoism and elitism of the climber, on one side, education, responsibility and the common-good on the other. Perhaps caught between a rock and a hard place, Simmel would both like to preserve the wild areas of the earth by increasing their exclusivity (and so become the playground for those with the physical and financial means to go there i.e. the fit and wealthy climber), and to flatten mountains and tame nature in the humanistic urge to make 'wilderness' available for all (accessible to the physically and financially weak). In emphasising such contrasting viewpoints Simmel captures an ambivalent aspect of modern technology. For in these illustrations technology is seen to be both an *enabling* and democratising force as it provides 'mass' access to otherwise exclusive areas; yet, it also emerges as a *disabling* and subduing force, not only of nature (as the dumbing-down of the Eiger into an effortless 'climb' suggests) but perhaps also a dumbing-down of the human senses: 'the ease of an open road… suggests an average sensibility'. Perhaps it is here that we confront a key tension in the relationship human bodies have with technology? From its enabling powers to 'open up' new horizons of space and time, to its disabling effects upon the human capacity to sense the distinctive spatial and temporal horizons within different environments,[5] modern technology becomes a double-edged sword. Technology both reveals and conceals. Technology both excites the senses and placates the senses. Technology can both be a means of escape and incarceration. Understood in this way, we can begin empirically to explore the desired limits of technology.

Drawing upon climbing discourses regarding technological innovations within climbing practices, the chapter explores (within a leisure context) this perceived ambiguity of technology as simultaneously enabling and disabling human embodied agency and intentionality. Technological innovations can thus facilitate both 'adventurous' and 'touristic' leisure. For example, Vester's (1987) analysis of 'adventurous activity' includes dimensions such as risk, coping, and low levels of routinisation, suggesting that adventurous leisure requires human powers of perception and action to be immanent if it is to be successfully executed. In contrast, touristic leisure, as Ritzer highlights, includes low levels of risk and coping, with a high level of routinisation. Human powers of perception and action can therefore be less involved or detached from the successful completion of the activity. In short, adventurous leisure often requires an active, purposeful and independent body, whilst touristic leisure engenders a more passive body often reliant upon others to facilitate recreation. With this Weberian ideal-type contrast as a guide, I now explore two styles of climbing leisure – what climbers commonly refer to as adventure or traditional climbing, on the one hand, and sport or bolted climbing, on the other.

Adventure climbing, sport climbing and 'falling-off' places

> If the perception of resemblance between distinct and different objects is exalting, the perception of difference between likes is appalling.
>
> (Ferguson 1992: 50)

The traditional style of rock climbing in the British Isles has been, and continues to be overwhelmingly, a style known as *adventure* climbing or 'free' and 'clean' climbing (see Wilson 1998 for an excellent overview). In most other climbing regions of the world different styles of climbing have predominated, such as 'aid' or artificial climbing and bolt-protected *sport* climbing. This division, while not always delineated as above, has existed in practice since the years prior to the First World War, when Austrian climbers began using pitons – a metal spike with an eye for threading rope or clipping a karabiner[6] that is hammered into the cliff – to facilitate their ascent of the larger Alpine faces (see Wilson 1981 [1975]: xii).

In his discussion of rationalisation and commodification within British rock climbing, Ian Heywood (1994) has highlighted 'protection' equipment as a key factor promoting the differentiation between adventure climbing and sport climbing. Climbing protection refers to the array of technical devices utilised by climbers when moving up a mountain or cliff, offering protection from the possibility of death or serious injury in the event of a fall. Heywood notes how the sport climber is 'unlikely to suffer serious injury however many times he or she falls, jumps, or rests on the [bolt] protection. The same could not be said for many adventure climbs' (1994: 185). Heywood thus delineates a significant difference between adventure climbing and sport climbing: sport climbing begins by nullifying a ready and obvious hazard of a cliff or mountain environment by reducing the consequences of falling, be it death or serious injury. In the language of the ecological psychologist James Gibson (1986), sport climbing appears to annul the cliff or mountain environment as a place that affords 'falling-off', as a place that affords injury (Gibson 1986: 37).[7] Two immediate benefits or affordances of sport climbing thus become the ability to open up new areas for climbing, along with a perceived diminution in the psychological traumas of climbing: for example, the sense of feeling one's body to be at risk when exposed on a cliff. As one climber who preferred sport climbing told me: 'It's safer. You can concentrate on the movement without fear to screw your head up'.

The Italian climber Paolo Vitali (1997) captures this sense of transforming the cliff environment into a relatively safe recreational space, when he wrote to the British adventure climbing community:

> I have never climbed in the UK but I have read certain articles indicating a consensus opinion that routes, both long and short, should be left in their original state. I have to say that your persistence, in the UK, in refusing any kind of sure and lasting protection baffles me! After all, you no longer climb with hemp ropes ... Since climbing styles inevitably evolve over time, I find your continued resistance to bolts perplexing.
>
> (1997: 181)

Bewildered by the adventure climber's apparent scant regard 'for sure and lasting protection', Vitali wonders why adventure climbers make use of some technological innovations in climbing equipment but not others? Why do adventure climbers refuse the safest protection device yet invented for climbing? The bolt is a piece of climbing protection inserted into holes made by a cordless drill carried by the climber. Attached to the bolt is a hanger or hole through which a karabiner can be placed in order to protect the climber (see Figure 1). This process of protection enables the sport climber to explore hitherto uncharted areas of cliff by facilitating progress across blank areas of rock, bringing with it an unprecedented level of safety and predictability into the climbing experience. Sport climbing brings as Vitali suggests 'sure and lasting protection', and offers the possibility for

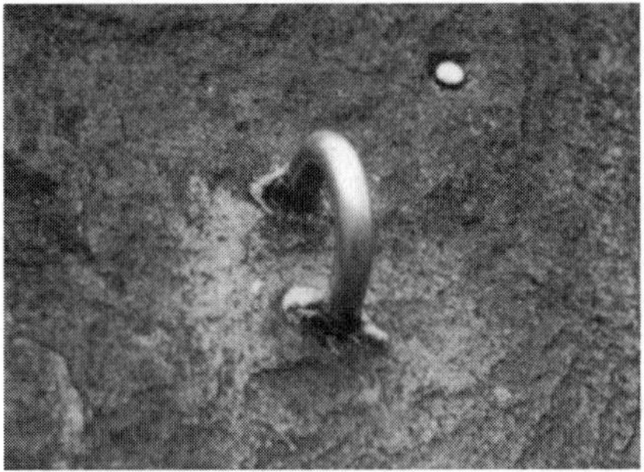
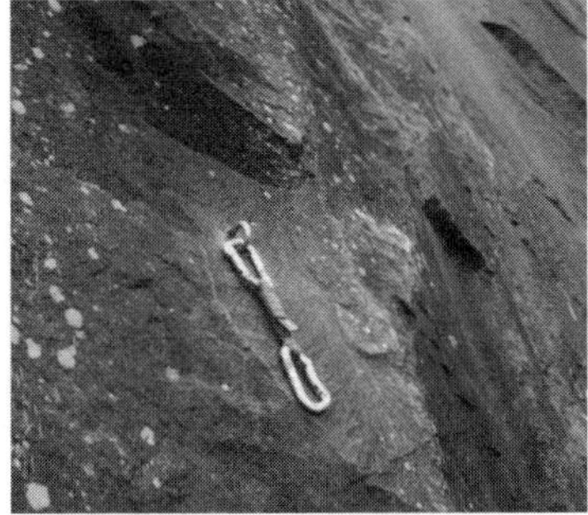

Figure 1 The bolt – the protection technology of sport climbing

climbing any cliff regardless of topographical detail while hermetically sealing the cliff environment as a relatively safe and predictable space.

A related benefit of sport climbing is that the bolted climb presents fewer occasions when the direction of the climb becomes difficult to ascertain. Indeed, sport climbs are often bolted in such a way so as to avoid the potential for getting lost or losing the route. Again, in reducing the necessity for the sport climber to develop navigational and route-finding skills, greater concentration can be given over to the kinaesthetic requirements of the route. Vitali (1997) admits as much when he outlines his methods for creating a new sport climb:

> My approach to climbing new routes has changed during the last few years … Today I try to identify as much as I can with potential repeaters of my routes and, conversely, I bear in mind how I myself, as a repeater, would like to find the routes. In general, *I try to make my new routes basically safe*. To be specific, I supply two bolts at belays and one bolt for protection at the beginning of each pitch; in this way, the most dangerous falls are prevented. The hardest moves of a climb still have to be climbed, of course, but, where possible, I avoid long run-outs [sections without protection]. On the easier sections, *where it is very possible to stray off-route, I often put in a bolt 'for direction'*. On the compact slabs of the Mello and Qualido [in Italy] these directional bolts are very useful, because it is quite possible to make a catastrophic and irreversible move to a 'dead point' from which there is no way forward
>
> (1997: 182–183, emphasis added)

The sport climb, then, attempts to minimise orientational hazards. This is beneficial to the sport climber who can, instead, concentrate solely upon the technical moves required by the climb. There is no need to scan the rock ahead in an attempt to work out the direction of the climb when a bolt has been preplaced to indicate the way. Sport climbers then, revel in a style of climbing that facilitates greater levels of technical kinaesthetic difficulty (indeed most climbers are able to complete harder moves when sport climbing than when adventure climbing). With the cliff subdued into accepting the safe and trouble-free passage of sport climbers, harder and more demanding routes have been created in order to quench the thirst for pushing the kinaesthetic limits of the climbing body. As a leading British sport climber of the 1980s, Ben Moon, once commented, 'I don't climb to be in beautiful places, I climb to do hard moves' (Grimes 2001), thus perhaps highlighting the rather utilitarian relationship sport climbers have with the cliff environment.

Sport climbing sets for itself the task of making the cliff as safe as possible so as to promote the technical limit or ability of the climber. In many ways it is a recreational practice with much in common with Ritzer's McDonaldised worldview. Geared towards maximum enjoyment with minimal risk, the sport climber begins each climb with the reassurance that preplaced and secure protection exists at equally spaced intervals along the route (often no more than two or three metres apart). Not only does this minimise the consequences of a fall but the very proximity of each bolt serves to direct the climber towards the next section of the climb. Sport climbers need not worry about getting lost on a cliff or falling very far. Sport climbing thus facilitates the expansion of certain kinaesthetic capacities (at the expense of others) – enabling the climber safely to push beyond their limit to the point of failure (falling) before trying again. The sport climbing environment thus affords a fourfold return for the climber: first, it enables the exploration of new rock (or rock that would otherwise deter the climber); second, sport climbing reduces the level of bodily risk when on vertical ground – indeed, statistically, sport climbing is less likely to result in a fatality than playing football (Carpenter 1998: 66); third, sport climbing facilitates the creation of technically harder routes, which, finally, extend even further the limits of climbing kinaesthetic ability. Since the 1970s, there has been a steady growth in sport climbing venues within the British Isles. However, such developments have not been well received by many adventure climbers who regard the spread of sport climbing to herald an age of 'theme park' climbing (Littlejohn 1997). Why might this be so?

As the precursor to the bolt protection of sport climbs, pitons[8] provided a valuable means of protection for the early twentieth-century British climber. The piton may not have prevented injury but it could certainly diminish the prospect of death. British climbers, however, responded with much ambivalence to the use of such equipment. For example, when I. A. Richards (the literary critic) forced the first piton into Welsh rock in 1918, one can sense his discomfiture when reflecting on hammering in 'this iron Finger of Fate' (Jones and Milburn 1986: 27). Similarly, when in 1936, a group of German climbers were invited to climb on British rock as an exercise in good-will between two countries increasingly at loggerheads politically, the exercise merely served to highlight the opposing ethics of British and continental climbing styles. The German climbers pioneered a quality route of some difficulty up the South Buttress of Tryfan in North Wales. The result was the appropriately named *Munich Climb*. However, in creating the route the climbers had placed three pitons to protect their ascent. Two were removed; the third left in place as a permanent installation. When news got out of this act of 'desecration', local climbers vowed to remove the offending object and climb the route cleanly (i.e. without using the installed protection). This was done a fortnight later by the leading climber of the day, John Menlove Edwards; thus 'British honour [had been] duly vindicated' (Perrin 1993: 138-139). Yet, two years later, Edwards himself would admit to using a piton when establishing a climb on the Snowdonia cliff of Lliwedd (Perrin 1993: 169). By the end of the decade, Colin Kirkus, who along with Edwards, pioneered the hardest routes in Wales during the 1930s, wrote an article for the *Wayfarers' Journal* entitled 'The Ethics of Ironmongery'. It began:

> The piton has long been prevalent in Central Europe and now it is winging its way to this country like a germ of a deadly disease or the beginning of a glorious climbing renaissance ... who shall say which?
>
> (Dean 1993: 223)

Kirkus highlights the ambiguous tension between the opportunities and the decrements which new technologies present to the climber. As a leading climber of his day, Kirkus could understand the desire to forge ahead with ever more demanding routes assisted by the added security of the piton, though he was equally aware of the dangers of its misuse: 'ordinary rock-climbing may tend to die out; that every slight difficulty may be overcome with pitons ... And when the Piton Age has come – Goodbye to the peaceful age of natural exploring!' (Dean 1993: 225). For Kirkus, the British style of traditional adventure climbing typified a form of 'natural exploring' where dangers and difficulties were to be overcome by a mixture of body skills and commitment as opposed to technological innovations. My own ethnographic research with British climbers – and reflection on my own climbing practices – suggests that such a belief continues to hold sway (Lewis 2001). For example, when climbing club members living in the Northwest of England were asked if they preferred adventure climbing or sport climbing, 70 per cent of respondents stated that they preferred adventure climbing, citing the following reasons:

> I would prefer to take my own responsibility for protection and it adds a little more to the whole experience.
>
> Bolted climbing in France can be fun but adventure climbing is more natural.
>
> Adventure climbing offers a spirit of discovery and one remembers such routes much more than bolted ones.
>
> Adventure climbing is the original way and still the best.
>
> Adventure climbing is more skilful. The outcome is less certain. It's more exciting. And it's not contrived and artificial.
>
> Bolted routes offer little opportunity for route-finding skills to be used, minimising the sense of 'adventure'.
>
> I prefer adventure climbing. The challenge of climbing a mountain and having the ability to self-protect anywhere. That is, you're carrying the right kind of gear all the time.
>
> Adventure climbing because a higher level of experience and skill is needed to place protection than to clip into a bolt.
>
> Adventure climbing seems fairer.

The continued desire for traditional adventure climbing appears to emanate out of its perceived 'more natural' and 'uncertain' characteristics. Deemed as the 'original way' of exploring cliffs, adventure climbing is felt to offer a 'more skilful' and 'exciting' experience than can be had from the 'contrived and artificial' routes of sport climbs. Adventure climbers emphasise a desire for letting nature dictate the path or route of the climb and for providing possibilities for securing protection. For example, during their ascent the adventure climber has to scan the nearby rock for suitable areas where they might temporarily place pieces of protection to safeguard the party's progress from the consequences of falling (see Figure 2). Such a style of climbing 'seems fairer' and its challenges add to the overall climbing experience. As Pete Livesey, one of the great climbers of the 1970s, reflects upon the skills of placing protection:

> The important thing in ropework is having the strength not just to climb the route but to hang around long enough to select and place your belays [protection], and then have the strength to go on climbing afterwards. It's like a game of chess – being two or three moves in advance the whole time – and there's considerable skill involved putting the runners [protection] in place.
>
> (Hankinson 1988: 196)

The placing of protection on an adventure climb is ultimately dependent upon the climber's own ingenuity and expertise despite the array of contemporary specialised protection equipment (see Figure 3). Fissures and points of weakness in the rock vary enormously and even when protection is available, it will never be possible to mass-produce equipment that will fit each and every crack on adventure climbs. Therefore, if the cliff doesn't provide the climber with points of weakness within which protection can be placed, then they climb unprotected, often for some distance until a suitable natural feature presents itself. The protection technology of adventure climbing is thus designed with the sole purpose

Figure 2 The adventure climber with a rack of protection equipment

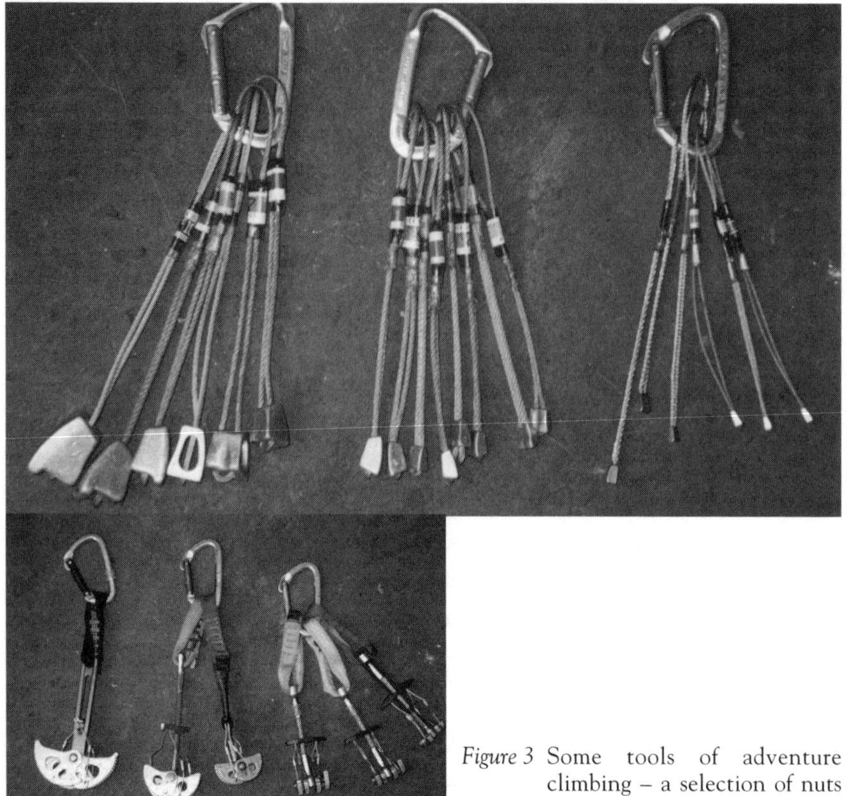

Figure 3 Some tools of adventure climbing – a selection of nuts (top) and 'friends'

of utilising the natural characteristics given on each climb (see Figure 4). If there are no natural fissures or points of weakness in the rock, then there is no protection. As Mick Fowler (2000), perhaps the most talented of contemporary adventure climbers, recently reflected when confronting a protectionless section of a climb he was pioneering in the Garhwal Himalaya:

> A bolt would solve the problem but Steve [his climbing partner on the ascent] and I have strong views on such things. Bolts can solve almost any protection problem. They do not require any weakness in the rock or any skill to place. They destroy the traditional challenge of mountaineering … Either way, on the Arwa Tower we had no bolts and no intention of using any. In retrospect, we would be able to say that we faced up to the full challenge of the face. At the time, it just felt downright frightening.
>
> (Fowler 2000: 26)

For the traditional British adventure climber the natural topography of the cliff dictates the marginalities of risk and safety on adventure climbs. And in order to

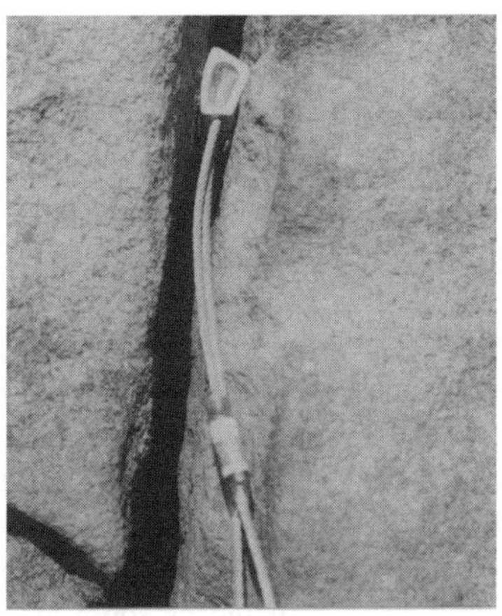

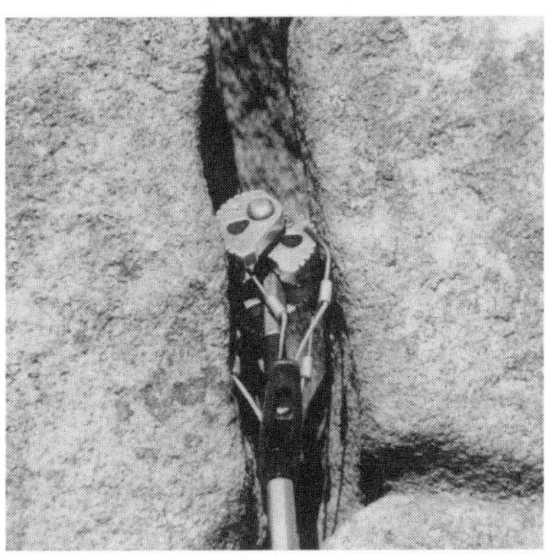

Figure 4 Working with what nature provides – a nut (top) and friend temporarily placed in cracks

protect the special qualities of British adventure climbing this superiority is in need of preserving. In refusing bolts, the adventure climber keeps open a far greater possibility for death – as Fowler intimates above. Doubt, contingency and risk remain in the repertoire of the modern adventure climber's imagination and constitute key ingredients in the recipe for adventure climbing.[9] This has prompted Ian Heywood (1994) to conclude that 'there is about the notion of adventure climbing something fundamentally at odds with the outlook and values belonging to the process of rationalisation as it has been understood and described by writers from Weber onwards' (1994: 185). This sensibility, a desire for 'deep play',[10] illustrates the radical and visceral nature of adventure climbing: of the voluntary and desired bodily risk adventure climbers initiate when they put hand and foot onto rock. British adventure climbers, it seems, are prepared to die for their leisure experiences.

Between 1906 and 1944, the Fell and Rock Climbing Club of the English Lake District suffered twelve fatalities out of an average membership of 500; between 1945 and 1980, when membership levels averaged 900, only three fatalities occurred (Hankinson 1988: 210). There is very little doubt that the fewer fatalities of the post-1945 era are due to the improvements in climbing equipment and protection devices, which, when coupled with the now cleaner rock and greater detailed route-descriptions offered by modern guidebooks, has made climbing a far safer proposition. While Heywood (1994) has argued that such specialised materialisation in equipment signifies an increase in the rationalisation of British adventure climbing, with the differences between adventure climbing and sport climbing now being merely one of degree (1994: 181, 185–187), the present chapter holds that adventure climbing, by continuing to proffer experiences of risk, uncertainty and 'natural exploration', remains a qualitatively different form of leisure practice to sport climbing. Let me explain.

For all its emphasis upon the commercialisation and rationalisation of contemporary British climbing, Heywood's argument ultimately tells us very little about how British climbers relate to the technology they use when climbing, and how they negotiate specific relationships with nature and technology in order to secure specific experiential rewards from their recreation. For if climbing has been guided by any single principle, above and beyond all others, then that principle must surely be the embodied experience of climbing itself? The direct deed? This phenomenological recognition is missing in Heywood's article which emphasises culture as material object, and climbing culture as an archaeology of rationalisation. While there is nothing inherently wrong with this perspective, it nevertheless serves to diminish the importance of culture as embodied activity, as practice and performance. Indeed, one might contest that embodied experience is the most pertinent and poignant constant between the climbing pioneers of yesteryear and the contemporary activist. Following the paths and climbs discovered by those who have gone before constitutes a choreographed history or 'kinetic museum' (Dawes 1996) for climbing bodies. A phenomenological approach to British climbing thus posits one or two ingredients as relative constants in the recipe for traditional adventure climbing. To experience the possibility of their own death and have the ability to protect themselves from such an encounter in the event of a fall is one such constant faced by the contemporary adventure climber. As a recent guidebook describes an adventure climb in the English Lake District:

> Modern technology has done little to enhance the protection from that available in 1922 [when the first ascent was made]. And as this was nil (apart from the stances) and given that the exposure is quite out of this world, it can be readily seen that a steady head, nerve and legs are desirable assets.
>
> (Reid and Ashton 1989: 234)

By demarcating a level of technology that is dependent upon the natural characteristics of the rock, adventure climbs continue to preserve the cliff environment as a 'falling-off' place. Adventure climbing continues to demand physical and psychological attributes from the climber. Consequently, *British climbing needs to be seen as a continual and embodied struggle with rationalisation, and not as unwittingly or passively succumbing to rationalisation* as Heywood suggests. To this extent, adventure climbing ruptures the teleological view of human history outlined by Weber. Indeed, from the hubris of rationalisation emerge ways of living where the iron cage of progress and the domination of nature are no longer deemed categorical imperatives. And so, contra Ritzer, we can, and do, escape a world of McDonald's and Disney. But how might such recreational pursuits be won and maintained in modern societies?

Messner, Heidegger and the limits to technology

In 1971, responding to the upsurge in bolted climbing in the European Alps, Reinhold Messner, the first climber to gain the summits of all fourteen of the world's 8,000m plus mountains, published an article that would hang like an albatross around the neck of the climbing world. Entitled *The Murder of the Impossible*, the article harangues climbing communities into considering the implications certain new technologies were unleashing within global climbing practices. 'Today's climber', warns Messner, 'carries his courage in his rucksack, in the form of bolts and equipment. Rock faces are no longer overcome by climbing skill, but are humbled, pitch by pitch, by methodical manual labour' (1978 [1971]: 300). Messner's fear was that technological innovations, in particular the drilling of bolts into the cliff to aid and safeguard the climber's ascent, would chasten the 'natural art' of climbing and subdue all remaining areas of unclimbed rock into the realm of human, nay technological, probability: 'why dare, why gamble, when you can proceed in perfect safety?' he asks (Messner 1978 [1971]: 301). For Messner, to murder the impossible is to destroy the ideal or spirit of climbing. Without a final frontier, a great unknown to pit one's endeavours against, much of the enigma of rock climbing would be lost. 'It's time we repaid our debts and searched again for the *limits of possibility*...' (1978 [1971]: 302–303), he argues. For Messner, the pondering gaze at swathes of unclimbed rock is essential to the vitality of any climbing community.

Messner directs his argument against the growing trend amongst climbers seeking to establish a *direttissima* line up a cliff. The direttissima pays little heed to the topographical characteristics of a cliff omitting the subtleties and nuances of erosion in favour of a direct ascent. Consequently, climber and nature no longer work together in establishing routes: 'sometimes the line of weakness wanders to the left or to the right of this line; and then we see climbers ... going straight on up as if it weren't so, striking in bolts of course' (1978 [1971]: 300). In contrast, Messner advocates that a climb should only exist 'so long as the mountain permits it', demanding that the climber should only use what the rock, what the cliff environment provides, in order to assist and protect the climber. In short, nature facilitates and becomes a co-participator within the leisure experience. And so, if the route does not provide the climber with points of weakness within which protection can be placed, then the climber will have to proceed unprotected if they want to complete the route. Adhering to the guidance of natural topography is one way in which cliffs will remain unclimbed until a climber bold enough (for there would be no protection) and agile enough (for hand and footholds would be difficult to establish), would be prepared to climb it. To deviate from this path, Messner argues, is to herald a time when 'Ambitions are no longer built on skill, but on equipment' (1978 [1971]: 300, 301). For adventure climbers, sport climbing heralds such an era: a time when the craft-skills of climbing are no longer embodied practices, but are instead preplaced or bought and carried in the rucksack.

Historically, the climber negotiated a passage up a cliff face by utilising the natural features of the rock: crack-lines, grooves, chimneys and ledges on which to rest, all facilitated the climber's progress.[11] Following natural lines of weakness instilled a feeling that the cliff 'allows' or invites itself to be climbed; that nature 'intentionally' creates various paths in the rock to encourage human beings to climb (see Figure 5). This notion that cliffs offer natural lines as prospective routes and that such routes *really were meant to be climbed*, habitually surface in climbing literature. Guidebook writers often use the phrase 'climb on "God-given" holds' to denote rock that, first appears holdless and unclimbable, is, on closer inspection, inundated with a succession of perfect hand and foot-holds enabling ascent (Reid and Ashton 1989: 122). In contrast, Messner describes the bolt-protected climber: 'Stubbornly, bolt by bolt, he goes on. His way, and none other, must be *forced* on the face' (1978 [1971]: 300; emphasis added). Unlike the adventure climber working with the topography of the cliff in order to create a climb, the sport climber is felt to be imposing himself or herself upon the cliff in order to 'force' a route.

There are interesting parallels between Messner's critique of the direttissima and the later philosophy of Martin Heidegger (on the applicability of Heidegger to discussions of a rationalised lifeworld, see Weinstein and Weinstein 1999; for a summary of Heidegger's later 'nature' philosophy, see Young 2002). Both espouse a relationship of disclosure between human beings and the world. Messner demands that a climb should follow naturally occurring pathways, existing only where 'the mountain permits it'. This understanding of climbing as a revealing activity is akin to Heidegger's claim that in order for human beings to dwell 'authentically' or ecologically on this earth, we must cultivate ourselves as 'shepherds of Being' who employ a willingness to 'let things be'. That is, to encounter things as they present themselves to us and to receive them in their very otherness. To dwell is to accept things as they are. In *The End of Philosophy* Heidegger (1973) writes: 'It is one thing just to use the earth, another to receive the blessing of the earth and to become at home in the law of this reception in order to shepherd the mystery of

Figure 5 The 'natural path' of the adventure climb – Max on Jean Jeanie, Lancashire

Being and watch over the inviolability of the possible' (109). Just like Messner's rebuke for climbs that murder the impossible and reduce the climbing experience to bland certainties, Heidegger proposes a world of limits – the 'inviolability of the possible' highlighting the need for sacred spaces that must not be transgressed.[12] Consequently, our use, or our proper use, of nature should not entail its conquering or debasing; to use something properly 'is to let it enter into its essential nature, to keep it safe in its essence' (Heidegger 1968: 187). In this context, cliffs should remain falling-off places.

As I outlined above, this preserving of the cliff environment is largely maintained by the protective 'nuts' and 'friends' employed by adventure climbers and serves to highlight a further comparison between Heidegger's philosophy and the ethos of adventure climbing. In his famous essay, 'The question concerning technology' (1993 [1977]), Heidegger explores the essence of technology as an all-pervading process towards reduction and manipulability – a process Heidegger calls *Gestell* or 'enframing'. Space curtails a full delineation of Heidegger's philosophy of technology, however some tentative connections and interpretations with the technologies of adventure and sport climbing can be made. Beginning with the bolt, we note that it does not harness nature but controls nature by 'setting-upon' the cliff, regulating and securing the rock for risk-free sport climbing (1993 [1977]: 321). The technology of sport climbing reveals the topography of the cliff environment as something that must be overcome, controlled and subordinated to rational order.[13] When bolted, cliffs become manipulated as 'standing-reserve', stockpiled and ordered to the requirements of the sport climber who, demanding 'maximum yield at the minimum expense' can fall all day and yet still reach the top of a climb. Bolt technology challenges the essence of a cliff as a falling-off place, highlighting the process of 'enframing' as it encloses, manipulates and makes certain the outcome of all climbs. If climbing were a culinary experience, sport climbing would exist alongside the Big Mac burger. In contrast, and noting how the equipment design of adventure climbing is geared towards working in tandem with, and maximising the use of, hitherto existing features of the cliff: naturally occurring cracks, flakes, spikes and blocks provide the template for protection design, Heidegger might refer to adventure climbing protection technology as being 'built into' the cliff – much like the old wooden bridge that joined the banks of the River Rhine (1993 [1977]: 321).

In favouring the irregular and meandering rock climb that weaves a natural course up a mountain (by following lines of weakness), instead of the enforced regularity of the direttissima, Messner revealed an aesthetic that favours the imperfections of nature, for they, in turn, create the imperfections or the irregularities in the climber's route, and prove, if you like, the coming together or synchronicity of natural design and the spirit of human endeavour. Thus, for adventure climbers it is nature – or at least, it should be nature that dictates where humans can and cannot climb – and not the innovations in technical hardware. In contrast, for sport climbers nature becomes what Heidegger calls a 'calculable complex': a cliff environment upon which sport climbers can accurately predetermine the successful outcome of a climb. But this control comes at a cost, for Heidegger argues that in rationalising and subduing nature one experiences a withdrawal of truth:

> the unconcealment in accordance with which nature presents itself as a calculable complex of the effects of forces can indeed permit correct determinations; but precisely through these successes the danger may remain that in the midst of all that is correct the true will withdraw.
>
> (Heidegger 1993 [1977]: 331)

Directing this line of thinking towards leisure and, in particular, to distinctions between adventurous and touristic leisure experiences, not only does the sport climber suffer a loss in meaningful contact with their environment, they also lose meaningful contact with their own body.[14] In foregoing the capacity to 'bring forth' other skills – the navigational and self-protecting skills of the adventure climber, for instance – that might enable the sport climber to 'enter into a more original revealing and hence to experience the call of a more primal truth' (1993 [1977]: 333), the sport climber remains a stranger, excluded from the cliff environment (perhaps typified by Moon's earlier comments regarding the utility and not the inherent beauty of a cliff).

By paying heed to the experiential impact of technology within climbing and noting the propensity for sport climbing to be swept away into an excessive ordering of the cliff environment, cultivating it into 'standing-reserve', adventure climbers grasp the essence of technology and 'the possible rise of the saving power' (Heidegger 1993 [1977]: 337). For Heidegger, the saving power lies in the body – that is, via embodied experiences do we most readily observe and question the pros and cons of technology (see also Levin 1985):

> never too late comes *the question as to whether we actually experience ourselves as the ones whose activities everywhere, public and private, are challenged forth by enframing*. Above all, never too late comes the question as to whether and how we actually admit ourselves into that wherein enframing itself essentially unfolds.
>
> (1993 [1977]: 329, emphasis added)

In emphasising embodied experience, Heidegger intimates that the perceptual and aesthetic qualities of 'releasement' and 'openness' to an environment, disclose to us a praxis, a movement by which possibilities for dwelling ecologically in a world that is, and will of necessity have to continue being in some significant capacity, a technologically-driven one (after all, the 'nuts' and 'friends' of adventure climbing are also immersed in networks of technological rationality). By listening to the reverberations of our bodies' in-the-world we can begin to delineate a sparing and preserving of temporal and spatial experience that is not enframed by technology. We might begin to do this by following the lead of adventure climbers and impose limits – limits defined by certain embodied experiences – as to the degree of control and mastery we exert over our environments. For if, as Buzard (1993) perceptively asserts, 'all tourists are anti-tourists, then perhaps anti-tourism has become a way of responding to the nature of that society the tourist must come home to' (1993: 154), then the adventure climber is prepared to forego some of the safeties and certainties of modernity, in order to experience a deeper and more enriched lifeworld where natural forces provide mutual support and encouragement to human fulfilment. These qualities are felt to be lacking both in the everyday environment and the receational space of sport climbing – 'a synthetic substitute offering "virtual adventure" where once we had the real thing' (Littlejohn 1997: 187). And so, in accepting a limit to their control over nature, and therefore embracing a perceptible bodily risk more readily into their recreational experiences, British adventure climbers regain the compunction to *be* with their bodies and to *be* with their environments.

Conclusion: ecological protest and the embodiment of nature

> In wild places, bolts are litter.
>
> (Littlejohn 1997: 187)

The relationships between bodies and environments, and the subjectivities and sociational identities that emerge from processes of 'perceiving a value-rich ecological object' (Gibson 1986: 140), pave the way towards defining the adventure climber's sensibility when entering the cliff or mountain environment. If, as Gibson postulates, an affordance 'points two ways, to the environment and to the observer' (1986: 141), and that basic affordances of the environment are 'commensurate with the body of the observer' (1986: 143), then we must surely pay heed to the cultural and bodily practices developed by adventure climbers as they seek to enter into the most equitable of reciprocal kinaesthetic experiences possible with the mountain environment.[15] As Nick Crossley (1995) has noted:

> to have acquired a body is precisely to be able to adapt and apply it in accordance with the demands of particular situations. It is only in the abstract imaginary of the human sciences, the catalogues and museums constituted through academic writing, that techniques assume a generalised, atomised and decontextualised form.
>
> (1995: 137)

From such a perspective, Heywood's thesis that the differences between adventure climbing and sport climbing is 'just one of degree' (1994: 188), is indicative of this pathology and suffers as a consequence. Similarly, and evoking the spirit of Durkheim's (1961 [1912]) 'collective effervescence', Mellor and Shilling (1997) underscore the sociological significance of bodily experiences as having:

> the potential to transform people's experience of their fleshy selves and the world around them. The somatic experience of the sacred, 'something added to and above the real', arises out of these transformations, and expresses a corporeal solidarity between people which can bind them into particular sectional groups …
>
> (Mellor and Shilling 1997: 1)

Mellor and Shilling highlight that people can be drawn together by the 'somatic experience of the sacred', developing a sense of mutuality based upon specific corporeal experiences of nature which are then clothed within a distinctive culture. The power of corporeal and visceral impulses to guide and direct human behaviour should never be underestimated (Loewenstein 1996). To be sure, there are few practices as corporeal and visceral as adventure climbing. This chapter has presented adventure climbing as one such somatic experience of the sacred and reaffirmation of our corporeal existence. From Descartes to Disney World the corporeality of human beings has become a grotesque presence in need of constant discipline and control (see Foucault 1977; Ritzer 1993; Ritzer and Liska 1997). Yet, for Bakhtin (1984 [1965]), 'grotesque' bodies could resist subordination so long as they remained in sync or in rhythm with the natural environment. The grotesque body of adventure climbing is a body that blurs the boundaries between self and other, between subject and object, between animate and inanimate being; a body that accepts the natural affordances of an environment. This might well be a contemporary expression of what Mellor and Shilling (1997) would call an 'immanence of the sacred', in this instance a meeting with nature upon even terms – terms upon which both human being and nature have the potential to extend themselves upon the other. As Vester (1987) writes: 'If leisure is commercialized and rationalized and if adventurous activities are infiltrated by industrial standards, little room is left for risk, daring, and uncertainty' (1989: 246). Yet, adventure climbing purposively seeks to maintain levels of risk and uncertainty. Consequently, when regard is given to the phenomenological experience of climbing there appears to be a continuation of sharp differences between adventure climbing and sport climbing.

Adventure climbers choreograph and practise their climbing activities in such a way so as to escape or withstand rationalising tendencies within climbing practices by judiciously maintaining the cliff and mountain environment as a place that affords 'falling-off', providing a leisure experience laden with risk, embodied coping strategies and low levels of routinisation. By assessing technological innovations within a corporeal and experiential framework, adventure climbers demarcate an optimal limit to which technology should transform the cliff environment. Both physically (as in the sport climbers' permanent installation of bolts) and metaphysically (in the sport climbers' transformation of the sacred 'abode of the dead' (Reid 1992; Bernbaum [1988] 1997) into a profane, commodified and inconsequential recreational space), adventure climbers practise a recreation where the *safe* limits of technology exist upon the margins of the *unsafe* limits of the body. In resisting the perceived safeties and certainties of sport climbing, exponents of British adventure climbing appear to embody a profoundly ecological relationship between themselves and the cliff environment (for an appraisal of the ethics of high-altitude mountaineering, see Cullen 1987). Exercising embodied freedom along with the intuition and desire to abide with one's environment have emerged as central themes of adventurous leisure explored in this chapter and serve to highlight the continuing possibilities for leisure to engage critically with everyday life. Indeed, it is perhaps this 'heaviness of being' and morality of responsibility that serves to distance British adventure climbing far from the madding and 'guiltless' sport climbing crowds of postmodern leisure outlined by Rojek (1995: 140). Having been co-present for much of modernity, the temporal and spatial experiences of British adventure climbing not only provides a truly grounded muse for cultivating an intellectual and practical space for a critique of non-adventurous and ecologically disastrous leisure, but to broader issues of global sustainability for a technologically-driven world. Perhaps it is time to apply the principles of ecological and radical leisure to the conduct of everyday life?

Notes

1 First popularized by the account of Thomas Gray and Henry Walpole's 1740 sojourn (see Schama 1995: 448-449; Withey 1997), the crossing of the Alps as part of the European Grand Tour habitually enforced a degree of 'mountain adventure' upon those intent upon reaching Italy.

2 Of course, there are numerous factors that impact upon the way we do things – class, gender, age, race, etc. In this respect, climbing cultures are no different. For more on gender and climbing, see Angell 1988; Birkett and Peascod 1989. For more on class and climbing, see Cook 1978; Darby 2000.

3 More apposite, perhaps, to the world of postmodern leisure is the burgeoning arena of indoor climbing – where 'climbers' pay to perform safe gymnastic exercises upon bolt protected moulded plastic walls in centrally-heated venues.

4 However, both Jarvis (1997) and Taylor (1997) provide persuasive historical arguments supporting a 'radical space' for outdoor recreation.

5 For Virilio (1995), speed has become a key aspect of experiencing the contemporary environment or lifeworld. And speed kills: 'Acceleration has effaced the distinction between here and there. All that is left is a mental confusion of near and far, present and future and real and unreal. What we have today is the mixing of history, of histories, and the hallucinating Utopia implanted by techniques of communication' (1995: 55).

6 Initially the British climbing community similarly frowned upon the use of karabiners. Irving (1935) has written of the lack of an English name for the German karabiner: 'It is, in fact, decidedly un-English in name and in nature' he muses provocatively (1935: 121).

7 Affordances are what an environment or object provide, both positively and negatively, to an animal. Affordances refer not only to the physical properties of things, or the phenomenal qualities of subjective experience, but to the ecological properties of an environment or object; that is, affordances are ecological to the extent that they are properties of the environment relative to the animal (Gibson 1986: 127–143). A path affords walking; a cave affords shelter, etc. Gibson's work runs contrary to much of the orthodoxy within psychology. In eschewing the mind-body dualism of Descartes and the notion that perception is primarily a mental exercise, Gibson postulates that the mind is but a part in a broader 'network of sensory pathways that are set up by virtue of the perceiver's immersion in his or her environment' (Ingold 2000: 3).

8 The use of pitons and pegs remain a grey and nebulous area within adventure climbing (as do the leaving of threads and slings as in-situ protection). By having preplaced protection on a climb the 'commitment factor' is severely reduced, for the following climber need not 'hang around' to arrange their own protection thus reducing fatigue and the potential for failure. While the hammering of pitons into existing points of weakness such as cracks makes it an action of a less imposing will to dominate an environment as one would implement when drilling in a bolt (for one is still working with the topography of the cliff), there is, nevertheless, still a considerable sense of forcing technology into rock. It too is semi-permanent and leaves a noticeable scar when finally removed. The current attitude amongst British climbers is to leave existing pegs on climbs until they rust away and not to replace them. The use of pegs is now discouraged and the semi-fossilised peg found on many a climb becomes not only a relic of a previous ethic but a highly suspect form of protection. Moreover, cracks often repel pitons with glorious uncertainty. Pegs and pitons perhaps typify the extremity of adventure climbing technology (and one which contemporary British climbers are moving away from); they are not, however, of the same calculable rationality of the bolt placed by the sport climber.

9 The Yorkshire Gritstone climbing guidebook employs a 'P' (protection) grade to inform the climber of the seriousness of the climb they are contemplating and what the consequences of falling might entail. At the extreme end, a 'P3' climb intimates with the typical gallows humour emblematic of adventure climbing culture: 'Dire consequences. Do not fall on these nasty numbers because you're going to have to be lucky to walk away from a P3 lob [fall]. Get full life insurance now' (Musgrove 1998: 12).

10 First developed by Jeremy Bentham, 'deep play' typifies a situation or activity within which the participating individual stands to lose far more than he or she would gain if successful (see Geertz 1973: 432–433).

11 By the 1930s the hitherto accepted practice of taking points of aid on a climb, either through judicious use of the rope or by employing one's partner for a 'leg up' or shoulder, increasingly gave way to a purer ideal of a free and clean ascent by linking one's body solely to that which nature provided for hand and foot holds. This sensibility shines through during accounts of Menlove Edwards' first free ascent of Sca Fell's Central Buttress in 1931. Regarded as the hardest route yet established in the British Isles, the climb had repelled a free ascent for nearly twenty years when Edwards 'made his magnificent lead up the Flake' (Dean 1993: 90).

12 This sensibility is illustrated by the climbing practice of avoiding the summit of peaks that provide sacred abodes for the deities of those living in the valleys below. For example, when Charles Evans led the first successful attempt to gain the summit of Kanchenjunga in 1955, the climbing party refrained from setting foot on the highest summit (there are five) out of respect for local beliefs (Bernbaum 1997: 20). Subsequent ascentionists have continued in this tradition.

13 An interesting parallel here is the contemporary motorway, which also forces itself through the landscape irrespective of natural obstacles. The M3 at Twyford Down in Hampshire – where a hillside was obliterated to maintain the efficiency of the motorway – is a classic case in point.

14 The philosopher and psychologist, Erich Fromm (1949), captures this sense of increasing alienation emanating from increases in rationalisation when he wrote: 'Man must accept the responsibility for himself and the fact that only by using his own powers can he give meaning to his life. But meaning does not imply certainty; indeed, the quest for certainty blocks the search for meaning. Uncertainty is the very condition to impel man to unfold his powers' (1949: 45).

15 From an academic or intellectual standpoint there is very little that can be done to verify such claims of truth or ecological consciousness. We simply do not possess the means to distinguish the climber who 'really' harmonises with nature or experiences a Zen-like moment of transcendence from one who merely fakes it. Heelas' advice that

the researcher remains 'agnostic with regard to the ultimate truth of what is taking place' seems an appropriate caveat here (Heelas 1996: 6).

References

Adler, J. (1989) 'Origins of sightseeing' *Annals of Tourism Research* 16: 6–29.

Angell, S. (1988) *Pinnacle Club: A History of Women Climbing*, Leicester: Cordee.

Bakhtin, M. (1984 [1965]) *Rabelais and His World*, Bloomington: Indiana University Press.

Bernbaum, E. (1997) *Sacred Mountains of the World*, Berkeley, CA: Univerity of California Press.

Birkett, B. and Peascod, B. (1989) *Women Climbing. 200 years of Achievement*, London: A & C Black.

Bryman, A. (1995) *Disney and His Worlds*, London: Routledge.

Buzard, J. (1993) *The Beaten Track: European Tourism, Literature, and the Ways to Culture, 1800–1918*, Oxford: Oxford University Press.

Carpenter, S. (1998) 'Sheer heaven' *Observer* 11/10/98: 66–8.

Cohen, S. and Taylor, L. (1992) *Escape Attempts*, London: Routledge.

Cook, D. (1978) 'The mountaineer and society' in K. Wilson (ed.) *The Games Climbers Play*, London: Bâton Wicks.

Crossley, N. (1995) 'Body techniques, agency and intercorporeality: on Goffman's Relations in Public', *Sociology* 29: 133–49.

Cullen, R. (1987) 'Expeditions, efficiency, ethics and the environment', *Leisure Studies* 6: 41–53.

Darby, W.J. (2000) *Landscape and Identity. Geographies of Nation and Class in England*, Oxford: Berg.

Dawes, J. (1996) *Best Forgotten Art*. Connabell Ltd T/A HB Promotions.

Dean, S. (1993) *Hands of a Climber: A life of Colin Kirkus*, Glasgow: The Ernest Press.

Donnelly, P. (1993) 'Subcultures in sport: Resilience and transformation' in A.G. Ingham and J.W. Loy (eds) *Sport in Social Development – Traditions, Transitions and Transformations*, Illinois: Human Kinetic Publishers.

Donnelly, P. (1996) 'The local and the global: globalisation in the sociology of sport', *Journal of Sport and Social Issues* 23: 239–57.

Durkheim, E. (1961 [1912]) *The Elementary Forms of Religious Life*, London: Allen and Unwin.

Ferguson, F. (1992) *Solitude and the Sublime. Romanticism and the Aesthetics of Individualism*, London: Routledge.

Foster, S. L. (ed.) (1995) *Choreographing History*, Bloomington and Indianapolis: Indiana University Press.

Foucault, M. (1977) *Discipline and Punish: The Birth of the Prison*, London: Penguin Books.

Fowler, M. (2000) 'Arwa Tower', *High Mountain Sports* 211: 22–6.

Frisby, D. (1997) 'Introduction' in D. Frisby and M. Featherstone (eds) *Simmel On Culture: Selected Writings*, London: Sage.

Fromm, E. (1949) *Man for Himself. An Enquiry into the Psychology of Ethics*, London: Routledge.

Fuller, P. (1985) *Images of God: the Consolations of Lost Illusions*, London: Chatto & Windus.

Geertz, C. (1973) *The Interpretation of Cultures*, New York: Basic Books.

Gibson, J. (1986) *The Ecological Approach to Visual Perception*, Hillsdale, NJ: Lawrence Erlbaum Associates.

Grimes, N. (2001) 'Over the moon', *High Mountain Sports* 222: 28–31.

Hankinson, A. (1988) *A Century On The Crags: The Story of Rock-Climbing in the Lake District*, London: J.M. Dent & Sons Ltd.

Heelas, P. (1996) *The New Age Movement: The Celebration of the Self and the Sacralization of Modernity*, Oxford: Blackwell.

Heidegger, M. (1966) *Discourse on Thinking*, trans. J. Anderson and E. Freund, New York: Harper and Row.

Heidegger, M. (1968) *What is Called Thinking?* New York: Harper and Row.

Heidegger, M. (1973) *The End of Philosophy*, trans. J. Stambaugh, New York: Harper and Row.

Heidegger, M. (1993 [1977]) 'The question concerning technology' in D.F. Krell (ed.) *Basic Writings: Revised and Expanded Edition*, London: Routledge.

Heywood, I. (1994) 'Urgent dreams: climbing, rationalization and ambivalence', *Leisure Studies* 13: 179–94.

Ingold, T. (2000) *The Perception of the Environment. Essays in Livelihood, Dwelling and Skill*, London: Routledge.

Irving, R.L.G. (1935) *The Romance of Mountaineering*, London: J.M. Dent & Sons.

Jarvis, R. (1997) *Romantic Writing and Pedestrian Travel*, London: MacMillan Press.

Jary, D. (1999) 'The McDonaldization of Sport and Leisure' in B. Smart (ed.) *Resisting Rationalization*, London: Sage.

Johnston, B. and Edwards, T. (1994) 'The commodification of mountaineering', *Annals Of Tourism Research* 21(3): 459–78.

Jones, T. and Milburn, G. (1986) *Welsh Rock: 100 Years Of Climbing In North Wales*, Glossop, Derbs: Pic Publications.

Lefebvre, H. (1979) 'Work and leisure in daily life' in A. Mattelart and S. Siegelaub (eds) *Communication and Class Struggle: Capitalism, Imperialism*, New York: International General.

Levin, D. M. (1985) *The Body's Recollection of Being: Phenomenological Psychology and the Deconstruction of Nihilism*, London: Routledge.

Lewis, N. (2000) 'The climbing body, nature and the experience of modernity' *Body & Society* 6(3): 58–80.

Lewis, N. (2001) *The Climbing Body: Choreographing a History of Modernity*, unpublished thesis, Lancaster University.

Littlejohn, P. (1997) 'The great alpine theme park', *The Alpine Journal* 102(346): 184–87.

Loewenstein, G. (1996) 'Out of control: visceral influences on behaviour', *Organizational Behavior and Human Decision Processes* 65 (3): 272–92.

Mellor, P.A. and Shilling, C. (1997) *Re-Forming The Body: Religion, Community and Modernity*, London: Sage.

Merleau-Ponty, M. (1962) *The Phenomenology of Perception*, London: Routledge.

Messner, R. (1978 [1971]) 'The murder of the impossible' in K. Wilson (ed.) *The Games Climbers Play*, London: Bâton Wicks.

Musgrove, D. (ed.) (1998) *Yorkshire Gritstone*, Yorkshire Mountaineering Club. Leicester: Cordee.

Perrin, J. (1993) *Menlove: The Life Of John Menlove Edwards*, Glasgow: The Ernest Press.

Reid, R. L. (1992 [1988]) *The Great Blue Dream. Inside the Mind of the Mountaineer*, London: Hutchinson.

Reid, S. and Ashton, S. (1989) *100 Classic Climbs: Lake District*, Ramsbury, Wilts.: The Crowood Press.

Ritzer, G. (1993) *The McDonaldization of Society: An Investigation into the Changing Character of Contemporary Social Life*, Thousand Oaks, CA: Pine Forge Press.

Ritzer, G. & Liska, A. (1997) '"McDisneyization" and "Post-Tourism": Complementary perspectives on contemporary tourism' in C. Rojek and J. Urry (eds) *Touring Cultures*, London: Routledge.

Rojek, C. (1995) *Decentring Leisure. Rethinking Leisure Theory*, London: Sage.

Schama, S. (1995) *Landscape and Memory*, London: Fontana Press.

Simmel, G. (1997 [1991]) 'The Alpine journey' in D. Frisby and M. Featherstone (eds) *Simmel On Culture*, London: Sage.

Taylor, H. (1997) *A Claim on the Countryside. A History of the British Outdoor Movement*, Keele: Keele University Press.

Urry, J. (1990) *The Tourist Gaze: Leisure and Travel in Contemporary Societies*, London: Sage.

Vester, H-G. (1987) 'Adventure as a form of leisure', *Leisure Studies* 6: 237–49.

Virilio, P. (1995) *The Art of the Motor*, trans. J. Rose, Minneapolis, Minn.: University of Minnesota Press.

Vitali, P. (1997) 'Bolting in the Alpine environment' *The Alpine Journal* 102(346): 181–83.

Weinstein, D. and Weinstein, M. A. (1999) 'McDonaldization enframed' in B. Smart (ed.) *Resisting Rationalization*, London: Sage.

Wilson, K. ed. (1975; 2nd edn 1981) *Hard Rock: Great British Rock-Climbs*, Granada Publishing.

Wilson, K. (1998) 'A future for traditional values', *The Alpine Journal* 103(347): 175–88.

Withey, L. (1997) *Grand Tours and Cook's Tours. A History of Leisure Travel 1750–1915*, New York: William Morrow & Co. Inc.

Young, J. (2002) *Heidegger's Later Philosophy*, Cambridge: Cambridge University Press.

5 Surfing

From one (cultural) extreme to another

Douglas Booth

> [...] the surfing lifestyle really lends itself to the very fringe of society – it's such a free-and-easy lifestyle, and it has so much to do with individual freedom—an almost irresponsible kind of freedom. [S]urfers are edge-riders. We've made a decision ... to live on the fringe of society and not be active citizens and participants in society, unless we want to. The act of going surfing is a very selfish endeavour. It's an experience that has nothing to do with anything except you and the ocean, period (Bill Hamilton, surfboard shaper and legendary rider).
>
> (Kampion 2000: 79 and 81)

Deeply intertwined with popular images of bright sun, yellow sand, blue water, rolling breakers and healthy tanned bodies, the appellation 'extreme' would appear a misnomer when applied to surfing. This chapter claims otherwise. It argues that extreme is a valid adjective in light of the irreverent and 'fratriarchial' nature of surfing culture and associated lifestyles, and given the fact that surfing culture bestows the greatest prestige and honours on big-wave riders, those who risk life and limb in violent masses of water that break with ferocious intent.

Section one traces the history of surfing and its development as an irreverent culture. This is best understood in the context of the prevailing countercultures of the 1960s and 1970s. Opposition to all forms of institutionalised power was a hallmark of the countercultures which embraced 'anti-authoritarian gestures,  iconoclastic habits (in music, dress, language and lifestyles), and ... [a] critique of everyday life' (Harvey 1989: 38). Section two examines surfing as a fratriarchial culture that largely excludes women and in which men interrelate and bond by putting women down. Although women have taken up surfing in greater numbers over the last five years, there is precious little evidence of them breaking down the fratriarchial structure of surfing culture. Lastly, section three describes some of the dangers associated with big-wave riding – the risks of drowning in cauldrons of turbulence, of having bones smashed and flesh torn open – and analyses those risks as a sociological system for the allocation of social prestige.

Extreme public profile: The development of an irreverent culture

'Rediscovered' at the turn of the twentieth century, it was not until the mid-1950s that the ancient Polynesian art of surfing once again became popular. Technology was the main obstacle to the development of surfing in the first half of the twentieth century. Made of solid wood, heavy and cumbersome, early surfboards were not only difficult to transport, they were impossible for all but the highly skilled to ride. In the 1950s, Californian surfers produced shorter, lighter and highly manoeuvrable boards made of balsa wood (later polyurethane) and fibreglass. These malibu boards made surfing more accessible. Surfing burgeoned in California and quickly diffused around the Pacific rim, assisted by peripatetic surfers, Hollywood beach films (romantic musicals and comedies: *Gidget* [1959], *Ride the Wild Surf* [1964]), surf music (a thundering guitar-based sound played as single-note riffs: Dick Dale's 'Miserlou' [1962], the Chantays' 'Pipeline' [1962], the Astronauts' 'Baja' [1963]), 'pure' surf films ('travelogues' with footage of surfers riding waves: *The Big Surf* [1957], *Slippery When Wet* [1958], *Surf Trek to Hawaii* [1961], *The Endless Summer* [1964]), and specialised surfing magazines (*Surfer*, *Surfing*, *Surfing World*).

The hedonistic and irreverent culture adopted by young surfers offended many of their elders, members of a generation whose life perspectives were forged in depression and world war. Social commentators in the 1950s and early 1960s condemned surfing as an indolent, wasteful, selfish and institutionally unanchored pastime. The surfer style, the trademark of which was long bleached hair, surfers' argot, humour and rituals, and their nomadic lifestyle rendered them socially irresponsible. Bruce Brown, producer and director of *The Endless Summer*, remembers well parents and non-surfing peers chiding him for 'wasting time' and urging him to 'do something useful' (Kampion 1997: 21). As a boy, Greg Noll, who later became a surf cinematographer, equipment manufacturer and renowned big-wave rider, recalls one particular exchange with a school principal:

> 'What do you guys do down there at the Manhatten Beach Surf Club? What are your goals, what do you want to become?' I told him that I wanted to surf, I wanted to make surfboards, I wanted to go to Hawaii, I wanted to see the world and have a good time. From the principal's point of view, that qualified me as most likely to end up a beach bum and never amount to shit.
>
> (Noll and Gabbard 1989: 31)

In Australia, New Zealand and South Africa, the newly-emerging surfing culture confronted a well-established surf lifesaving movement with club-based structures and its own culture that emphasised discipline and teamwork via beach patrols and organised sporting competitions. Surfers in these countries attracted particularly bad publicity and press. One Australian observer called surfers 'useless': they 'cruise from beach to beach looking for the best surf' and 'pay no rates or fees of any kind, frequently not even parking fees' (Titchen 1966). Others denounced 'long-haired' surfers who 'took over footpaths for their boards, public toilets for changing rooms, made unofficial headquarters of public facilities', and passed loud 'rude' and 'foul' remarks at girls (*Manly Daily* [Sydney] 15 October 1965; *Daily Telegraph* [Sydney] 13 February 1964). The principal of one Sydney high school warned that surfing, along with 'the wearing of jeans, lumber jackets, gaudy sweaters and socks and casual footwear', could adversely affect boys (*Manly Daily* 18 December 1962). Local councillors were especially vociferous in their attacks. 'Those there [at Manly] last weekend were badly dressed', Councillor J. Illingworth charged: 'their hair was longer than that of Alderman Mrs A. M. Ambrose. They were drinking wine. They blocked the stairways from the beach and were hustling people on the promenade' (*Manly Daily* 7 October 1965).

Some surfers attempted to negotiate a more acceptable cultural style and expression by defining themselves as sportspersons. Concomitantly, they established new regional and national associations, and organised competitions to take surfing into the mainstream sporting world. Initially, they appeared to have succeeded. Hoppy Swarts, the inaugural president of the United States Surfing Association noted with pride that competitions had 'helped develop a new image with the public – the public has come to respect our surfers in the same way as they respect other athletes' (*Surfer* May 1968: 27). A Sydney newspaper echoed Swarts' sentiments, declaring that surfers had 'matured' since they had formed an official body and that they now had 'the right to promote their sport' (*Manly Daily* 15 May 1964). Big business and vested political interests flocked to the sport of surfing. Sponsors of the first official world surfing championships held at the Sydney coastal suburb of Manly in May 1964 included Manly Council, Ampol (Petroleum) and TAA (Trans Australian Airlines). They were blunt about their motives: 'Manly will get a lot of publicity from international television coverage of the event', said Mayor Bill Nicholas (*Manly Daily* 16 April 1964). The championships were a phenomenal success – an estimated crowd of 65,000 watched Australian Bernard 'Midget' Farrelly win the crown. A senior Ampol representative described surfing as 'the fastest growing sport in Australia' and pledged his company's ongoing support (*Manly Daily* 19 May 1964).

But organised competition required formal rules, and codification was no simple matter with surfing styles reflecting regional variations, particularly between California and Australia: Australians wanted to slash and conquer waves, Californians sought waves for artistic expression. Debate over style fuelled dissension over judging methods and scoring, and led to accusations of corruption, cronyism and nepotism (Booth 1995: 193–5). The result was a significant decline in competitive surfing in the late 1960s.

Not all the political pressures on surfing culture emanated from within. The countercultures also influenced the development of surfing. Amalgams of alternate, typically utopian, lifestyles and political activism, the countercultures emphasised self-realisation and encouraged individuals to pursue their dreams through a distinctive new-left politics. Soul-surfing – riding waves for 'the good of one's soul' – articulated this new politics and conjoined surfing with the countercultures. Soul-surfers scorned organised surfing as a form of institutionalisation.

Kimo Hollinger captures well the general animosity towards competitive surfing. He was at Waimea Bay, Hawai'i when a contest began:

> The kids started paddling out with numbers on their bodies. Numbers! It was incongruous to the point of being blasphemous. I wondered about myself. I had been a contestant and a judge in a few of those contests when it all seemed innocent and fun. But it never is. The system is like an octopus with long legs and suckers that envelop you and suck you down. The free and easy surfer, with his ability to communicate so personally and intensely with his God, is conned into playing the plastic numbers game with the squares, losing his freedom, his identity, and his vitality, becoming a virtual prostitute. And what is even worse, the surfers fall for it. I felt sick.
>
> (Hollinger 1975: 40)

Soul-surfers applied increasingly esoteric interpretations to surfing: waves became dreams, playgrounds, podia and even asylums, and the 'surfari' – the search for perfect waves – became an endless pursuit. Surfing signified self-expression, escape and freedom. Australian surfer Robert Conneeley (1978: 18) described surfing as 'the ultimate liberating factor on the planet'; fellow traveller Ted Spencer (1974: 10) claimed that he 'dance[d] for Krishna' when he surfed; and former world champion turned soul-surfer Nat Young (1970: 7) believed that by the simple virtue of riding waves, surfers were 'supporting the revolution'.

The countercultures transgressed middle-class tolerance. According to the media, surfers' long hair and beards, and their supposedly unwashed and soiled bodies, signified lack of discipline, self-indulgence and decadence. Sydney's *Sun Herald* (19 April 1971) called them 'jobless junkies'. Many surfers did consume drugs and some were members of drug networks comprising investors, organisers, traffickers and dealers (Jarratt 1997: 70–3 and 78–84; Kampion 1997: 127–32). Nonetheless, the tabloid media's depictions of surfers too often descended into gross caricatures.

The countercultures were unsustainable. Yippy leader Jerry Rubin's immortal words, 'people should do whatever the fuck they want' (Silber 1970: 58), could not reconcile alternative independence with an interdependent society. Adherents of the countercultures presented 'philosophical' environmentalism and Eastern mysticism as panaceas, but neither engaged the state nor addressed the problems of political economy. Drugs, a key source of counterculture enlightenment, might have given surfer Ted Spencer (1974: 9) 'an insight and an appreciation of the energy of ... underlying things' but, as David Caute (1988: 40) points out, 'the claimed journeys to "inner truth" degenerate, on inspection, into puddles of vomit' – or, in the case of several renowned surfers, long periods of heroin addiction. Lastly, as the young aged they discovered new priorities, particularly after the resolution of major political issues, notably the withdrawal of troops from Vietnam and the end of conscription, and the onset of economic recession in the 1970s.

Yet, paradoxically, the countercultures contributed to the development of professional surfing. The work-is-play philosophy of the countercultures encouraged one group of surfers to establish a professional circuit in the belief that it would offer them an economic avenue to eternal hedonism. But the professional circuit also introduced into surfing culture an irreconcilable tension. Implicit in all professional sport is a system of embodied ethical values and attitudes which Bryan Turner (1984: 111–2) calls 'managerial athleticism'. In short, all professional athletes must carefully manage the public presentation of their bodies to convey acceptable images, especially to potential corporate sponsors. In particular, they must demonstrate that they are self-disciplined, hard working, conscientious and determined. Thus, in trying to achieve images of 'authenticity and responsibility', the new governing associations implemented codes of conduct that compelled members to present a respectable face to sponsors and the public. Consumption of recreational drugs in particular became taboo, much to the chagrin of some surfers who suddenly found themselves disciplined by peers who were also consumers.

While it is no coincidence that many of the public criticisms directed at surfers quietly evaporated after professionals established institutional structures with explicit disciplinary functions and policies, most surfers still subscribed to the irreverent culture of the early founders. Even today, surfers continue to question the place of competition and professional surfing in particular: manicured images portrayed by professional surfers to win broad public appeal simply do not resonate with a culture that shuns institutionalism in all its guises. 'As soon as those assholes in the seventies tried to turn "surfing the artform" into "surfing the sport," surf culture suffered', complains Kit (*TransWorld Surf* 8 August 1999), a correspondent whose words echo the sentiments of thousands and illustrate that surfing is a very different, if not extreme, culture.

Irreverence, nonetheless, does not in itself explain how surfers identify with, and relate to, each other. The following section explores this issue in more detail.

Extreme relations: the surfing fratriarchy

A collective conscience, based on common understandings and experiences, is the essence of all culture. Surfbathers, for example, are conjoined in the first instance by their experiences of the 'motion of the waves', 'the instability of the sand beneath their feet', 'the sting of spray in their eyes' and 'the sudden weight of costumes filled with water and sand' (Lenček and Bosker 1998: 141). Among surfers, the common experience is a much rarer moment of transcendence in which the subject (the surfer) and the object (the breaking wave) merge as one. Surfers agree that unity with a wave, especially getting 'tubed' (locked in the cylinder created when the breaking crest pitches in front of the wall) is an orgasmic experience. Deep in the tube boardriders discover 'surfing's secret', a realm that 'tilts the otherwise ordinary planes of … existence', where time has no meaning, where fear merges with joy in a rush of adrenalin, and the racing heart of danger and the ecstasy of dance become one (Tomson 2000: 15). Such experiences 'fuel the dreams' of every surfer and put the pastime at the centre of many surfers' lives as they build lifestyles around the pursuit of the 'green room'.[1]

But common experiences do not explain the peculiar relations and patterns of bonding in surfing that, for all intents and purposes, is a highly individualistic activity. Despite common interests and purposes, surfers regularly treat others 'as if they were not there, even though they are interacting with them, often in an intense way. Verbal communication is rare during a surfing session, except between one or two friends while waiting for waves' (Pearson 1979: 152). In a seminal study, Kent Pearson highlighted surfers' use of non-verbal intimidation as a form of interaction. For example, when an individual surfer or group of surfers hinders another who is paddling to catch a wave, the latter 'may steer a collision course, thereby requiring evasive action on the part of those in the way' (Pearson 1979: 153; Zane 1992: 87–92).

Although surfing is a relatively informal pastime, surfers frequently congregate in small groups at specific local surf breaks. They jealously protect their territory against outsiders and 'kooks' (beginners). Recently, one self-proclaimed enforcer wrote to *Tracks* and publicly warned kooks 'not to step out of line, in or out of the water' at his break. Otherwise, he threatened, 'I'll be all over you' (Cherry 2000: 18). Locals generally recognise social hierarchies that provide a sense of order in the water. 'I've spent fifteen years surfing here to earn the right to get a set', explains one Narrabeen (Sydney) local, and 'so as long as anyone who paddles out here understands that, there'll never be any drama. I had to fight hard to get [a] spot out there and it was a heavy apprenticeship' (Abraham 1999: 53).

Local surfers bear many of the characteristics of sporting fratriarchies or brotherhoods. Sociologist John Loy offers some particularly interesting insights into these traits. First, sporting fratriarchies 'represent "where the action is" in [Erving] Goffman's sense of engagement in "activities that are consequential, problematic, and undertaken for what is felt to be their own sake". As Goffman points out, such action situations involve character contests, special kinds of moral games, in which contestants' moral attributes, such as composure, courage, gameness and integrity, are displayed, tested and subjected to social evaluation' (Loy 1995: 266–7). Second, 'they are in large measure modern tribal groups' (Loy 1995: 266–7). Elaborating on the latter, Loy (1995: 267) argues that 'modern tribal groups provide young men comradeship, a sense of community, an experience of excitement and adventure, and a release of youthful aggression through innocuous, if often immature, physical exploits'.

Third, sporting fratriarchies 'all have, albeit in varying degrees, established codes of honour and violent performative masculine styles' (Loy 1995: 267). Such codes and styles are critical means by which men gain membership of a fratriarchy and subsequently bond with each other. Initiates seeking membership of a fratriarchy frequently face different kinds of 'ordeals and abusive behaviour' such as 'bodily mutilation, physical testing, and verbal hazing' (Loy 1995: 270-1). While the literature contains relatively few examples of extreme forms of male bonding among surfers, such practices do occur. In the not so distant past, older surfers at Narrabeen regularly tied younger surfers to the 'grommet' pole, locked them in the rage cage (a wire basket used by lifesavers to detain stray dogs), or simply buried them to the heads in the sand. In one particular instance 'they tied Robbo and Skiddy's arms behind their backs and buried them up to their necks about two metres apart, facing each other with only their heads sticking out of the sand. They had to have a spitting competition. They had to hack gollies at each other's heads. Robbo lost so they got his scum dog, Bandit, that used to hang around the carpark and shimmied Robbo's face with Bandit's arse' (Abraham 1999: 53).

Masculine style also helps explain the traditional paucity of female surfers. In theory, the individualistic nature and non-club based structure of surfing should have facilitated strong female involvement in surfing; in practice, women found themselves shunted to the cultural margins. Fred van Dyke, an Hawaiian big-wave rider in the 1950s and 1960s, says women were solely 'props':

> You took the best looking woman you could find, sat her on the beach so she could watch everything you did, then you went out and bragged to your friends about her. So she'd sit on the beach all day, get sunburned and dehydrated, and the guy would come in and get pissed off because she didn't see his best ride. That was the scene. It was machismo to the nth degree.
>
> (Warshaw 1997: 111)

According to Loy (1995: 267), 'fratriarchies foster male domination in at least three ways: they bring men together, they keep men together, and they put women down'. Among many young male surfers, women are sexual objects and 'scoring heavily' is an important means to build credibility among peers (Noll and Gabbard 1989: 17; Young 1998: 25–6).

Women surfers concur with these accounts. American Margo Oberg remembers standing around fires after surfing sessions in the early 1960s and 'all the guys would be telling dirty, chauvinistic jokes' (Kempton 1981: 39). In 1963, a group of boys approached a young American Jericho Poppler (who would later help organise women's surfing) and demanded to know where she was from: 'I told them, "Oh, I just live down there and I have three brothers" and they told me, "You're pretty good, but why don't you come back when your tits are bigger"' (Douglas and Glazner 1999: 25). Australian Gail Couper says women surfers were regularly 'harassed and put down' in the 1970s; she even claims to have been punched on one occasion (Stranger 1998: 6–7). As a young teenager Pam Burridge thought she was one of the surfer boys. She soon realised otherwise: 'if they were being derogatory towards women, it was other women not me. Then it slowly dawned on me that that was not in fact true. It's like a family you're not allowed to belong to' (Stell 1992: 91).

Has surfing culture changed? Some commentators suggest so. They point to a sudden influx of women into surfing in the late 1990s as evidence of a new culture less hostile to women. Among the conditions explaining women's new found interest in surfing are the revival of longboards, the buoyancy and stability of which make it easy for beginners to catch waves and to learn basic skills, and the appearance of a dynamic female role model, American Lisa Andersen who won four consecutive professional world titles between 1994 and 1997. Supporters and peers maintain that Andersen's aggressive and radical surfing style helped resolve the long-running debate among women surfers over an appropriate female riding style and ultimately gave women surfers legitimacy among men (Schwab 1999). Andersen's reign also coincided with a restructuring of the women's professional surfing circuit and with more liberal attitudes towards the marketing of feminine sexuality in sport. The former, combined with more aggressive riding styles, assisted the commercial and administrative development of the women's professional surfing; the latter has resulted in younger female surfers using sexual images to entice sponsors in the belief that athleticism and feminine sexuality can co-exist comfortably (Andersen 1996: 87; Jones 1999).

In addition, the mid-1990s witnessed the launching of new magazines (*Surfing Girl*, *Chick*, *Wahine*, *Shred Betty*) and surf clothing lines devoted to women. One item of clothing, more than any other, has been identified for its positive influence on women's surfing – the female boardshort (*Wahine* 2, 2, 1996: 2; Jones 1999). Cultural perceptions of women as ornaments who merely decorated the beach meant that manufacturers did not consider producing appropriate clothing for active female surfers. Rather women's beachwear – highcut bikini bottoms and flimsy bra-tops – were 'inextricably linked to the commercialization of the female body and the commercialization of sexuality' (Hargreaves 1994: 159). 'What do you do', pleaded 'Penis Envy' in a letter to the surf magazine *Tracks* (May 1995: 15), 'when you're out there trying to learn how to surf and all you can do is keep checking your costume to make sure its not up your crack?' (To which an unsympathetic male editor replied: 'occupational hazard I'm afraid.') Boardshorts specifically cut for the female figure solved the problem instantaneously. 'Now we can actually go surfing' and not have to worry about fixing costumes, enthused Lisa Andersen (1996: 87), adding that old-style swimsuits had prevented her from performing radical manoeuvres. Observing the advance, legendary female surfer Linda Benson dolefully mused, 'I would have given anything to have the boardshorts that they are making now' (Bystrom 1998: 84).

While these conditions imply sweeping cultural change, closer analysis reveals little firm evidence of a new gender order in surfing. Longboards may facilitate learning to ride, but shortboards remain the dominant equipment and their mastery requires time, patience and distinct skills. In reality, longboards and shortboards underpin two distinct cultural genres of surfing. Those who refer to professional surfers as role models, ignore the traditional animosity between professional surfing and popular surf culture. The manicured images portrayed by professional surfers to win broad public appeal, simply do not resonate with grassroots surfers who, as seen above, are vitriolic in their condemnation. Professional female surfers may take a more relaxed approach to sexuality and see no contradictions in the concept of feminine athleticism. However, the historical legacies of the issue remain unresolved. The use of female sexuality to sell women's professional surfing will undoubtedly increase visibility and thus sponsorship, but it also detracts from their athleticism. The lines between athleticism, sexuality and eroticism are extremely fine and even finer in the context of a male-dominated culture where any presentation of the female body as a sexual object merely reinforces negative stereotypes of women.

Absence is a form of discouragement and the limited coverage of women in traditional male-dominated surfing magazines effectively denied them access to 'the symbolic resources needed to identify as surfers' (Stedman 1997: 77). Not surprisingly, then, women are enthusiastically consuming the new surfing magazines: 'I am so thrilled to see this empowering magazine for women', wrote one correspondent to the women's surf magazine *Wahine*. 'Finally a magazine that portrays women as strong and capable rather than the usual images of us as wimpified, clueless and not to be taken seriously. Vogue, Cosmo[politan] and *Glamour* could learn something from your style' (Clay 1999: 12). Yet, even the women's surfing magazines send skewed and contradictory messages to young girls, a fact not lost on several correspondents who have criticised the incongruity of fashion pages and advertisers' reliance on one particular body type. 'I think the whole fashion thing is lame. If I wanted info on skincare and what kind of clothes I should wear to the beach and be 'hip', I'd read *Seventeen*', Jesska Carilli protested in a recent edition of *Wahine*. 'Please stick to surf related articles, not girlie-surf related articles', she begged the editors (Carilli 1999: 18). Similarly, Kristin Borges accuses *Wahine* of maintaining the status quo with respect to female body shape. 'Show us women from more diverse backgrounds', she urges, or 'at the very least, let's see gear made for a wider variety of body types and aesthetic preferences' (Borges 1999: 12).

Loose-fitting, baggy boardshorts are a long way from tiny, flesh-revealing bikinis and undoubtedly they hold little appeal for heterosexual male voyeurs. Nonetheless, it is not clear that they represent a radical departure from the past. The fact that they are worn in advertisements by young models with firm, nubile bodies merely reinforces 'narrow definitions of femininity and sexuality and marginalizes or masks alternatives'. As Jennifer Hargreaves reminds us, the potential of diverse images to free women from a host of social constraints remains limited by 'a powerful heterosexual code' (Hargreaves 1994: 165 and 169). In fact, there is no evidence of a correlation between increased sales of female boardshorts and more active women surfboard riders, any more than there was a correlation between the production of sports-bras (that relieved chaffing and cutting the skin) and an increase in female runners in the 1970s. Just as many non-running women wear sports bras, so boardshorts are fashionable items of street-wear among girls and young women with no aspiration to surf or participate in surf culture.

Thus, much of the evidence that suggests the possibility of a new gender order in surfing is superficial. Indeed, many women still find the gender imbalance in surfing daunting. One female correspondent recently called it 'an intimidating sport' purely on the grounds of 'the large number of male participants' (Tran 1998: 18). Women also continue to complain about the male-focused, sexist surfing media: 'I was paging through [another surfing magazine] yesterday and while devouring those tasty travel pics, stumbled across [an advertisement] asking for photos of the "Biggest Set in North America", and they weren't talking waves. How disappointing, how discouraging to be reminded again of how women are [often] perceived in male surf culture' (Wood 1998: 19).

Finally, sporting brotherhoods are, according to John Loy (1995: 267), agonal fratriarchies, that is, male-dominated groups that emphasise the pursuit of prestige through physical prowess. The key question here is, how, precisely, do surfers allocate prestige and status?

Extreme riding: corporeal capital, prestige and big-wave surfing

Evidence shows that surfing is a particularly safe activity with the rate of injury no higher than that for fishing![2] Yet, while surfing is a comparatively safe activity, its record rests more on the fact that the overwhelming majority of participants do not venture into big-waves. Indeed, when the big swells arrive, excuses pour forth to explain absences – 'doctor's appointment', 'collecting the kids', 'work commitments', 'family engagements' (Finnegan 1992: 56). Renowned big-wave rider Ken Bradshaw observes that 'the crowds on the beach may have increased' over the last half-century, 'but the number of guys in the water on a big day has stayed about the same' (Noll and Gabbard 1989: 147). (Similarly, while their numbers escalated in the late 1990s, very few women venture into big surf. Among the better-known exceptions are Linda Benson, Betty Depolito, Maria Souza, Layne Beachley and Sarah Gerhardt.) Referring to Waimea Bay, long the shrine of big-wave riding, Bradshaw notes that the only time crowds appear is when the waves break under 18-feet: 'the first set that hits 25-feet, that's it, you're suddenly down to six or eight guys (Noll and Gabbard 1989: 146–7).

While all surfers intrinsically know that, in the words of surf-film cinematographer Bruce Brown, 'it takes a lot of guts to go out there when the waves are breaking bigger than a house' (Noll and Gabbard 1989: 78), many of the dangers are not immediately apparent, especially from the shore. For example, nearly all big rideable waves break on coral reefs, the depth of which is not always easy to decipher; surfers need an acute sense of alertness, skill and timing to avoid being pitched into a serrated coral head (Young 1998: 395). Deep holes formed by coral polyps also pose unique dangers: 'blasted' into these pitch-black caverns, it is easy to become disorientated and entombed (Wolf 2000: 81–2). Being caught in the impact zone of a big wave, and churned by its turbulence like a rag-doll in a washing machine, is an extreme hazard. Greg Noll compares entanglement in a collapsing 25-foot wall of water with 'going off Niagara Falls without the barrel'. He estimates the chances of drowning at 'about eighty percent' (Noll and Gabbard 1989: 5). After wiping-out on such a wave at Makaha, Hawai'i, in 1969, Noll found himself trapped in the impact zone. Even after diving to twenty feet under the oncoming walls of whitewater, Noll was still 'thrashed': 'These waves were so big and there was so much pressure in them that, each time I went under, the pain from the pressure in my ears was almost unbearable. In waves like these, if you can't equalise the pressure by popping your ears, you can lose an eardrum. I ... tr[ied] to remain orientated towards the surface and let the turbulence carry me away from the main break' (Noll and Gabbard 1989: 5). Surfers dance in the jaws of the impact zone. It is a game of dice. Catching a wave, for example, requires the surfer to paddle in front, and sometimes directly underneath, the breaking lip; the slightest mistake – catching an edge of the board, losing balance, hesitating – means being catapulted into the impact zone.

While most explanations of the contemporary surge in extreme sports focus on individual temperaments and the apparent psychological need for individuals to find meaning by risking their lives, Bradshaw's comments above alert us to the sociological factors. Big-wave riders are surfing's warrior caste; riding giant waves bestows the greatest prestige. Indeed, irrespective of the era and performance in organised competitions, surfers have always reserved the most prestige for those who show excess courage in big waves. Ancient Hawaiian legends, for example, recount the big-wave riding feats of Kelea, Mamala, Hauailiki, Umi-a-liloa and Holoua. When the first wave in a set of tsunami washed him, his house and all of his belongings out to sea, Holoua pulled a plank from the side of his house. He used this to ride the next wave in the set, a 50-footer, back to the shore (Finney and Houston 1996: 76–7).

In riding big waves, surfers demonstrate skill, strength, endurance, cunning and, above all, courage. These traits constitute what Pierre Bourdieu calls corporeal, or physical, capital (Bourdieu 1984; Booth and Loy 1999). The real value of corporeal capital rests on the ability of an owner to convert it to other forms, notably prestige, or the recognition of individual merit.[3] In all sporting cultures, prestige is a resource for which there is intense competition. While the primary function of a culture is to build social consensus, this does not necessarily mean the elimination of the competition for prestige. On the contrary, competitors who continue to compete are the building blocks of cultural groups (Barnes 1995: 147; Horkheimer 1964: 176–7).

The competition for prestige among surfers often leads to extreme situations as oceanographer and big-wave rider Ricky Grigg and professional surfer Jeff Hackman have both testified. A member of the first small group of surfers in the modern era to ride the giant waves on the North Shore of Oahu, Hawai'i, Grigg recalls the competitive spirit and behaviour it evoked:

> You got damn scared at times. You got so scared you needed each other to do what you were doing. I've been real scared at Waimea ... I've taken off on waves at Waimea that I probably wouldn't have, had [my peers] not been watching.
>
> (Noll and Gabbard 1989: 146)

Hackman describes the 'single most electrifying' event of his surfing career occurring just prior to a contest held in 25–30 foot waves at Waimea Bay. Hackman and his fellow contestants were in the water waiting for surfers competing in the previous heat to return to shore and for their heat to begin. A set approached and 'T-Bone', a young local and member of the water patrol responsible for safety and marshalling, started paddling for a wave:

> The wave just jacked up and it was huge. It started to suck him up the face and he was at the moment of commitment. We were all so close we could see the expression on his face. He just faltered his paddling rhythm for a split second and I could tell he was wondering. Suddenly we're yelling ... at him to go, go! I'll never forget that look on his face, a mixture of apprehension and pride. I mean, what's he gonna do? Every surfer in the world that he respects and admires is watching him. Suddenly he's hanging there in space, and at that moment he knew he wasn't going to make it. He just plunged, fell out of the sky, landed on his board and the both of them got sucked back over the falls again. There was a split second where he knew he wasn't going to make that wave and where he could have pulled back, but he didn't. He pushed it too far, but he knew he had to or it wasn't worth a damn thing.
>
> (Jarratt 1997: 125)

Recently, the dimensions of big-wave riding have been radically redefined. Using finely tuned – and regularly tested and flushed! – jet skis, a small band of devotees are towing each other, like water skiers, into massive 40 and 50-foot waves that break on Hawaii's outer reefs. As well as specially shaped and weighted surfboards with cushioned straps for their feet, tow-in equipment includes a battery of safety equipment from neck braces to hospital grade oxygen.

In the quest for prestige and honour, tow-in surfing has sparked intense debate. Critics call tow-in surfers 'phonies' and label it 'cheating'. They charge that without a 'take-off and drop' the tow-in brigade evades the most dangerous part of surfing. Critic Dave Parmenter elaborates:

> Did you ever see the movie *Hatari*? They're hunting rhinos in Kenya and they have this special truck with a seat on the hood, and as they go alongside the rhino at 50mph, the guy in front drags him with a noose. To me surfing is having the rhino charge you, and you're there by yourself in a pair of trunks. It's Greg Noll, a solitary guy facing his ultimate fear, and here comes a big black one around the point. You have to choke back that fear, turn around, match the speed of the wave and choke over that ledge. These tow-in guys have the truck, and they're chasing right along with the rhino, at its speed. They're going faster than the wave right off the bat. Plus it's motors and noise, the smell of octane – that doesn't appeal to me at all. And this extreme surfing, you've got to have a partnership, your gear, your walkie-talkies. I've never thought of surfing as teamwork.
>
> (Jenkins 1997: 111)

Laird Hamilton, the undisputed king of tow-in surfing, rejects these arguments. The real issue, he says, is 'high performance and efficiency'. Being towed-in allows the surfer to get deeper into the tube, while footstraps enable the rider to 'do a bunch of slick stuff'. Moreover, towing allows surfers to 'ride the wave twice as far and be back to catch another wave' quickly. Thus, it is 'totally superior' with respect to both physical exertion and the actual time spent riding. Hamilton insists that tow-in surfing is the future: 'I'm here to surf, OK? I've done enough wiping out. I want to make the wave now. Most guys think tow-in surfing is weak, or it's not manly or something, which is great. Killer. They'll just be that much farther behind when they see the light' (Jenkins 1997: 114–15).

Parmenter is certainly correct when he refers to tow-in surfing as fundamentally changing surfer relationships by introducing support teams and teamwork. Traditionally, surfers have emphasised their individuality and relied totally on their own skills. They never expected anyone to look after their interests. Indeed, when Mark Foo drowned after wiping-out on a relatively small 18-foot wave at Maverick's, near San Francisco, in 1994, his body floated for two hours before being discovered, despite the fact that a photographer captured his last wave and wipeout on film.

Of course, even if a surfer is in trouble, peers are not necessarily in a position to help. Close friend and Makaha lifeguard, Richard 'Buffalo' Keaulana, tracked Noll's movements in the water after he wiped out in 25-foot surf in 1969. 'Good ting you wen make 'em Brudda', Keaulana told Noll as he crawled out of the water, 'cause no way I was comin' in afta you. I was jus goin' wave goodbye and say "Alooo-ha"' (Noll and Gabbard 1989: 9). By contrast, assistance is a critical ingredient of tow-in surfing where the survival of surfers trapped in the impact zone depends on their partners driving through – risking their own lives and equipment – to collect them. But even when partners arrive, things can go wrong. On one pick up, Michael Willis's partner stalled the ski in the trough of a monster wave that crashed over the pair. Amid the turbulence, Willis became entangled in the towrope and was dragged 400 metres by the ski with the line progressively tightening and cutting deeper into his leg muscle. Although he survived, the mishap cost Willis two weeks on crutches (Carroll 1997: 24).

Not surprisingly then, choosing a partner is no light matter. 'Being there in a crisis' is Laird Hamilton's sole criterion:

> I can't tell you how many guys I thought were my friend, but when a really heavy situation came down and they didn't come and get me, I never looked at 'em the same. … and they know that. Not a thing they can do about it. It's like a brand (makes a sizzling noise). And there won't be another chance … They didn't cross the fine line, where it goes from courageous to the next level.
>
> (Jenkins 1997: 116)

Towing-in has expanded the boundaries of extreme surfing, allowing surfers to circumvent the physical forces that prevent them from paddling into waves over 30 feet. (At this height the water travelling up the face of the wave moves faster than surfers can paddle.) Wave size and speed, in short, are no longer physical barriers in surfing. But towing-in has not altered fundamental cultural conditions. The grassroots politics of access to tow-in breaks and the competition for prestige are as intense as ever. Indeed, towing-in has compounded the thorny dilemma faced by every surfer who prefers solitude and peace to publicity, but who simultaneously needs publicity to bolster their prestige.

Conclusion

Is surfing an extreme pastime? Analysis of the criteria used to allocate prestige in surfing, together with the irreverent and fratriarchial nature of its culture, certainly appear to justify the label extreme. But does this analysis hold when surfing is compared with other physical activities and pastimes? Other sporting and physical cultures reserve the most status for, and award the highest honours to, those with the greatest corporeal capital; fratriarchial beliefs and practices continue to pervade other sporting and physical cultures; and larrikinism (fighting, obscene language and songs, nakedness, drunkenness and vandalism against property), which is prevalent in highly respected and institutionalised sports,[4] is surely a form of irreverence.

Seen in this light, the question remains what makes surfing extreme? The answer is threefold. First, surfers are pure hedonists who, unlike mainstream sportspeople, make no claims about the social utility of their activity. Second, surfing does not have an institutional structure in which members can hide their irreverent or anti-social conduct. Ironically, many established sports ignore the anti-social behaviour of their members; some even sanction it as non-threatening youthful exuberance or cathartic behaviour. Third, surfers define themselves as different. As one surfer wrote recently in a surf magazine, 'we [should] encourage surfing to be publicly damned … People don't have to fear us – they just have to NOT WANT TO BE US, not want to identify with a label that spells sick, perverted deviant' (Stedman 1997: 81). In other words, extreme is ultimately a matter of cultural context.

Notes

1 Some surfers believe 'just sitting' in the ocean is beneficial, 'even if no waves are caught': 'Being so close to nature enhances inner peace, well-being, calmness, self-assuredness and general happiness' (*Tracks*, May 1993: 13). While others claim that 'piling into a car with a couple of mates and heading off to your favourite stretch of coastline for a few days of surf, fun and adventure is one of the purest, most liberating aspects of the surfing lifestyle. No parents, teachers or girlfriends' (Sutherland 1995: 115).

2 The average surfer incurs four injuries (deep cuts, sprains, fractures, and so forth) every 1,000 days of riding (Renneker *et al.* 1993: 274). Most injuries happen in waves under four feet high as a result of surfers colliding with their own surfboards or the ocean bed. Shark attacks, drownings and deaths are extremely rare, although in the mid-1990s a spate of accidents saw the deaths of three experienced big-wave riders: Mark Foo, Donnie Solomon and Todd Chesser.

3 Social theorists agree that prestige is a 'prime force in human society' (Goldschmidt 1992: 48; Barkow 1975: 553–72). In his analysis of heroes, William Goode describes prestige as 'a system of social control that shapes much of social life': 'All people share

the universal need to gain the respect and esteem of others, since without it they can not as easily elicit the help of others'. Moreover, 'all individuals and groups give and withhold prestige and approval as a way of rewarding or punishing others' (Goode 1978: vii).

4 For the case of rugby see Dunning and Sheard (1979); for the case of surf lifesaving see Booth (2001).

References

Abraham, P. (1999) 'Paradise or bust', *Deep* (Summer): 42–57.

Andersen, L. (1996) 'Interview', *Tracks* (March): 86–7.

Barkow, J. (1975) 'Prestige and culture: A biosocial interpretation', *Current Anthropology*, 16, 4: 553–72.

Barnes, B. (1995) *The Elements of Social Theory*, London: UCL Press.

Booth, D. (1995) 'Ambiguities in pleasure and discipline: The development of competitive surfing', *Journal of Sport History*, 22, 3: 189–206.

Booth, D. (2001) *Australian Beach Cultures: The History of Sun, Sand and Surf*, London: Frank Cass.

Booth, D. and Loy, J. (1999) 'Sport, status, and style', *Sport History Review*, 30, 1: 1–26.

Borges, K. (1999) 'Letter', *Wahine* (Fall): 12.

Bourdieu, P. (1984) *Distinction: A Social Critique of the Judgement of Taste*, London: Routlege.

Bystrom, C. (1998) *The Glide: Longboarding and the Renaissance of Modern Surfing*, Palm Beach, Queensland: Duranbah Press.

Carilli, J. (1999) 'Letter', *Wahine* 5, 3: 18.

Carroll, N. (1997) 'Yikes!' *Good Weekend* (Supplement to the *Sydney Morning Herald*), 6 December: 24–8.

Caute, D. (1988) *Sixty-Eight: The Year of Barricades*, London: Hamish Hamilton.

Cherry , S. (2000) 'Letter', *Tracks* (January): 18.

Clay, T. (1999) 'Letter', *Wahine* (Fall): 12.

Conneeley, R. (1978) 'Interview', *Tracks* (April): 15–19

Douglas, T. and Glazner, E. (1999) 'The real gidget', *Wahine*, 5, 2: 20–33.

Dunning, E. and Sheard, K. (1979) *Barbarians, Gentlemen, and Players : A Sociological Study of the Development Of Rugby Football*, Oxford: M. Robertson.

Finnegan, W. (1992) 'Playing doc's games', *The New Yorker*, 24 August: 34–59.

Finney, B. and Houston, J. (1996) *Surfing: A History of the Ancient Hawaiian Sport*, Rohnert Park, CA: Pomegranate Artbooks.

Goldschmidt, W. (1992) *The Human Career*, Cambridge: Blackwell.

Goode, W. (1978) *The Celebration of Heroes*, Berkeley: University of California Press.

Hargreaves, J. (1994) *Sporting Females: Critical Issues in the History and Sociology of Women's Sports*, London: Routledge.

Harvey, D. (1989) *The Condition of Postmodernity: An Inquiry into the Origins of Cultural Change*, Oxford: Basil Blackwell.

Hollinger, K. (1975) 'An alternative viewpoint', *Surfer* (August/September): 38–40.

Horkheimer, M. (1964) New patterns in social relations, in E. Jokl (ed.) *International Research in Sport and Physical Education*, Springfield, IL: Charles C. Thomas.

Jarratt: P. (1997) *Mr Sunset: The Jeff Hakman Story*, London: General Publishing.

Jenkins, B. (1997) 'Laird Hamilton: 20th century man', *The Australian Surfer's Journal*, 1, 1: 84–121.

Jones, R. (1999) 'Girls surf market overview', *TransWorld Surf Business Magazine*, 1, 2, www.transworldsurf.com.

Kampion, D. (1997) *Stoked: A History of Surf Culture*, Los Angeles: General Publishing.

Kampion, D. (2000) 'Up a lazy river with Bill Hamilton', *The Surfer's Journal* (Early Spring): 72–88.

Kempton, J. (1981) 'Margo', *Surfer* (July): 36–42.

Lenček, L. and Bosker, G. (1998) *The Beach: The History of Paradise on Earth*, New York: Viking.

Loy, J. (1995) 'The dark side of agon: Fratriarchies, performative masculinities, sport involvement and the phenomenon of gang rape', in K. H. Bette and A. Rutten (eds) *International Sociology of Sport Contemporary Issues: Festschrift in Honour of Günther Luschen* Stuttgart, Naglschmid.

Noll, G. and Gabbard, A. (1989) *Da Bull: Life Over the Edge*, Berkeley, CA: North Atlantic Books.

Pearson, K. (1979) *Surfing Subcultures of Australia and New Zealand*, Brisbane: University of Queensland Press.

Renneker, M., Star, K. and Booth, G. (1993) *Sick Surfers Ask the Surf Docs and Dr Geoff*, Palo Alto, CA: Bull Publishing Company.

Schwab, F. (1999) 'Inspirational waters', *Los Angeles Times*, 22 July.

Silber, I. (1970) *The Cultural Revolution: A Marxist Analysis*, New York: Times Change Press.

Spencer, T. (1974) 'Interview', *Tracks* (August): 9–12.

Stedman, L. (1997) 'From gidget to gonad man: Surfers, feminists and postmodernization', *ANZJS*, 33, 1: 75–90.

Stell, M. (1992) *Pam Burridge*, Sydney: Angus and Robertson.

Stranger, M. (1998) 'Deconstructing gender in the pursuit of thrills: An alternative approach to sexism in surfing culture', unpublished paper.

Sutherland, M. (1995) 'Surf trippin', *Tracks* (September): 115.

Titchen, J. (1966) Letter to Warringah Shire Council, 14 March, Warringah Shire Council, Parks and Baths, File 20A.

Tomson, M. (2000) 'The horror: Deconstructing Teahupoo', *The Surfer's Journal* (Summer): 10–27.

Tran, Y. (1998) 'Letter', *Wahine* 4, 4: 18.

Turner, B. (1984) *The Body and Society*, Oxford: Basil Blackwell.

Warshaw, M. (1997) *Above the Roar: 50 Surfer Interviews*, Santa Cruz: Waterhouse.

Wolf, D. (2000) *Sleeping in the Shorebreak and Other Hairy Surfing Stories*, Manhattan Beach, CA: Waverider Publications.

Wood, D. (1998) 'Letter', *Wahine* 4, 4: 19.

Young, N. (1970) 'Letter', *Tracks* (October): 7.

Young, N. (1998) *Nat's Nat and That's That*, Angourie, New South Wales: Nymboida Press.

Zane, W. (1992) 'Surfers of Southern California: Structures of identity', unpublished MA Thesis, McGill University.

Part II

Ambivalent masculinities

Identity and difference

6 Taking risks

Identity, masculinities and rock climbing

Victoria Robinson

Introduction

The social significance of sport at both local and global levels, in traditional and extreme, or alternative forms, has become increasingly apparent through theoretical concern with sporting identities (see for example Donnelly and Young 1988; Messner and Sabo 1990; Coakly and Donnelly 1999; McKay *et al.* 2000). These studies are informed by investigations of shifting, flexible and multiple hegemonic masculine identities that have emerged in the sociological and cultural studies literature (see Connell 1995).

There have been a number of studies done on men, masculinities and identities in relation to sport (see for instance Sabo and Messner 1994 and McKay *et al.* 2000). Connell also argues that '(i)n western countries, [...] images of ideal masculinity are constructed and promoted most systematically through competitive sport' (Connell 1987: 85). However, as de Garis (2000) contends, most research on masculinity ideology in sport has been confined to young males in mainstream organised sports. Non-mainstream or marginalised sports have been neglected. But this is changing and there have been an increasing number of works which seek to expand the study of 'new sports' (Wheaton and Tomlinson 1998; Wheaton 2000a, 2000b), or 'whiz sports' (Midol and Broyer 1995). These sports are supposedly less about competition, status, bravado and arguably more individualistic, potentially less gendered and more about co-operation.

However, there are still few detailed grounded studies available, which explore from the viewpoint of the everyday experience of participants, the specific culture of extreme sports. Rock climbing, for instance, has not been analysed in any major and sustained way. Though there is some theoretical work on rock climbing, for example Donnelly and Young (1999), Lewis (2000 and this volume), Donnelly (2003) and Dornian (2003), the sport has so far received little sustained critical attention in relation to other extreme or 'risk' sports such as windsurfing or skateboarding (Wheaton and Tomlinson 1998; Wheaton 2000a, 2000b; Borden 2001). I am therefore chiefly concerned here with investigating the diversity of masculine identities in the sport of rock climbing which I define as an 'extreme' sport. (This is because of the possible injury involved in participating as well as the risk taking by some of the participants involved in the sport.) My research on climbing challenges the optimistic, if not simplistic, dichotomies of 'new' and traditional sporting activities. I take issue with the idea that extreme sports necessarily allow for a more relaxed sporting masculine ideology whilst more commercial sports do not. As well, the fact that climbing can be seen as more commercial than previously also needs to be noted.

In this chapter, I will theoretically contextualise my study of men, masculinities and climbing, then use the data from my interviews to interrogate recent debates around sporting bodies and gendered notions of risk and competition. I will also propose that a concept I am developing of 'mundane extremities' can inform debates around the extreme and the everyday in the sport of rock climbing. Lastly, I will investigate shifting masculinities in relation to other sports, specifically in relation to age and gender, arguing that with the latter, exploring patterns of intimacy can be useful to see if gender relations are changing in any substantial manner.

Rock climbing is one of the fastest growing extreme sports in the UK. Though more men engage in climbing, it is a risk sport which is participated in by women and men. Recent figures from the British Mountaineering Council (BMC), reveal a notable increase in female members. In 1999 the BMC had 13,000 individual members with 12 per cent being female. In 2000 that had increased to 24,000 members, with 18 per cent of that total being women. Though I am concentrating on 'traditional' rock climbing, climbing as a sport is very diverse in terms of the forms it can take. Traditional climbing, using ropes, involves placing protection into the rock to allow an ascent to be made (though 'soloing' means the rock is climbed without the aid of ropes or other protection). This form of climbing can encompass short or long routes which can be completed within minutes or days, for example, with big wall climbing. With traditional climbing, either on rock or ice, the fear is that the protection that a climber has placed themselves may not hold. Added to this is the possibility of being 20 or 30 feet above the last piece of protection placed, so falling off a route can have serious, even fatal consequences. Mountaineering involves longer routes and is traditionally associated with adventure, risk and danger, the public's imagination increasingly fuelled by global coverage of ascents of the world's highest peaks.

Sports climbing is generally judged to be less hazardous than traditional climbing and, as a consequence, less 'pure' by some in the climbing world. Sports climbing consists of climbing routes which have been equipped with bolts drilled into the rock. More routes can be climbed in a day with this safer style of climbing. The proliferation of bolted sports climbing, albeit in selected areas, has provoked much debate in the climbing world about its desirability (see Lewis, this volume). Some enthusiasts argue that bolting devalues the climbing experience and, as a consequence, sports climbing is sometimes seen as a pale imitation of traditional climbing, the latter seen as the 'real thing'. (see Donnelly 2003 for an analysis of 'adventure' climbing and 'sport' climbing. He sees the debates around these as part of the rich anarchic nature of the sport of climbing.) Though seen as a 'risk' sport, climbing is in some forms, becoming more commercialised than it has been through increased sponsorship of climbing expeditions, to the appearance of artificial crags, known as climbing walls, in many British cities. Though initially conceived of as a training aid for the ' real thing' there are now a whole generation of climbers who have learnt to climb indoors, never having been on a rock face. This creation of an artificial climbing arena was followed by organised competition climbing, league tables and an international competition climbing circuit. (See Dornian 2003 for an argument why indoor competition climbing is the ' best sport in the world' (286) and Lewis, this volume, for a very different view of sports climbing and British adventure climbing.) In contrast, the subculture of bouldering is a style of climbing a few feet off the ground, without ropes or harnesses and using thick mats as crash pads to break falls. This form of climbing takes place indoors and outdoors. In practice, many climbers will climb inside on climbing walls, as a way of training to increase strength and stamina and will also climb outdoors in a variety of styles.

Rock climbing as a sport has some interesting parallels as well as points of departure with other extreme sports. For instance, as Iain Borden argues, skateboarding is a sport which produces space, time and self, which for its practitioners '[...] involves nothing less than a complete and alternative way of life ' (Borden 2001: 1). Many of the climbers I spoke to saw climbing in this way. Climbing fits into a conception of an extreme or risk sport as a 'lifestyle' sport, partially because of the diversification of the sport as I have outlined above, as well as the increasing popularity of climbing across different age groups and genders and its increasing commercialisation. However, given the very real dangers associated with some aspects of climbing, the notion of climbing as a 'lifestyle' sport may not encapsulate climbing in all its forms, for example when real injury or death can occur. Therefore, rock climbing needs to be recognised in all its subcultural elements; traditional climbing, sports climbing, competition climbing, big wall climbing and soloing for example, as a diversifying and rapidly changing sport.

Eric Dunning (1999) argues that sport has been marginalised in attempts to come to grips with the social production of masculinity and that this can be linked to some theorists' insistence on linking sports with 'hobbies' and 'conceptualizing it as separate from 'the everyday world" (220). My focus here is on whether and how rock climbing, as a new 'lifestyle' sport, challenges traditional hegemonic sporting masculinities, allowing for more fluid and flexible gendered identities within a sporting context to be developed than previously. My argument is based on data obtained from a number of semi-structured interviews with British climbers.[1] I have investigated in these interviews how the sport of rock climbing is experienced and practised at the everyday level. The everyday experiences of men in specific sporting subcultures were problematised, so that the contradictions of their embodied experiences could be exposed and potentialities in relation to shifting identities explored. In this initial study, I documented how the subjective experience of masculinity is affected by age and gender for instance, and how certain forms and practices of masculinity are produced, primarily in traditional climbing. My research contributes to the study of everyday cultures by considering climbers as reflexive actors involved in the creation of diverse, fluid and contradictory identities. The analysis illuminates the ordinary and extraordinary aspects of everyday experience and cultural practices in a climbing sub-culture. In addition, I problematise the relationship of the extraordinary with the ordinary in everyday culture, by proposing a concept of 'mundane extremities' to explore certain aspects of the climbers' experiences.

Situating the study of men, masculinities and rock climbing

Within a sociological and cultural studies framework, particularly from feminist and critical studies of men and masculinities perspectives, a central assumption is that sport has been seen as a site of cultural struggle and cultural resistance in relation to gender (Hall 1997). Climbing is seen in my investigation as a cultural practice, and one which can be interpreted through a 'circuit of culture' (identity, representation, production, consumption and regulation) (du Gay *et al.* 1997). This allows, as Woodward (1997) utilising du Gay *et al.* asserts, a full understanding of the cultural artefact (or practices) under investigation. The circuit allows also for the different aspects to be investigated separately and to be seen as interrelated. So for instance, here I am concerned particularly with identity, but also how a climber's identity might be linked to representations.

Though I am concerned with the everyday experiences of the male climbers, it is important to note how extreme sports have been conceptualised in the context of globalisation. In his study of globalisation Maguire (1999) identifies in the latest phase of globalisation an increase in a variety of sports cultures. Global processes are now seen as characterised by the organisation of diversity and not uniformity; '(n)ew sports such as windsurfing, hand-gliding and snowboarding have emerged and 'extreme sports' have become the cutting edge for some devotees of peak experiences' (Maguire 1999: 87). Relating this to a study of the every day, I am concerned with how practices in an extreme sport such as rock climbing both reveal the extraordinary, 'cutting edge' experiences of its participants and how those ordinary and extraordinary experiences can be problematised.

Beal (1995, 1999) states in relation to the subculture of skateboarding 'sport has also been analysed as a place where dominant values and norms are challenged and where alternative norms and values are created' (1995: 252). If sport is used by a diversity of people to express, manipulate and negotiate their identities, as well as to challenge the way they are identified by others, and to assist in the creation of new social identities (MacClancy 1996), it is also crucial in the maintenance and reproduction of a specifically masculine identity. Elaborating on this idea, Dunning (1999) sees sport simultaneously as one of the most significant sites of resistance against, and challenge to, but also of production and reproduction, of traditional masculinity.

My primary concern with the everyday experiences of male climbers needs to be situated in terms of the theorising of the everyday. The importance of the everyday has a long history in the context of sociology and can be defined as a 'largely taken for granted world that remains clandestine, yet constitutes what Lefebvre calls the "common ground" or "connective tissue" of all conceivable human thoughts and activities' (Gardiner 2000: 2). Whilst Chaney (2002) suggests that the everyday acts as a space for 'other ways of being' that can be envisaged; and, in tracing the significance of changes, everyday life and what is orderly or disorderly about it needs to be closely investigated. He sees the 'common experience of normality' as giving people's lives order and stability and is what makes experiences meaningful. In contrast to this, my work is conceived with problematising precisely what a 'common experience' of the normal and everyday is for different people.

The everyday is conceived of by Highmore (2002), as potentially having an extraordinary element to it, which can be characterised as mysterious or even bizarre. The exceptional can be found in our everyday lives and it forms the contradictory and paradoxical nature of the everyday. However, my analysis seeks to problematise this idea, for in extreme sports the everyday nature of the practices which constitute these, suggests that the 'exceptional' is very quickly routinised and comes to consist of largely standardised activities.

Gardiner's (2000: 8) view that ' (i)ncreasingly, the "everyday" is evoked in a gestural sense as a bulwark of creativity and resistance, regardless of the question of assymmetries of power, class relations, or increasingly globalized market forces' needs to be borne in mind if gendered (sporting) relations are also to be seen as sites of power and dominance in the context of feminist and other criticisms (see Creedon 1994). This point is also important to bear in mind for any critical examination of the fluidity and possibilities of change in hegemonic masculinities, so that any shifts identified in sporting masculinities are seen in the continuing context of gendered and other power relations.

Taking risks: competing bodies

For the study, I conducted ten semi-structured interviews with British male rock climbers who had climbed worldwide. The climbers were from Yorkshire, Derbyshire, Wales and Dorset. All were white and in their twenties and thirties. Though my emphasis is on rock climbing, some of the climbers were also mountaineers.

As a climber myself and living in Sheffield (often referred to as the 'climbing capital' of the UK because of its proximity to diverse climbing routes and the large numbers of people who climb), I had access to a wide variety of climbers for my study and the climbers were also British Mountaineering Council officials, roped access workers, 'professional' climbers, traditional and world class competition climbers and/or worked in the climbing industry. Mainly, the climbers were part of a national 'scene'. Many of them knew each other, or had heard of each other by 'reputation'. As I climb and I knew some of the climbers personally, I had insider access both to finding my sample and to some prior knowledge of some of the interviewees in personal and social situations.

I have utilised visual material as stimulus in the interview process. This was either in the form of photographs I had of others climbing, or photographs from climbing magazines, where some of the rock climbers I interviewed had been featured. Many of the interviewees will have taken photographs of themselves and other climbers. I was mindful of Nettleton and Watson's (1998) suggestion of the importance of visual prompts in using a range of methods for accessing lay accounts of the body, as well as Benyon's (2002) stress on the importance of the visual as a research method in accessing masculinities and male subjectivities. The utilising of visual matter as stimulus in the interview process met with varied levels of responses. Some were not happy to talk about their self image either in photographs they had of themselves or pictures/articles of themselves in climbing magazines. Some were uneasy and seemed to think they were bragging about their climbing exploits to me. The most useful outcomes from using the visual material was that I was able to further explore the notion of the denial of overt competition in climbing, how the climbers managed their reputations in the climbing world and their own body image. For instance, one said in relation to being on the cover of a famous British climbing magazine:

> It is definitely good seeing yourself when you are in a powerful position …cos the thing is I'm never ever defined like some of the other people are so I always think I look fat. There's only a couple of times when I've seen myself on… on… on photographs, where you think, god I'm thin and ripped.
>
> (27-year-old climber)

This competitive aspect of climbing, which could be construed in terms of a status consciousness for climbers, will be explored in more detail later in the chapter.

A predictable and central finding of my study was the importance of the body, which is understandable, given that it is the body which has perhaps captured the imagination of those writing on men, masculinities and sport more than anything else. In relation to bodies, embodiment and everyday cultures, Nettleton and Watson (1998) argue that it is surprising, given the centrality of the body in relation to everyday life, that there has been little empirical research into how humans experience their body, particularly research which prioritises '[…]engaging ordinary men and women in talk about their personal bodily experiences' (1998: 2).

Challenges also remain in theorising the role of the body in relation to structure, agency and material practice (Backett-Milburn and McKie 2001). These challenges can be undertaken by a recognition that aspects of the body such as training routines, dieting and body image relate to men's everyday experiences of 'being men'. It is through taking account of people's perceived sense of agency in everyday situations that we can start to unpack ideas such as how, through sport, different cultures construct an image of ideal masculinity, a global archetype of manliness. Whether and how ordinary, and extraordinary, everyday practices disturb such archetypes is an issue to consider.

The climbers I interviewed who would be regarded, and who regard themselves, as a sporting 'elite', were openly obsessed with training regimes, dietary habits, and body image, thus supporting arguments that men in general are becoming more body conscious, some even anorexic, and that it is more socially acceptable to voice such concerns (see Williams and Bendelow 1998). All the climbers interviewed were concerned with weight gain in relation to their climbing. All but one, who was 'naturally thin', had dieted to different degrees. There was even an element of covert competition in terms of who dieted the most extremely or effectively:

> The thing is. It's such a crucial thing. You lose sixteen pounds and you're ten percent stronger. It can be really obsessive, but it does work as well. I've been ridiculously obsessive at times. I used to weigh potatoes. I'd go on a 1000 calories a day diet.
>
> (29-year-old climber)

At the same time, we need more empirical evidence of how people experience their bodies in different ways according to their gender. In relation to climbing, Lewis (2000) has examined the climbing body in detail, specifically the hands of a climber, but does not differentiate the climbing body or body parts, in gendered terms. Starting to analyse the climbing body in terms of what is perceived as 'masculine' or 'feminine' climbing styles, movements and skills in terms of everyday practices and how this connects to a gendered sense of self, as well as examining training regimes and dieting habits would elaborate on work already done on bodies and body practices, in specific sporting environments. My data revealed that some male climbers particularly associated 'slab climbing', where the style of climbing calls for balance and nimbleness, with women climbers, who were seen as more suited to this type of climbing.

The gendered notion of 'risk' and competition was another particularly interesting finding. This provided material to both support and add to the findings of other studies of sports. The notions of risk, violence in sport and injury have been looked at in relation to masculinity and identity. (For example Curry and Strauss 1994; Young *et al.* 1994; Dyck 2000.) Young and White (2000: 126) argue that 'the cultures of some sports continue systematically to produce high injury rates not only because of the financially driven emphasis on winning but also because of the connection between aggression and the process of masculinization'.

But how is risk negotiated in individualistic and (supposedly) non-competitive sports like climbing for example? If it is common, as Young *et al.* (1994) assert in male-defined sports such as athletics, that willingness to risk injury is as highly valued as demonstrating pure skill, how does this translate into more individualistic 'extreme' sports? In relation to skateboarding, Borden (2001: 53) quotes young male skateboarders talking about the pain, danger and bodily injury involved in a new sport and links this to the 'competitively collective nature of the group' created by an extreme set of individual attitudes and actions. Male bonding is created by such injuries through an aggressive masculinity.

The reactions of the rock climbers I interviewed to sports injuries supports Young *et al.* (1994) who argue that privileging forceful notions of masculinity are highly valued and serious injury is framed as a masculinising experience. One climber, who had never been able to climb properly for more than nine months in a year without having an injury which stopped him climbing for up to six to eight weeks said:

> I probably take risks with what I do... It's one of those sports where you learn by your mistakes... But also I don't give up. So I keep trying something, trying something, keep trying something until I either do it or my body's falling apart... till your fingers are bleeding whatever. I just keep going... I like being obsessive.
>
> (35-year-old climber)

Young and White's (2000) conclusion that men expose themselves to risk and injury because the rewards of hegemonic masculinity remain meaningful for them, despite the attendant dangers attached to this, needs to be investigated in diverse sporting contexts to assess whether the potential/actual/symbolic rewards are the same for all men. In relation to climbing, a pertinent question to consider is how does risk taking in relation to potential death, take on its meaning in relation to masculine identities?

An article by Neil Lewis (2000) explores the experience of the 'marginal situation of death' in relation to rock climbing and argues that adventure rock climbing embodies the possibility of witnessing the death of others and anticipating one's own death in real life and in the imagination. Such notions of risk in extreme sports need to be examined, but in a gendered sense for it to be fully appreciated how consideration of these new sports adds to our understanding of the extraordinary in everyday life. Furthermore, it needs to be asked whether all climbing subcultures, for example, sports climbing, embody the possibility of death in the same ways.

Mundane extremities

At one level, the risk taking features and the possibility of death in climbing situations can be conceptualised as representative of the extraordinary aspects of ordinary and everyday living. However, this conceptualisation can be problematised and the implied binary rejected. Climbers are increasingly represented in the media as obsessive thrill-seekers engaging in a risky, even crazy, extreme leisure pursuit. Certainly, as I have acknowledged, risks are taken, particularly by those climbers determined to achieve a high standard of climbing in terms of the grade of climbs they can achieve. But for others, including many of those climbers determined to climb at hard levels, minimising the risk is all important. The point is to live to climb another day, in a way ordering and controlling what they see as an ordinary aspect of their life, not the extraordinary as climbing may be perceived as being in the non-climbing world. What the male climbers I interviewed have indicated to me is how mundane the activity of climbing was for them. The idea of 'mundane extremities' captures this.

Many of the climbers I interviewed implied or stated that wanting to escape the mundane by doing something extreme had to be continually worked at, with the result that the extreme aspects of climbing had to be continually reinvented, for example by climbing ever harder routes, or engaging in more and more potentially risky activities such as big wall climbing abroad. The extreme continually shaded into the mundane. One climber spoke about always wanting to be 'chasing a moment':

> Yeah, trad climbing is more, is about the fear, trad climbing is about overcoming fear, and it's just about being out there, and hoping you get that thing. I've talked to a few people about this, and a lot of people seem the same thing, you're chasing, I think, yeah, it's probably that you're chasing one moment all the time. Who was it I was talking to? An interview with somebody and they said the same thing, you're chasing a moment and you get it maybe two or three times in a year, where you're absolutely on form and you're just not scared at all, and you're just flowing, and the whole thing is a joy, and the rest of the time, you're in that nether world of half, of like, one minute you're having a great time, next minute you're shit scared and not enjoying it.
>
> (35-year-old climber)

These chased moments of transcendence occur infrequently and are only a small part of the extreme activity, which consists of practices and feelings which are mundane in that context.

If climbing as a pursuit is often taken up to put the rest of the world in perspective, or to escape the ordinariness of much of everyday living, the mundane and everyday aspects of life were seen to be needing to be re-adopted by some climbers, when getting older did not allow for them to climb at the level they wanted, or when priorities such as relationships and families were changed throughout the life course. The more mundane aspects of life, represented by paid employment, relationships and family responsibilities, were seen as necessities when they got older and could not climb as hard or as often. Consequently, their positions in relation to the mundane and the extreme shifted considerably through the life course. Such transitions, according to some of the climbers I interviewed, were not always desired or easy. The embracing of the ordinary was seen as a necessity, not necessarily a welcome choice or act of agency.

Some of the climbers also refused the label of 'the extreme' in relation to the sport of rock climbing and in doing so, were reflecting on the meaning of an 'extreme' sport across different sporting contexts. This showed that a continuum of the extreme in relation to different sports is necessary to assess participants' relationships to ideas of the extreme and what it means both for individuals and for cultural perceptions of climbing as a dangerous and risk activity. When one climber, previously a professional competition route setter, was asked if he thought climbing to be an extreme sport he replied:

> I mean, yes, it's an extreme sport, but no more so than canoeing is. You [...] kill yourself canoeing, [...] live and learn, or you go canoeing on the River Derwent or on a lake or something like that, that's not an extreme sport, but the top end is. It's the same with climbing, it's not an extreme sport, but I don't really know what that, the definition is meant to be.
>
> (38-year-old climber).

His view, was that all sports had their 'top end' of the spectrum that was more risky, more exciting, more extreme. The response from someone else was very different, however, and distinguished between 'the most dangerous' and other sports around the idea of risk management:

> It's all about risk management, or risk taking. You see, for me, the thing that I do, which is the most dangerous things I do, is go motorbike riding, which is far more dangerous than climbing. Go to the hospitals, it's just ludicrous, it's ridiculously dangerous, so, yeah, but then again, I have put myself in quite a few positions, where you think, ah, you've blown this or you're going to die or break your legs, or, oh what am I doing here, you know. So, yeah, and you can be really, and you can injure yourself quite badly in a very short fall, and you can be really unlucky, but because I know it's [...] you don't think of it as being that dangerous.
>
> (35-year-old climber)

Often the climbers I interviewed commented that mountaineering, as opposed to rock climbing, was a more dangerous and risky activity, because the chances of death or serious injury were perceived as more likely, and most of them personally knew another rock climber or a mountaineer who had died or been seriously injured. There is the recognition that climbing can be a dangerous sport and a climber can either manage risk to minimise the possibility of injury or death, or court risk as part of the management of an extreme experience. Their responses to my questions revealed less about differences between extreme sports and more about whether they perceived their own climbing practices as more or less risky. The concept of what is extreme, then, is not fixed and is rather a relational concept in regard to (shifting) subject positions and particular everyday practices when engaging in the sport.

Shifting everyday masculinities

Studies which connect a concern with hegemonic masculinities to less achievement orientated sports have been concerned with skateboarding and windsurfing, for example Beal 1995 and 1999 and Wheaton 2000b and Chapter 7, this volume. My study on climbing can substantiate and add to these investigations and contribute further to a knowledge of masculine identities.

Becky Beal (1995, 1999) acknowledges that a variety of subgroups skateboarded, and that there were those who wanted to skate professionally and those who rejected the sport's professionalisation, demonstrating 'a continuum of hegemonic to counter-hegemonic behaviour' (1999: 255). This is similar to climbing which is currently in the process of diversifying as a sport, so that there are sponsored competition climbers, climbers who climb for a living and those who view climbing as purely a leisure activity. The climbers I interviewed were aware of such divisions and also categorised them. A central distinction being that for the 'elite' climbers, other climbers who 'only climbed at weekends' or whose level of climbing skill was perceived to be lower than their own were classed as 'bumblies'.

Beal recognises that numerous individual and daily resistances occur in mainstream sport, but chooses her subcultural form of resistance because it entails ritualistic patterns which go beyond individuals testing the limits of organised sports practices. Others for instance, Salisbury and Jackson (1996), have asserted that in relation to boys' sporting activities, alternative sports such as climbing, canoeing, outdoor pursuits and orienteering will allow boys who hate the often humiliating and pressurised climate of team games to have personal challenges, as such sports can offer confidence building and self esteem. Boys can find their own comfortable levels with no comparative pressure being brought to bear. But this assumed and unproblematised dichotomy between team competitive sports and more individualised 'relaxed' ones needs to be further explored through different sports and through empirical research..The men in my sample often saw climbing as having a competitive element, but tended to deny competition as existing between each other:

> It's not me versus you, it's us versus that, be it the problem or route or whatever.
>
> (36-year-old climber)

> You just totally compete with yourself.
>
> (35-year-old climber)

But when pressed on this, the same climber said:

> Everyone thinks I'm really competitive, but I'm not ... when there's competition I climb a hell of a lot better.

The existence of competition between different climbing subgroups is borne out by my experience of climbing, where people are 'sandbagged' into thinking a route is easier than it is, and so are set up to fail. This is done sometimes as a joke, and sometimes more seriously.

What Beal does not do (1999) is to look at participants who manage to have links with different subgroups within the subculture, where a competitive ethos may differ. What would be useful is to look at the relationships between different subgroups through individuals who 'cross over'. For example, in climbing, though there are diverse groups who range from the professional to the 'bumblies', there are those climbers who link the elite groups with bumblies – whose climbing partners may come from either/or both subgroups. Through this examination, the notion of competition, and specifically the notion of a status hierarchy in different sporting contexts, can be broadened out. How different masculinities relate to specific subgroups would also be interesting to investigate.

Belinda Wheaton's studies on masculinity, identity and windsurfing culture (2000b and Chapter 7, this volume) are concerned, amongst other things, to look at how competing masculinities are negotiated within a sporting environment and how this can broaden out recognised boundaries of sporting masculinities. A central research question for her is whether gendered relations, in particular sporting masculinities in a specific sports culture, are re-negotiated and/or reconstructed, and her chosen conceptual framework of hegemonic, plural and contested or competing masculinities, are useful in exploring masculinities in the context of other extreme sporting cultures such as rock climbing. There were similarities to my study and how the data could be interpreted in her recognition that age and life experiences were key variables in terms of how the windsurfers interviewed competed with and related to each other, as well as providing a context for how they conceptualised and made sense of their own sporting achievements.

For instance, many of the older climbers I spoke to conceptualised a 'golden age' in the 1980s in Britain, where many climbers were on the 'dole' and honed their climbing talents sometimes to world class standard. Areas such as Sheffield in Yorkshire and Llanberis in North Wales were known centres of the sport, where climbers who climbed at a range of grades formed close subcultures, sometimes over a period of years. These times were often conceptualised by a number of climbers as a period in which they had no responsibilities in terms of paid work, family responsibilities, or relationships. These times were mourned as passing because of wider changes in society, often defined by the connection of climbing becoming more commercialised in a material world and because of their own sense of ageing. Many had taken jobs in connection to the climbing world to maintain those links as they got older. As one 39-year-old climber said: 'I have my job because I want to be involved in climbing'. Another, after talking about getting older, the passing of 'the golden age' of climbing for him and new found responsibilities of paid work said:

> One day you enjoy the fact that you're dead scared. Then the next day you enjoy the fact that you are really strong. And the next day you enjoy the fact that you're just having some banter at the crags with people ... And it's different when you're sixteen as to when it feels like now. Now sometimes it just feels like the only time I can shut off completely from the world.
>
> (35-year-old climber)

In addition to this, climbing can be defined as a performance with the climber performing for themselves and usually an audience. The climbing 'gaze' is often between older males, who stare with a variety of feelings towards up and coming climbers younger and fitter and more reckless than themselves. What is the relationship between men's aging bodies and their changing masculine subjectivities? Such questions point to the fluidity and changing disruptions of masculinities and male subjectivities in the context of the everyday.

Theorists of masculinity have been accused of studying masculinity at the expense of gendered power relations between the sexes. There is evidence, as McKay *et al.* (2000) state, that this tendency is being rectified, but as they argue, we continue to need studies of both 'men's' and' women's' sports but need to be more aware of taking into account unequal power relations in single gender sport contexts. The studies by Beal (1995, 1999) and Wheaton (2000a) look at newer, less traditional sporting environments to examine men's attitudes to women participants. Beal's (1999) findings that of the 41 skaters interviewed, only four were women and other women associated with the sport were 'skate betties', stands in interesting comparison to Wheaton's 'windsurf widows' or, here, climbing 'belay bunnies', women who don't often climb but who hold the ropes of their boyfriends to ensure that they can climb safely. With an increasing number of female rock climbers already referred to, some pushing hard at the grades, men's attitudes to increased female participation needs further analysis. In the interviews I conducted, a significant aspect of identity for those I interviewed was gender difference in terms of male climbers comparing themselves to female climbers, where there were diverse responses to women climbing better than themselves.

In the framework of her identification of this specific sport as a 'male heterosexual arena', through men's attitudes to both female participants and those labelled ' beach babes', Wheaton's findings (Chapter 7, this volume), on female and male windsurfers, revealed diverse attitudes to women windsurfers ranging from respect and acceptance to negative attitudes. Borden (2001: 263) found that skaters are mostly young men in their teens and twenties, with 'broadly accommodating dispositions towards skaters of different classes and ethnicity', but here too, gender relations are problematic, with female skaters being discouraged by convention and including sexist objectification. Older skaters were also seen to face prejudice whilst homophobic attitudes and homosocial masculinity were created in a skateboarding environment.

The climbers interviewed also revealed diverse attitudes to being asked if they thought women climbers faced prejudice:

> It's a mixture. I mean some they'll get preferencial treatment, but they'll get a lot of bad reaction, analysing exactly how they did it [the climb] much more than they'd analyse men.
>
> (26-year-old climber)

Others rarely, if ever, climbed with women, though this was seen in relation to the fact that they would not climb with anyone who climbed at a lower standard than themselves. It was just that, for these climbers, there were not many women climbing at the higher grades.

Another interesting and related aspect of those interviews, concerns the light thrown by men 'doing intimacy' in this extreme sport, on debates around the emotions intimacy and trust. Lynn Jamieson (2002) argues that intimacy should be thought of as a set of practices and that it is through these that how men are 'doing intimacy' differently can best be perceived, while Williams (2001) wonders if gendered emotional stereotypes are breaking down around a pluralisation of masculinities. In this context, men's views on, and relationships with, women climbers, can reveal much about changing patterns of intimacy and emotional relations.

One interviewee had climbed with a former girlfriend who has an international reputation and climbs harder grades than him. He commented that he had more arguments when climbing with her than with any other partners (though she has a reputation for being very tempestuous as a person). This is however, perhaps related to his comment that the normally protective attitude towards women climbers displayed by many men, was absent from their relationship because of the standard she climbed at.

Another, on the other hand said categorically:

> I wouldn't, I just refuse to go out with girls, because, you'd always, for me my time was precious and the last thing I would do with anybody, girls, boys, was go pandering to them, like, oh, come on, you can do this problem, come on, it's only. Fuck off, I'm not interested, you know, I'm just really not interested.
>
> (35-year-old climber)

He justifies this by saying that he would not climb with anyone who climbed at lower grades than himself, but the terms he uses are unintentionally revelatory, with 'girls' and 'boys' and 'pandering', suggesting a very patronising approach. However, it should also be noted that the same climber, when talking about a woman climber who climbs at a very high standard, also said:

> we went on an (ice) climbing trip together and we were both absolutely rubbish. I'd been once, she'd never been, we borrowed all the stuff, we had no idea what we were doing and where we were going, and it was, and I was just, don't [...] we might as well just soldier on, and she was bursting into tears [...], but after like a year later, it was completely the other way round. I was just like, 'oh, get me out of here, I don't like this, get me to the top', sort of thing.

In this extract, it was through climbing with a woman who was better than himself that he could admit his fear and feelings of vulnerability. The question of if, how and to what extent masculinities are pluralising in positive and more democratic ways can be explored through a consideration of extreme sporting activities in which women are beginning to enter and become competent in. Ordinarily, and in mundane ways within the extreme, men's emotions are made explicit and are 'handled' within the practices that constitute these. Women's entry into this sport disrupts those practices and renders the mundane, and the extreme, problematic.

Conclusion

Through analysis of my data, I have identified some central emerging issues and questions around the body, the notion of risk, competition, age and gendered relations. I would also argue that to investigate sporting masculinities in a more diverse and comprehensive way than has been done previously, a problematising of the extreme and mundane aspects of sports as they are practised at local and everyday levels, from the viewpoint of the people involved, is necessary. In doing this, debates specifically around intimacy and the emotions can be utilised and therefore expanded.

The importance of studying gendered relations in terms of shifting masculine identities was particularly obvious in exploring male climbers' attitudes to climbing with women. Here, there was evidence to support the argument that men have diverse and often contradictory attitudes to more female climbers entering the sport. Further study could extend the analysis to women climbers who climbed at different levels and with both male and female climbing partners. Such a focus could illuminate the everyday for instance in asking what, if any, are the gendered differences between women and men climbers in taking calculated risks in their everyday sporting practices and routines to achieve a sporting goal, or dealing with pain and injury? Or if and how do women and men deal differently with competitiveness in climbing situations given that women are now climbing harder grades?

For further and more detailed consideration of the everyday, a comparative study of individual men in their different contexts and habitats; the sporting world and their sense of their masculine selves, as well as how they feel at work, in their families and in relationships, could be undertaken. As Giulianotti observes in his study of men and football, masculine identity is complex and multi-faceted : 'Outside football, they adopt other masculine roles as partners, parents, children, workmates and social friends' (1999: 156). Whilst in relation to a more alternative sport, Borden (2001) argues that through graphics, words and ideologies, skateboarders reject the external world, especially paid work and the family. How does that rejection inform their relationships and family connections outside of a sporting context? Meanwhile, de Garris (2000), found egalitarian practices in the gym, for example, male boxers accepting female boxers, but no such evidence of egalitarian practices being extended to other areas of their lives. Any future research with male climbers, either through interviews or participant observation which prioritises the investigation of the everyday in grounded empirical studies, would allow the charting of men's increasingly shifting and enmeshed relationship to both public and private spheres.

Wheaton's conclusion (Chapter 7, this volume), that her research demonstrates that windsurfing is not a site for a radical 'new' embodied masculine identification, but that men's relationships with women and other men are complex and variable is borne out in my study. Clearly, climbing forms part of the changing discourse of identity and masculinities, but more research needs to be undertaken to explore in detail if climbers challenge traditional/dominant notions of gender roles, identity and power, or merely appear to re-invent them, while in reality they are reconstructing existing ones.

Gardiner's view is that daily life contains '... redemptive moments that point towards a transfigured and liberated social existence.' (2000: 208), that can generate new forms of personal identity. This can be explored through analysis of men's (and women's) need to scale rocks and mountains and through their own very different stories of why they do something which seems extraordinary, as well as unfathomable, to most people.[2]

Acknowledgements

I would like to thank Elizabeth Silva, Liz Stanley and Kath Woodward for their help and comments on earlier versions of this work.

Notes

1 This research was funded by the Open University, Pavis Centre in the context of their National Everyday Cultures Programme.

2 This chapter has emerged out of a working paper published by the Open University (Robinson 2002) and a PhD (by published work) awarded by the University of Manchester, UK in 2003. See Robinson (2003).

References

Backett-Milburn, K. and McKie, L. (eds) (2001) *Constructing Gendered Bodies*, Basingstoke: Palgrave.

Beal, B. (1995) 'Disqualifying the official: An exploration of social resistance through the subculture of skateboarding', *Sociology of Sport Journal*, 12, 3: 252–67.

Beal, B. (1999) 'Skateboarding: an alternative to mainstream sports' in Coakly, J. and Donnelly, P. (eds) *Inside Sports*, London: Routledge.

Beynon, J. (2002) *Masculinities and Culture*, Buckingham: The Open University.

Borden, I. (2001) *Skateboarding, Space and the City: Architecture and the Body*, Oxford: Berg.

Chaney, D. (2002) *Cultural Change and Everyday Life*, Basingstoke: Palgrave.

Coakley, J. and Donnelly, P. (eds) (1999) *Inside Sports*, London: Routledge.

Connell, R. W. (1987) *Gender and Power*, Cambridge: Polity Press.

Connell, R.W. (1995) *Masculinities*, Cambridge: Polity Press.

Creedon, P. J. (ed.) (1994) *Women, Media and Sport: Challenging Gender Values*, London: Sage.

Curry, T. J. and Strauss, R. H. (1994) 'A little pain never hurt anybody: A photo-essay on the normalization of sport injuries', *Sociology of Sport Journal*, 11: 195–208.

de Garis, L. (2000) ' "Be a buddy to your buddy": Male identity, aggression, and intimacy in a boxing gym' in McKay, J., Messner, M. and Sabo, D. (eds) *Masculinities, Gender Relations and Sport*, London: Sage.

Donnelly, P. (2003) 'The great divide: Sport climbing vs. adventure climbing' in Rinehart, R.E. and Sydnor, S. (eds) *To The Extreme: Alternative Sports, Inside and Out*, Albany: State University of New York Press.

Donnelly, P. and Young, K. (1988) 'The construction and confirmation of identity in sports subcultures', *Sociology of Sport Journal*, 5: 223–40.

Donnelly, P. and Young, K. (1999) 'Rock climbers and rugby players: identity construction and confirmation' in Coakley, J. and Donnelly, P. (eds) *Inside Sports*, London/New York: Routledge.

Dornian, D. (2003) 'Xtreem' in Rinehart, R.E. and Sydnor, S. (eds) *To The Extreme: Alternative Sports, Inside and Out*, Albany: State University of New York Press.

du Gay, P., Hall, S., Janes, L., Mackay, H. and Negus, K. (eds) (1997) *Doing Cultural Studies: The Story of the Sony Walkman*, London: Sage / The Open University.

Dunning, E. (1999) *Sport Matters: Sociological Studies of Sport, Violence and Civilization*, London: Routledge.

Dyck, N. (ed.) (2000) *Games, Sports and Cultures*, Oxford: Berg.

Gardiner, M. E. (2000) *Critiques of Everyday Life*, London: Routledge.

Giulianotti, R. (1999) *Football: A Sociology of the Global Game*, Cambridge: Polity.

Hall, S. (ed.) (1997) *Representation: Cultural Representation and Signifying Practices*, London: Sage / The Open University.

Highmore, B. (2002) *Everyday Life and Cultural Theory*. London: Routledge.

Jamieson, L. (2002) 'Contextualising friendship and relationships across the life course' (unpublished paper), Research on Families and Relationships Conference, University of Edinburgh, November, 2002.

Lewis, N. (2000) 'The climbing body, nature and the experience of modernity', *Body and Society*, 6, 3–4: 58–80.

MacClancy, J. (1996) *Sport, Identity and Ethnicity*, Oxford: Berg.

Maguire, J. (1999) *Global Sport: Identities, Societies, Civilizations*, Cambridge: Polity.

McKay, J. Messner, M. and Sabo, D. (eds) (2000) *Masculinities, Gender Relations and Sport*, London: Sage.

Messner, M. and Sabo, D. (eds) (1990) *Sport, Men and the Gender Order*, Champaign, US: Human Kinetics Publishers.

Midol, N. and Broyer, G. (1995) 'Toward an anthropological analysis of new sport cultures: The case of whiz sports in France', *Sociology of Sport Journal*, 12: 204–12.

Nettleton, S. and Watson, J. (eds) (1998) *The Body in Everyday Life*, London: Routledge.

Robinson, V. (2002) 'Men, masculinities and rock climbing', Pavis Papers in Social and Cultural Research, Buckingham: The Open University.

Robinson, V. (2003) 'Everyday heterosexualities and everyday masculinities: The mundane and the extreme', PhD Thesis, (by published work), University of Manchester: UK.

Sabo, D and Messner, M. (1994) 'Changing men through changing sports: An eleven point strategy' in Messner, M. and Sabo, D. (eds) *Sex, Violence and Power in Sports: Rethinking Masculinity*, Freedom, CA: Crossing.

Salisbury, J. and Jackson, D. (1996) *Challenging Macho Values: Practical Ways of Working With Adolescent Boys*, London: Falmer Press.

Wheaton, B. and A. Tomlinson (1998). 'The changing gender order in sport? The case of windsurfing', *Journal of Sport and Social Issues*, 22: 252–74.

Wheaton, Belinda (2000a) '"New lads"? Masculinities and the "new sport" Participant', *Men and Masculinities*, 2, 4: 434–56.

Wheaton, Belinda (2000b). 'Just do it: Consumption, commitment and identity in the windsurfing subculture', *Sociology of Sport Journal*, 17, 3: 254–74.

Williams, S. (2001) *Emotion and Social Theory*, London: Sage.

Williams, S. J. and Bendelow, G. (1998) *The Lived Body: Sociological Themes, Embodied Issues*, London: Routledge.

Woodward, K. (ed.) (1997) *Identity and Difference*, London: Sage.

Young, K. and White, P. (2000) 'Researching sports injury: Reconstructing dangerous masculinities' in McKay, J. Messner, M. and Sabo, D. (eds) *Masculinities, Gender Relations and Sport*, London: Sage.

Young, K., White, P., and McTeer, W. (1994) 'Body talk: Male athletes reflect on sport, injury and pain', *Sociology of Sport Journal*, 11, 2: 175–94.

7 'New lads'?

Competing masculinities in the windsurfing culture*

Belinda Wheaton

> What is a Real Man? A Real Man is strong, tough, aggressive, and above all, a winner in what is still a Mans' World. [...] He must be willing to compromise his own long-term health by showing guts in the face of danger, by fighting other men when necessary, and by 'playing hurt' when he's injured. [...] his aggressiveness will net him the ultimate prize: the adoring attention of conventionally beautiful women. He will know if and when he has arrived as a Real Man when the Voices of Authority – White Males – *say* he is a Real Man. But even when he has managed finally to win the big one, has the good car, the right beer, and is surrounded by beautiful women, he will be reminded by these very same Voices of Authority just how fragile this Real Manhood really is: After all, he has to come out and prove himself all over again tomorrow.
>
> (Messner *et al.* 2000: 390)

Introduction: masculine identities in transition

Late-modern societies are widely claimed to have given an increasingly prominent role to the leisure industries, and new consumer activities (Featherstone 1991). There has been a shift in emphasis away from 'production' to a more fragmented social order, one where culture and consumption have more central roles (Jameson 1991; Lash and Urry 1987; Giddens 1991). These sites of consumption, it has been argued, offer a potentially broader, and more differentiated range of masculine identities from those discourses and practices produced around work or career (Nixon 1996; Jackson *et al.* 2001; Whannel 2002; Edwards 1997). Mort (1988: 194) suggests that 'A new bricolage of masculinity' is the noise coming from the 'fashion house, the market place the terraces and the street':

> On the high streets, in the clubs, bars, brasseries, even on the terraces. It seems that young men are now living out fractured identities, representing themselves differently, feeling differently.
>
> (Mort 1988: 218–19)

* This chapter is an updated version of Wheaton, B. (2000) '"New lads?" Masculinities and the new sport participant', *Men and Masculinities*, 2: 436–58, retaining the empirical core of the original article.

Within this context, sport plays an increasingly important role, and as this chapter will illustrate, is a consumption practice that exemplifies these trends. Historically sport as a physical practice has been so closely identified with men, that it has become one of the key signifiers of masculinity in many Western societies (Connell 1995: 54).Yet, sport is increasingly experienced as a consumed 'leisure lifestyle', and so the meaning of masculinity is fought over in the playing, spectating *and* consumption of sport (Boyle and Haynes 2000; Messner *et al.* 2000; Tomlinson 2001). As Boyle and Hayne underline, on today's terraces 'a preoccupation with fashion sits alongside the more "traditional" forms of fan identification' (Boyle and Haynes 2000: 136). The period between the 1960s to the 1990s has seen an explosion in new sports forms and practices in Western societies, as well as transformations in existing sport's arrangement and cultures (see Chapter 1). Examples range from the fitness movement to the recent upsurge of lifestyle sports activities; however my focus in this chapter is windsurfing, one of these new non-urban individualised forms of lifestyle sports. This chapter explores the creation of sporting masculine identities within the windsurfing culture. The empirical basis for this discussion is extensive ethnographic research which focused on a windsurfing community centred around Silver Sands beach on the south coast of England.[1]

Masculinity and embodiment in lifestyle sports

Lifestyle sports appear to be broadly associated with the countercultural social movements of the 1960s and early 70s and subsequent social development (as documented in Chapter 1). Windsurfing, like other lifestyle sports cultures that have emerged during this historical epoch, evolved in opposition to dominant sporting cultures, and in particular the institutionalisation of sport in late modernity. The activity grew out of surfing and sailing cultures in the later 1960s and retains many of their cultural characteristics. Like surfing it is less institutionalised than more traditional 'modern' sports; has fewer formal rules and regulations, less formal restrictions and exclusion policies, and tends to be opposed to traditional forms of competition, also promoting a participatory ethos (see Booth 2001 on surfing).[2] Windsurfing does exist in institutionalised forms, most apparent in its inclusion in the yachting category in the 1984 Olympic Games (initially for men only). However, the Olympic craft is different to the short-board used by the majority of participants; furthermore, the pinnacle of sporting success tends to be associated with the wave acrobatics, slalom racing, and freestyle tricks promoted and administered by the Professional World Windsurfing Association.

These, and other characteristics differentiate windsurfing from more traditional rule-bound, competitive and 'masculinised' sport cultures that tend to be marked by combative competition, aggression, courage and toughness. Historically, traditional institutionalised sports cultures have been a central site for the creation and reaffirmation of masculine identities, and the exclusion of women (Messner and Sabo 1990). As Connell outlines:

> The institutional organisation of sport embeds definite social relations: *competition* and *hierarchy* among men, *exclusion* or *domination* of women. These social relations of gender are both realised and symbolised in the bodily performances. Thus men's greater sporting prowess has become a theme of backlash against feminism. It serves as symbolic proof of men's superiority and right to rule.
>
> (Connell 1995: 54 emphases added)

For Connell (1995: 54) sports centrality in defining masculinity in Western culture is due to the association between maleness, skill and strength. 'What it means to be masculine is, quite literally, to embody force, to embody competence' (Connell 1983: 27). Furthermore, Whitson suggests that it is those sport cultures where 'force' is most evident that celebrate 'a physically dominating, hegemonic masculinity' and are thus most likely to be part of the defence of the existing gender order (Whitson 1994: 363). By contrast, he argues that 'new sports' like skateboarding and mountain biking, may offer physical practices and sites of identities that encourage 'femininity and masculinity to be embodied in a variety of shapes and ways that allow power to be embodied in ways not tied to domination or gender' (1994: 368). These individualised activities may offer new opportunities for the development of personal skill, strength, and pleasure in physicality, for those men who do not shine in more traditional competitive sports, and in particular traditional team games (Whitson 1994, 1990). Similarly Midol and Broyer (1995: 208) assert that in these new sports the body has a 'new status' associated with 'gender liberation, characterised by its blurred boundaries.' They reason that body movements, although energetic, emphasise rhythm, grace, imagination and fluidity. Physiques are slender; their muscularity honed for efficiency rather than visibility (1995: 208). Rather than a Hemingwayesque battle *against* nature, the focus is on harmony with the environment; the 'masculine' realm of adventure, risk and danger is combined with the aesthetic and 'feminine'. In this chapter I explore embodiment in windsurfing, examining whether this is a cultural space in which sporting masculinities are re-negotiated and re-constructed.

The windsurfing culture: 'it's a man's world'

The windsurfing sport, and its culture, is clearly dominated by men. According to survey data (Profiles Survey 1994), women constituted only 13–30 per cent of British 'regular' windsurfers, of which there are an estimated 300–400,000. Between 80 to 90 per cent of the windsurfers who used Silver Sands, a coastal location, were male. They were all white, the youngest aged eight, the eldest over sixty; the majority however, were aged 30–40, which was also the largest age group in the survey data (Profiles Survey 1994). Windsurfing is a sport that is conducted in specific geographical locations, often inaccessible by public transport; it places great demands on the participant's time, and to progress involves considerable capital expenditure. British windsurfers tended to be socio-economically privileged; there was a bias towards the professional classes. Nevertheless participants in the Profiles survey represented all socio-economic groups. Correspondingly men's occupations at Silver Sands included a range of professions, including: students, bar tenders, truck drivers, builders, salesmen, scientists, doctors and dentists, and those working in the media industries. The 'voices' presented in this chapter are not representative of all windsurfing men; they describe the participants who are active members of the subculture defining *themselves* as 'windsurfers,' not the occasional or 'vacation' participant.

The male domination and masculinisation of the windsurfing culture is apparent in the discourses in and of the sport, which address the heterosexual male participant. For example, a t-shirt worn by a young male windsurfer read: 'No wind, waves, girls – no future'. The t-shirt was promoting a particular brand of windsurfing sails. A salesman in a windsurfing shop suggested that a particular windsurfing product was 'superior' – he described it as: 'really powerful – it's a man's sail'. Images of windsurfing both in the windsurfing media and popular cultural mediated forms such as TV advertising, espouse the relationship between windsurfing participation and masculinity and the 'otherness' of women. Beach scenes depict beautiful, nubile, tanned, female bodies in skimpy bathing suits that signify sexuality and the marking of sexual difference (see Wheaton 2003). These representations mirror Mulvey's analysis of the 'pleasure of looking' in narrative cinema, in which she suggests that the organisation of spectatorship in relation to Freud's scopophilic drives, is split between active/male and passive/female (Mulvey 2000). These representations, the 'active masculine control of the look and the passive feminine object of the look' (Nixon 1997: 319), reproduce positions of sexual difference maintaining this power relationship. As Willis (1982) reasons, patriarchal ideology has become so implanted in popular consciousness that female inferiority in sport is seen as natural, the 'way things are'.

It is perhaps then surprising that the author is female, and specifically that a female field-worker gained access to this 'male world'.[3] However, due to my status in the subculture, based on my windsurfing proficiency and commitment to the sport (being a British wave sailing champion certainly ameliorated my subcultural credentials), I was able to participate in most sporting and social activities. I had almost full access to the men's activities and conversations, including the time that their female partners weren't 'welcome' in the group. I even had entry to the changing room – traditionally one of the most hallowed of male sanctuaries.

A framework for exploring lifestyle sport and competing masculinities

> But out there on the waves, there was an attitude. [...] It wasn't anti-female exactly, and it was more complex than that. But it put girls and women in their place, and that place in that 'naturalised order of being' was not out on the waves. Naturally, that was a place for boys to act out being real men. To conquer their fears. To conquer nature. To conquer each other. And, as a sort of afterthought, to not be a female.
>
> (Wenner 1995: 124)

Larry Wenner's (autobiographical) observation of surfing and windsurfing cultures in the USA is a useful starting point for discussing windsurfing masculinities, as it illustrates that although these are essentially cultural spaces where masculine identities are negotiated and defined, they do so in relation to both 'other' men, and to women. To understand the complexities and unevenness in men's exercise of social, economic and physical power a fluid model of gender oppression is required, that focuses 'on the processes and relationships through which men *and* women conduct gendered lives' (Connell 1995: 71). Further, taking Judith Butler's emphasis on gender as a socially regulated performance (1990, 1993), it is useful to examine how windsurfers *do* masculine identity work. Windsurfer's performance of identity ranged from story-telling to the consumption of material 'objects' like the windsurf board, and to a lesser degree adopting subcultural style (see Wheaton 2000). In this paper I focus on demonstrating sporting and sexual prowess as these are the markers of identity that are most pertinent to understanding the windsurfers' embodied masculinities.

Nevertheless, masculinity is a socio-historical construct, dependent on and related to other factors, and particularly 'class', ethnicity, sexuality, age and disability. It is therefore important to consider the plurality of masculinities that are produced in a particular cultural setting, and how the fluid and shifting subjectivities of individual men are 'addressed by a range of discursive masculine identifiers' (Nixon 1996: 13) such as father, worker, windsurfer, Southerner and so on. Certain aspects of the windsurfers' masculine identity were shared by most of the culture, such as being white and able bodied, however the *differences* in the ages, classes, and life experiences of the male windsurfers I observed affected the ways masculinity was negotiated and performed in the windsurfing milieu. In particular, as this paper will exemplify, there were marked differences in masculinities between the predominantly younger men I observed at the subculture's 'core' (both in the UK and abroad), and the experiences of the older, less committed participants.[4]

Thus as Connell (1995: 37) contends, we need to go beyond exploring diversity, acknowledging that there is a 'gender politics *within* masculinity'. Adopting Carrigan *et al.'s* (1987) concept of 'hegemonic masculinity' helps to determine how particular groups of men, and dominant versions of masculinity, occupy and sustain their positions of power over other forms of masculinities as well as over women.[5] Hegemonic masculinity however is not a fixed character type, but is a contestable position (Connell 1995). As Messner outlines, sport is an institution in which 'power is constantly at play' (Messner 1992: 13).

To expose these multiple and competing (re)constructions of masculinities within the windsurfing culture, and how particular versions compete to become dominant, or hegemonic, I will explore the extreme types of masculine identification. I examine what the windsurfers called 'laddish masculinity', which I contrast to 'ambivalent masculinity', to describe how windsurfing masculinities both reflect, and differ from, more traditional hegemonic sporting masculinities. Clearly, as Connell (1995) warns, collapsing multiple masculinities into typologies runs the risk of over simplification. However, in this paper I argue that the masculine identity named by the windsurfing participants, specifically 'laddishness', obscures a taken-for-granted masculinity that is more complex, more ambivalent, and potentially more progressive. That the latter masculinity is not 'labelled' by the windsurfers is significant. The lack of a label illustrates that this 'ambivalent' masculinity, which as I will demonstrate is the dominant form in this culture, is, because of its obviousness, culturally invisible. Yet like other oppositions it depends on its 'other' for meaning – identity is defined in terms of what it is not. One evident aspect of this masculinity 'invisibility' is its whiteness; as Frankenberg outlines, 'the white Western self as a racial being has for the most part remained unexamined and unnamed' (Frankenberg 1993: 17).[6] This paper will demonstrate that although characteristic of certain individuals, and prevalent in specific parts of the windsurfing subculture, laddishness was not the dominant identity. Nevertheless, despite the windsurfing culture's participatory ethos, competitiveness over subcultural status contributed to a culture of exclusivity. Sporting prowess, as I will illustrate, was an important aspect of peer approval, which was achieved in relation to 'other' men: men of other abilities, as well as men of different ages, sexualities and socio-economic categories;[7] and in relation to women.

'The lads'

> But here it's like a laddishness you get – like a boy's club, sort of thing. It's a macho thing [...] it's that they have to have to seem to be tough, hard, masculine, successful, attractive – to be able 'to pull'. [...] I think windsurfing men, it's still like footballing and all those things, you have to be a man.
>
> (Stephanie)

Despite windsurfing's counter cultural heritage and the 'feminised' appearance of some male windsurfers, such as long hair, lean not overtly muscular physiques, and wearing jewellery, traditional 'hegemonic' masculinity predominates at the 'core' of the subculture. The discussion will illustrate that assertive heterosexuality was the desired sexual identity for the 'laddish' male windsurfer, and that men distanced themselves from behaviour or activity associated with femininity and homosexuality. I will outline how competitiveness over sporting prowess, sexual conquests, and sexist attitudes to women, particularly characterising women as passive, and feminine, were all ways that 'the lads' asserted their 'laddish' masculinity.

Heterosexual prowess: conquests of women

Commentators in the 1980s described the chauvinistic and misogynistic character of surfing subcultures in Australia in which females were predominantly non-surfers; their role was as 'passengers, spectators' (Fiske 1989: 60). Further, Pennie (1981) claimed that surfers had among the most homophobic beliefs of any social group. In the late 1990s, despite the influx of women as participants, the culture in Australia, at least as expressed through the surfing media, has not substantially changed (Lewis 2003; Stedman 1997; Henderson 2001). As I will illustrate, there were similarities between the 'sub world' of the lads, (younger white male, core windsurfers) and the surfing subculture: among the lads 'real men' proved their heterosexuality to their male peers.

Miller (2001: 10) suggests that the gender politics of (mainstream) sport has become increasingly complex, particularly in terms of sexuality. During the fieldwork I only witnessed a few incidents of overt homophobia. Each of these events startled me, suggesting perhaps that explicit homophobia was not as widespread as in the surfing culture. It seems very probable that there were gay men who windsurfed. However, I did not meet any men who were 'open' about their homosexuality, perhaps indicating that gay men feared they might face some hostility. Moreover the windsurfing culture was unequivocally heterosexist in its address and values which marginalises homosexual women and men (Pronger 2000). Heterosexual masculinity, and the Othering of homosexuality was often marked though symbolic gestures and language. For example, male banter called less proficient men 'sissies' or 'gay' and involved verbal 'put-downs' of women, which even when said in jest, reinforces that this sports arena is a heterosexual male one (see also Beal and Wilson this volume):

> I stopped in at the windsurfing shop after sailing. I was complaining that I'd had a horrendous day, due to a new windsurfing board and the difficult conditions. Peter replied 'well if you will go sailing in men's conditions, what do you expect' [grinning as he said it].
>
> (Field notes)

Among the younger male windsurfers I observed that developing reputations of heterosexual prowess by 'telling stories' about sexual conquests, and/or being seen to successfully 'chat up' women, was prevalent especially among the professional male windsurfers. Peer approval seemed to be an important motive, first, as these conversations and events were in very public places; second, other men in the community ridiculed those men who didn't demonstrate their heterosexual prowess:

> I think he's inept with women – he doesn't actually know how to deal with them. They [the lads] take the piss out of him something rotten cause, he's always trying 'to pull,' and tries too hard and does it too aggressively and doesn't succeed.
>
> (Stephanie)

The lads' girlfriends tended to be the so-called 'girlies', usually non-windsurfers, or at least 'less serious' windsurfers than their partners (see Wheaton and Tomlinson 1998). It seemed important to these men that their girlfriends looked attractive and fulfilled the symbolic role of 'beach bunny', that of 'emphasised femininity' (Connell 1983). An extract from my field notes reads:

> Joe was one of the most elite wave sailors, and as such one of the most respected wave sailors in the community. His girlfriend was a non-windsurfer, a pretty (by dominant standards) blonde girl in her late teens. She was voted 'the sexiest chick around' by several of the other young wave sailors.

Many of these women, the 'girlies,' were aware of their ascribed 'decorative role' and that for their 'laddish' boyfriends having 'an attractive' girlfriend was part of the way they gained peer approval. Angela, the girlfriend of a prominent windsurfer, felt pressured to look attractive, 'look the part', which she described as 'a beach babe – blonde hair, breast implants. You know, a little Pamela Anderson.'[9] In this as in other sporting contexts women are characterised in terms of their appearance; their dress, style and demeanour emphasise their sexuality.

To summarise, 'laddish' masculinity was characterised by heterosexual prowess, reinforcing the 'naturalness' of heterosexuality, and a construction of male sexuality based on objectification and conquest.

Demonstrating sporting prowess

Competitiveness between men to demonstrate their masculinity through sporting prowess in more 'mainstream' institutionalised sports is well documented (Connell 1995). As Messner (1995) argues, sport teaches boys and men that 'being out there with the boys' or 'being mates' is not enough. Sport culture is very hierarchical with an incredible amount of importance placed on winning (Messner 1995: 108). Acceptance by other men is contingent upon being 'best' or at least very 'good'.

Combative competitiveness, however, depends on easily quantified measures. Windsurfing performance and prowess, like surfing, are very subjective; it cannot easily be measured by standardised or objectified measures such as who is the fastest from A to B. Being good or in subcultural argot a 'hot' or 'rad' sailor, was based primarily on his/her level of skill. Those who performed the most difficult manoeuvres, with the most style, and 'go for it' attitude, were accorded the most status. Nevertheless:

> As surfers are individuals, so are their styles on the water, and how do you compare such a thing as style? Along with beauty, 'best' is in the eye of the beholder.
>
> (Sam Moses in Noll and Gabbard 1989: x)

Recreational coastal windsurfers, like surfers, tended not to get involved with formal competitions;[10] such contest opposed the freedom and expression of the windsurfing lifestyle. When questioned about why they windsurfed, and in particular what had attracted them to the sport, the vast majority of participants of all abilities, and levels of involvement, stressed the individualistic, and anti-competitive nature and meaning they gave to their sports participation.

The majority of men who I interviewed denied that overt competition existed (the subcultural ethos or mythology), or that they as individuals were competitive. Yet despite claims that they windsurfed for intrinsic rewards, many windsurfers wanted some external recognition for their achievements. There was however no formal way of marking expertise, such as badges, certificates, or recognised achievement levels prevalent in more institutionalised sports cultures. In windsurfing the main form of 'external' reward was peer approval.[11]

'Beach cred'

So despite the participatory and anti-competition ethos, competitiveness between men over subcultural status or 'beach credibility' was prolific. At beaches around the coast the better windsurfers competed to be the 'local hot shot' by demonstrating their skill, and outperforming the other sailors:

> Silver Sands is a vast beach, yet people see it necessary to perform in one area, again vying for status.[…] it happens wherever you go – everyone wants to be the hot shot on the day.
>
> (David)

I am not suggesting that intense rivalry over status existed for all participants – it did not. Competitiveness was most apparent and prevalent among men, and specifically those men whose sense of self was most firmly embedded in the windsurfing activity, and younger men whose masculine identity was most fragile. I will discuss how this competitiveness between elite men to demonstrate their sporting supremacy excluded participants who were less skilled, less committed and less willing to take risk (being 'go for it') as well as reducing camaraderie and support among 'the lads'. Masculine identity work underpinned these subcultural status hierarchies; gender politics both between and especially within the sexes, was central to the existence of exclusion processes in the culture (see also Anderson 1999 in snowboarding; Beal and Wilson this volume in skateboarding).

Laddish core men competed rather than supported each other. The prevalent attitude among the lads was that a participant should be skilled enough to get him/herself 'out of trouble', or not be 'out there' (Field notes, Maui):

> You get this thing of acting hard I think – I mean I can go up there and start chatting to someone like Dan, or Ian or someone and then they'll just cut you dead and walk off. You know, the lads thing. […] What I've seen is people who are not very confident sailors come to a place like WideMouth, and completely be fazed by it.
>
> (Stephanie)

The exclusion of (less elite) individuals and groups was most prevalent among the 'core' elite windsurfer, thus was particularly evident in Hawaii, home to the world's elite wave sailors, and the windsurfers' Mecca. During a conversation with a professional wave sailor, Karl, and his girlfriend Lucy, he used the word 'Bods' as a derogatory term to describe those who were less skilled so 'got in the way' of more skilled windsurfers. While this specific term does not seem to have widespread use, it illustrates these exclusion processes inherent in this competitiveness over status. I interviewed Lucy, who explained Bods in more detail:

LUCY: Because it is their whole life, but that doesn't mean that someone should be less on the water because it isn't their whole life.

BW: Do you not think that is the attitude they do have?

LUCY: Yes, that is totally the attitude. Karl would say something like 'yes but I'm out there and I've got to learn these manoeuvres, and they are in the way' because they are thinking they have to get better for the next competition, but they have no right to either [...] They are really going for things and they don't think you should be out there sailing at 'The Point' unless you have that same mentality, and capability as well.

The elite wave sailors' attitude was that they had a greater claim to the waves, which caused hostility on the water (that I observed in Hawaii and Australia) including men jostling for space in the waves, verbal abuse and aggressive behaviour. In Hawaii, I witnessed several collisions and brawls between windsurfers. This aggressive way of protecting subcultural space has been widely documented as 'surf rage' or 'localism' in surf culture (Abell 2001; Booth 2001). Yet underpinning these expressions of localism, are exclusion processes based around the performance and (boundary) maintenance of masculine identity and status.

This competitiveness over status and subcultural space was most apparent among elite windsurfers. While the elite did value and acknowledge each other's skills, 'respect' was rarely expressed face to face, that is one windsurfer directly commenting on another's performance. Windsurfers did not overtly compete with their peers, nor did they overtly give praise. The closer to the symbolic core of the subculture participants were, the less likely they were to applaud their direct peers – the other windsurfers with whom they were vying over status. As James, an elite wave sailor, put it; 'It's nice when someone says you are sailing well, because, NO ONE ever says it'.

My own experiences are illuminating here. When learning to wave sail (a form of advanced windsurfing), I was constantly being told how well I was doing by the elite men at the beach. They admired my commitment, an important subcultural value. Yet, at the time I was improving most rapidly, they stopped giving me compliments. A male friend (an elite windsurfer), said he was not surprised that they had stopped complimenting me as my windsurfing ability had reached a similar level to some of them. As such I was considered 'one of them, one of the lads' (and arguably also a 'threat' to their masculinity – see on). Stephanie's experiences were similar:

> I think you see men like to be complimented, and they don't get it, so they compete with each other instead, or a lot of them do. [...] And I think as you

> do improve you get less compliments and less support from the men anyway, probably because they feel that you don't need it anyway. And I don't think they praise each other, and they start to treat you like one of them in that sense.
>
> (Stephanie)

For many laddish men there seemed to be a tension between demonstrating masculine sporting prowess and toughness while fostering support and friendliness between participants in a particular community, particularly among 'mates'.

Men's bodies on display

> Because people, people, are watching you all the time.
>
> (Joe)

'Being looked at' or 'watched' is a re-occurring part of the windsurfers' narratives. At the beach the gaze (both in terms of its capacity to discipline and desire) of the spectators, as well as 'other' windsurfers was focused on the windsurfers out on the water. As Michael, a professional man in his mid-thirties, explained, being watched made him feel uncomfortable, and was a hindrance to his progress while learning to windsurf:

> Every one used to look at the people who were crap, [...] like carrying your kit down the beach, I felt I should be 'a man,' trying to manage, to do it all right. As a beginner and as a young person I was self-conscious.
>
> (Michael)

Men were under the gaze of other men, specifically more proficient men. As Cara Aitchison (1996) observes, we are accustomed to the conception of the 'male gaze' in the sexual objectification of women, but less sensitised to notions of the 'male gaze directed at particular forms of masculinity rather than femininity in order to maintain male supremacy' (1996: 9).

Michael eventually realised that this gaze was predominantly focused on the advanced male windsurfers:

> As time went on I realised that people didn't look at the crap people. Now I don't care – I am arrogant enough not to care.
>
> (Michael)

As he got older, and more confident in his masculine identification, especially as a successful professional man who had status in his occupation, the need to demonstrate his masculinity in the sporting sphere decreased. Although windsurfing was a central site for the creation of masculine identities, it is not the only domain. Masculinities are fluid and learned/negotiated in a variety of settings such as the family, and work environments; the importance participants gave to the windsurfing community for the construction of their masculine status versus other contexts such as 'work' differed. The younger men tended to be the most competitive over status:

> As you get older it's more intrinsic – you do things that suit you. You are less insecure, don't need to prove yourself to other people.
>
> (Scott)

Likewise, those participants (young or old) who were exiting the subculture were noticeably less concerned about attaining peer status.

Men's relationship with and within a cultural milieu differs depending not just on age, but other social differences. Their reconstructions of masculinity take different meanings depending on their varying backgrounds. The windsurfers from lower social status backgrounds (in terms of their socio-economic background and educational levels) were more competitive over status. As Stephanie observed:

> it's a class thing I think as well, you get the working class sailor who gets good and becomes part of an elite. You get the middle-class ones who get good but they've got a life outside it as well.
>
> (Stephanie)

The professional, more educated, and middle-class men, as well as the more marginal participants were the least 'laddish men'. Correspondingly, those men who encountered 'laddish' masculinity in their work and home environments, irrespective of their age and windsurfing proficiency, were more likely to behave in a laddish way at the beach. The laddish culture prevalent at the core of this community is in part reflective of 'lad culture' prevalent among white middle-class men of this age group in British culture at that time (Whannel 2002). Nevertheless, as the remainder of the chapter will illustrate, laddish behaviour was not the most prevalent masculine identity in the windsurfing culture, and many male windsurfers actively disassociated themselves with 'lad culture'.

Ambivalent masculinity: camaraderie and support

Film representations of surfing, such as *Point Break*, or the cult movie *Big Wednesday* often signify surfing as an expression of 'male bonding'; sporting supremacy is subordinate to male camaraderie.[12] Mike Doyle, an ex-professional surfer, highlights this element of the surfing experience in his autobiography, an attitude still prevalent among parts of the surfing culture (see Booth this volume):

> Since my early days at Malibu, the part of surfing I cherished most was the friendship and camaraderie I shared with other surfers. [...] The point, at least for me, was never to prove how great you were, but to have fun with

> friends. If there was a competitive element involved, it was challenging each other to do better.
>
> (Doyle 1993: 166)

Socialising and camaraderie was an important part of the experience for many male windsurfers I interviewed. The majority of men at Silver Sands were supportive of each other, particularly if the conditions were difficult; this companionship (between men and women) was then most evident. For example, if someone performed a big jump, others nearby 'yipped' him/her; if a participant got hit by a wave and lost their equipment (so had to swim to the beach), a spectating windsurfer would rush into the shore break waves to rescue the kit from getting broken or damaged. Those who couldn't manage to get out through the shore-break were consoled and encouraged for their effort.

Even at the subcultures' core, men supporting and competing with each other coexisted. Messner (1995) similarly argues that for boys in organised athletic sports, there is a contradiction between developing 'positional identities' in the hierarchical and competitive sports world, while retaining a need for closeness and rapport with others: An 'important thread running through the development of masculine identity' he claims, ' is 'male's ambivalence towards intimate unity with others' (Messner 1995: 112). Yet as I have illustrated, in the windsurfing culture a feature of the windsurfers' (masculine) identity was to deny competitiveness (the anti-competition ethos). Central to the 'ambivalent masculinity' identity was a rejection of many values central to the dominant sport culture, such as the emphasis on competition and winning. These windsurfers embraced the meaning that 'being out there with the boys' *was* enough to be accepted in the windsurfing culture, that you don't need to be competitive, or good at sports to be a 'real man'. As John, a core man in his mid-thirties argued, men were appreciative of each other's achievements, and problems:

> They all wanted to be good – but it wasn't you know, I can do this, so, I'm better you know I'm a better person than you are. There was one guy who was trying to learn to do forwards, someone else was doing duck tacks, whatever. I mean they just try and do it, and they'd be really pleased if they could do it, and the other guys would be really pleased if they could do it. [...] So no, there was no real sense of competition out there at all.
>
> (John)

One way I tested out this emergent theory about 'ambivalent masculinity' was to ask interviewees specific questions about whether windsurfing was a 'macho' sport, and whether the men who windsurfed were macho. Despite the derisive associations with 'macho' for some women and men in Western cultures, being 'macho and hard' is still glorified in laddish sport culture, such as the football culture where (self) proclaimed 'hard' men like Vinnie Jones are still popular sport stars. 'Macho' therefore seemed to signify the 'laddish' type of masculinity associated with hegemonic forms of sporting masculinity (Whannel 1993), and would thus be the antithesis of this 'ambivalent masculinity' espoused in the windsurfing subculture. None of the men (and few of the women) I interviewed perceived that windsurfing was macho. One possible explanation for their refutation – a form of 'identity talk' – lies with the pejorative connotations of the word macho in Western cultures. Nevertheless, some men conceded that macho windsurfers existed 'elsewhere', and in particular that the image of the sport was of a macho masculinity.

Furthermore, it is interesting to illustrate the ways in which men actively attempted to disavow the macho identity. A conversation with Michael, a marginal participant in his mid-thirties, and his female partner was illuminating in this respect. I asked Michael if he would help a woman do her 'downhaul rope', the part of the rigging process[13] that requires strength:

> Yes. People struggle all the time. [...] But I feel that I ought not to be helping her.
>
> (Michael)

Michael argued that rigging is time consuming, and that people should learn to do it; 'proper windsurfers do rig up themselves' (Michael). I asked him if he would ask for help if hypothetically he was unable to do his own downhaul. Michael tried to circumnavigate the question, unwilling to answer it. At this point his partner, Claire, cut in on the conversation:

> He won't ask the other lions in the group. He might ask one of his mates, but he wouldn't ask Simon or John, the guys he identifies as the macho ones at beach. He'd use me as an excuse, getting me to pretend I needed my downhaul doing. It's just not the done thing to ask another man for help because they are not strong enough.
>
> (Claire)

Eventually, after being chastised by his partner, Michael admitted that he would rather ask one of the elite or strong women for help before asking one of the elite men. As Claire commented:

> Michael is really fighting this. He doesn't want to be seen as a macho man.
>
> (Claire)

Claire's narrative is informing, particularly her analogy of the 'pride of lions' that seemingly symbolises a predatory male competitiveness denied by the men themselves. However, despite Claire's insistence that Michael's 'macho denial' was deceiving, it nevertheless highlights that Michael reflexively and actively disassociated himself from macho masculinity.

I should however stress that the *majority* of the men in the community were not so competitive about their status, and thus were able to support each other much more than the elite lads did. Throughout the windsurfing subculture, support and competition coexisted between men; men's need to use sporting prowess, and heterosexual success, as 'symbolic proof' of their masculinity was variable. In the next section, I will further exemplify this argument by illustrating the different ways these non-laddish men 'supported' rather than excluded female windsurfers.

The exclusion of women

Connell (1995: 54) suggests that men's sporting superiority has been used by men to exclude women from the sport arena and in so doing, bolster their own masculinity as symbolised in bodily sporting prowess. That is, institutionalised sport has played an important role in the reproduction of male hegemony over women, as well as hegemonic masculinity. In this discussion I will examine female windsurfers' place in the subcultural status hierarchy, focusing on how these different groups of men viewed the role of women.

Wheaton and Tomlinson (1998) describe the complexities of women's experiences of windsurfing, and explore the status of women in the windsurfing culture ranging from the 'windsurfing widows' to the active women participants. To summarise, active women windsurfers claimed to share experiences depending on subcultural positionality not gender; being a windsurfer, particularly a committed, advanced windsurfer, superseded some women's identity as *female* windsurfers. My own location in the subculture as a female 'researcher,' discussed earlier, illustrates this relationship. Despite the lack of expectation for women windsurfers to be elite, they could and did gain status in the subculture as active participants, as 'windsurfers,' albeit gendered, heterosexualised and racialised participants. I will demonstrate that although some groups of men, 'the lads,' did attempt to exclude women from the windsurfing activity, relations between men and women within the subculture, as a whole was more variable and negotiated.

Men's narratives illustrate that female windsurfers were respected as active sportswomen (see Wheaton and Tomlinson 1998). For some men the attraction of the windsurfing culture was that it wasn't the 'beered up with the lads' scene:

> I'm not a very blokish person – I'm not a football team player, I don't like that kind of scene. I think women really add something to the sport. Without women it would be too blokish – horrible. [...] And the type of women involved tend to be quite confident, together women, I think, which I admire.
>
> (Scott)

Prevailing gender ideologies rather than the attitudes or actions of individual women contributed to the cultural myth of women's passivity. The predominantly middle-class men who formed the majority at Silver Sands did not regard women windsurfers as passive, sexualised objects, nor were they particularly concerned with demonstrating their heterosexuality:

> I come from a very male orientated background in civil engineering and building, and there is an awful lot of 'cor, look at her – I wouldn't fancy her'. And it is such a nice change the slightly more educated, more professional background you get with windsurfers, you don't get any of that.
>
> (Stephen, core windsurfer in his late twenties)

Likewise Jason claimed, 'more women around would be good, it would remove all competitiveness from the sport'.

The women I interviewed also ardently denied associations with windsurfing and 'macho' masculinity, or that windsurfing was particularly a 'male sport':

> Not in the sense that I have ever come across any resistance to me, as a woman, windsurfing.[...] No I don't think it portrays the macho image you associate with rugby or boxing or anything like that.
>
> (Emma, advanced, core windsurfer)

Although women's experiences differed – as did their perceptions of what constituted sexism and exclusion depending on predominantly their home and work environments – the majority of women who windsurfed at Silver Sands commented on the small minority of 'immature' or laddish men at that particular beach. All the interviewees (male and female) suggested that windsurfing was less differentiated along gender lines, and that there was less sexist banter about women, than most other male dominated active leisure cultures such as the golf club, rugby club and (boat) sailing club. As Sue, a pensioner, explained, the attitude of men in the windsurfing subculture was 'different' to other sports environments:

> I had never felt a second class citizen until I joined the golf club. But when I go windsurfing over to the lake, I just pop over and have an hour or so by myself, um, [...] you know, it's an entirely different attitude – they are very nice, very supportive.
>
> (Sue)

The following discussion of the 'forward loop', illustrates that even the most elite female windsurfers, who by their very presence seemingly challenged the male domain of elite sporting prowess, were not actively excluded by the non-laddish majority.

The forward loop

> There are more difficult tricks, but if you go down to the Hachery [...] or any of the other macho launch sites, all people ask is 'Can you loop? Is she looping?
>
> (Kay Kucera, advanced windsurfer in the USA)[14]

Alex was an extremely committed male windsurfer in his mid-twenties, who had travelled extensively, and worked as a windsurfing instructor to enable him to 'keep windsurfing'. His whole life and sense of self revolved around, and was embedded in windsurfing. As a 'core' young elite participant, one might expect him to be 'laddish'. Nevertheless, Alex was emphatic about his admiration and respect for elite and 'go for it' women. For example:

> [...] a lot of respect. But I'd have to make sure she wasn't better than me, cos I'd get pissed off. [he laughs] When I see girls doing forwards it really pisses me off, because it is a really gutsy manoeuvre, and it is something I am trying to do, and I've gone for it many times and hurt myself, so I think damn, I'm not going to be able to do it. Not that girls shouldn't be gutsy, just hats off respect. It's really impressive.
>
> (Alex, core male, aged 25)

Alex's example of 'forwards' or the 'forward loop' is particularly revealing. The forward loop is a very advanced and potentially hazardous wave sailing manoeuvre, essentially a forward somersault in the air. As feminists have illustrated, women are brought up to be cautious, to 'take care' of their bodies; embodied risk taking is associated with masculinity (see Beal and Wilson; Kay and Laberge, this volume). But the forward loop relies on the participant's courage, not just skill. Thus as Lisa Gosselin (1994: 59) reasons:

> Doing a loop – a 360-degree aerial with a sailboard – is considered the studliest thing of all to do. Loops are what separate the men from the boys, and, more important, the men from the women.

Whitson (1990) has argued in the analogous context of male cliff jumpers, that they needed to exclude women to preserve their sport as a 'proving ground for masculinity' (Whitson 1990: 24). However although Alex (above), partly resented the elite women windsurfers who had more courage (and skill) than himself, he also admired them as windsurfers. Even though being out-performed by a woman in such a 'gutsy manoeuvre' seemingly challenged the basis of masculine identity, for him it didn't. Unlike the cliff jumpers who needed to exclude women, Alex was encouraging of elite women windsurfers. Although his responses reveal some contradictions, he did not perceive that women's presence was a 'threat'. One interpretation is that the few active, courageous women who adopt this masculine attitude, do little to challenge the association of windsurfing with masculinity. However, Alex's narrative (and others) suggests a greater ambivalence in his attitude to the gender hierarchy, and resultant exclusion processes. Furthermore, Alex's attitude seems to support my thesis that the underlying attitude towards participation was being 'out there' showing commitment and 'attitude' but not competing. That Alex's masculinity was not wholly threatened suggests that just doing it, and especially 'going for it' was enough to prove his masculinity:

> My enjoyment is of pushing myself. When it is big, and you are still smacking the lip, then it really does put the adrenaline in you, which is the whole fun factor. I don't do it for anyone else. [...] I like sailing alone but also with mates. When you are out jumping and your mates are riding coming in, and you are just cheering everyone on.
>
> (Alex)

'Lads' attitudes to women revisited

There was nevertheless a conspicuous divergence in the acceptance of women windsurfers at the core of the culture among the laddish men. Women's role in the *lads' gender order* was not as sportswomen. The elite young core men's intolerance towards any participants who were less proficient, implicated women participants. As Lisa explained, reflecting on women's status in Hawaii:

> They don't mind the women being out there, but we are never going to be accepted like they are, however good they are, [...] Say to someone like Peter, yes Julie is good, but *good for a woman*. They [the men] never feel like the women are as radical as they [the men] are [...] but um. I think it is slowly changing a bit.
>
> (Lisa)

As already noted, the elite men – particularly in Hawaii – were protective of 'their space', the big waves in the Pacific that represented the ultimate wave sailing conditions. Women were perceived to be intruders, 'in the way', regardless of their *actual* windsurfing skill.[15] For these young men, 'serious' or 'competitive' windsurfing remained their, the elite men's domain. Their practices illustrate how in the non-institutionalised sphere of the windsurfing environment, men controlled women's , and less elite men's, leisure space in subtle, but effective ways.

Nevertheless the attitudes and behaviour of even the young men continually surprised me. For example, in a competition in which I participated, I tied third place with one of the young male competitors, Sandy. Other male competitors, and I, anticipated that Sandy would be embarrassed that he hadn't beaten a 'female'. Yet, the next evening in the bar, Sandy proudly proclaimed to his male peers, that he tied third place with me. Even in Hawaii, the epi-centre of status and thus competitiveness, I witnessed the elite men encouraging and assisting the elite women, acknowledging and admiring their skill and courage. Hostility and sexist attitudes co-existed with support and encouragement towards elite women windsurfers.

Conclusions

In the introduction I outlined the contention that masculine identities in Western cultures have increasingly centred on and around leisure consumption practices. Yet instead of providing new sites and possibilities for progressive masculinities, this shift towards consumption as the basis of identities saw the re-emergence and reassertion of a hegemonic white male English identity, repacked in the styles and practices of new laddism (Carrington 1998; Whelehan 2000). Likewise, claims about 'new men' in 'new sports' are also premature. Windsurfing is not a site for a radical 'new' embodied masculine identification. Nevertheless, this ethnographic research supports other claims that (in some) lifestyle sport, the 'recognised boundaries' of sporting masculinities are broadened (Beal 1996; Midol and Broyer 1995; Anderson 1999; Whitson 1994; Robinson, this volume). To summarise, this chapter has illustrated that a range of different masculinities are negotiated in the windsurfing culture, and that the prevalent masculinity – 'ambivalent masculinity' – was less exclusive of women and 'other men' than many traditional institutionalised sports cultures, or even work cultures. Windsurfing men, in the majority were not 'new lads'. Nevertheless, the younger male windsurfers enacted aspects of the emergent lad culture evident in the wider culture in which this sporting community is embedded. The laddishness and competitiveness over status was predominately confined to the core of the windsurfing culture, and to younger men, and those men working in manual or non professional occupations. The masculine identification based on the subordination of women as passive, sexual objects was strongest among younger, elite men. Nevertheless, even at the core there was a duality and contradiction between men wanting women to be excluded and those who support their involvement. Men and women emphasised the supportiveness, and camaraderie among and between men and women in the culture.

Sporting masculinity is not a single monolithic category; it varies over time and cultural spaces, is articulated in relation to other power inequalities (such as age, class, ethnicity and sexuality), and is subject to a continual process of contestation, reinterpretation and revision. Like Messner's (1992) subjects my interviewees revealed 'strains' in the sport/masculinity relationship. Perhaps the most important challenge to the dominant conception of sporting masculinities in windsurfing is the rejection of formal competitiveness, and the overt emphasis on 'winning' that is characteristic of the dominant athletic value system. Beal (1996) makes similar insights based on her observation of the skateboarding subculture in the USA (see also Thornton this volume; Kay and Laberge this volume). Despite the discrepancy between ethos and action at the core of the subculture, and the individuality of the activity, the windsurfing value system promotes having fun, improvement, support and fellowship between men, and between men and women, above winning and competing. As Messner (1992: 163) suggests, a value system, which 'elevates relationships above competition and winning' inverts and challenges 'the priorities that govern the dominant forms of sport'.

Windsurfing remains a key component of the gender order in society, especially in reproducing compulsory heterosexuality, yet there are clear contradictions between aspects of the culture and both traditional sporting masculinities the 'status quo of hegemonic masculinity' (Messner 1992: 171).

Windsurfing women and some windsurfing men are actively redefining notions of 'sport'; and their accounts point to a blurring of traditional ideas and embodied performances and experiences of masculinities and femininities in sport.

Notes

1 The 'formal' Ethnographic research was conducted during 1994–97. However my analysis is informed by my ongoing involvement in windsurfing (albeit as a less active participant and freelance journalist); and by subsequent research I've conducted in the windsurfing context (Wheaton and Beal 2003). The original research was based on participant observation based around a beach community in the south of England. The analytical themes that emerged from participant observation at the main setting were developed with 24 'formal' in-depth interviews with selected members of the British windsurfing community. Furthermore, observations and informal interviews were conducted at other windsurfing communities in the UK, and abroad, including the island of Maui in the Hawaiian Islands, the windsurfer's Mecca, and home to an international community of 'hard core' windsurfing addicts. For the purposes of anonymity and confidentiality some place names and all the names of respondents are changed – likewise some event dates are changed.

2 These characteristics have been documented in; surfing (Booth 1995, 2001) skateboarding (Beal 1995; Borden 2001); snowboarding (Humphreys 1997, 2003; Henio 2000) and the whiz sports (Midol and Broyer 1995). Bourdieu's (1984) thesis about new sports also proposes that competitions are incompatible with the ideals of new sport participants, although they exist as 'highly ritualised competition' (1984, 217) such as 'man's battle with nature'.

3 These issues around access, insider status and gender in the ethnographic process are discussed in Wheaton (2002).

4 In this chapter I use the terms culture and subculture somewhat uncritically. While it is not my intention here to contribute to a definition of subculture, there are ongoing polemics about the use of 'subculture' as a theoretical category. However I contend that subculture remains a useful analytical and descriptive category for mapping this sporting context.

5 Hegemonic masculinity is not without its critics. See for example Miller who suggests that the commodification of male sport stars in the 1990s has 'destabilized the hegemonic masculinity thesis' (Miller 2001: 52).

6 As has been explored in critical whiteness studies, white identities are characterised by their ' invisibility' and lack of labelling. Thornton (this volume) also illustrates that this 'unnamed general reference group' based on normative whiteness and heterosexuality, is a shared, but under studied, characteristic of other lifestyle sporting masculinities.

7 Although not explored in this paper, these competing masculinities were also observed in relation to men of different nationalities and ethnicities, particularly evident in the Hawaiian's context.

8 'To pull' in this context entails the young man successfully chatting up a female in the social setting, and then conspicuously leaving the room/location with her.

9 Pamela Anderson is the star of the Californian-set TV drama, *Bay Watch*.

10 Several different forms of organised competitions do exist, and were particularly popular among those who windsurfed on inland waters (lakes, reservoirs, etc.). However for the majority competition takes other forms, in particular gaining his/her peer respect, and that of the individual against the elements (the wind, sea and waves).

11 Although for elite participants media recognition was also an important form of status.

12 However this is not prevalent across all the surfing subcultural media. See Lewis (1998).

13 Rigging up is subcultural argot for putting the sail, mast and boom (which constitute the 'rig') together.
14 Quoted in *Women Sport and Fitness* 1994: 59.
15 Some elite men argued that this 'exclusion' was due to the 'lack of space' reflecting claims that surf rage and localism were also due to overcrowding at the premier wave sailing venues.

References

Abell, J. (2001) Values in a sporting sub-culture: An analysis of the issues of competitiveness and aggression in surfing. Masters thesis, University of Warwick.

Aitchison, C. (1996) Gendered tourist spaces and places: The masculinisation and militarisation of Scotland's heritage. *Leisure Studies Association Newsletter*, 45: 16–23.

Anderson, K. (1999) Snowboarding: The construction of gender in an emerging sport. *Journal of Sport and Social Issues*, 23: 55–79.

Beal, B. (1995) Disqualifying the official: An exploration of social resistance through the subculture of skateboarding. *Sociology of Sport Journal*, 12: 252–267.

Beal, B. (1996) Alternative masculinity and its effect on gender relations in the subculture of skateboarding. *Journal of Sports Behaviour*, 19: 204–220.

Booth, D. (1995) Ambiguities in pleasure and discipline: The development of competitive surfing. *Journal of Sport History*, 22: 189–206.

Booth, D. (2001) *Australian Beach Cultures: The History of Sun, Sand and Surf*, London: Frank Cass Publishers.

Borden, I. (2001) *Skateboarding, Space and the City: Architecture and the Body*, Oxford: Berg.

Bourdieu, P. (1984) *Distinction: A Social Critique of the Judgement of Taste*, London and NY: Routledge & Kegan Paul Ltd.

Boyle, R. and Haynes, R. (2000) *Power Play: Sport, the Media and Popular Culture*, Harlow: Longman.

Butler, J. (1990) *Gender Trouble: Feminism and the Subversion of Identity*, London: Routledge.

Butler, J. (1993) *Bodies That Matter: On the Discursive Limits of 'Sex'*, London: Routledge.

Carrigan, T., Connell, R. and Lee, J. (1987) Towards a New Sociology of Masculinity. *Theory and Society*, 14: 551–604.

Carrington, B. (1998) 'Football's coming home' But whose home and do we want it? Nation, football and the politics of exclusion in *Fanatics! Power, Identity and Fandom in Football* (ed, Brown, A.) London and NY: Routledge.

Connell, R. (1995) *Masculinities*, Cambridge: Polity Press.

Connell, R. W. (1983) Men's bodies in *Which Way is Up?* Allen & Unwin.

Doyle, M. (1993) *Morning glass: The Adventures of a Legendary Waterman*, Three Rivers, CA: Manzantia Press.

Edwards, T. (1997) *Men in the Mirror: Men's Fashion, Masculinity and Consumer Society*, London: Cassell.

Featherstone, M. (1991) *Consumer Culture and Postmodernism*, London, Newbury Park, New Delhi: Sage Publications.

Frankenberg, R. (1993) *White Women, Race Matters: The Social Construction of Whiteness*, London: Routledge.

Giddens, A. (1991) *Modernity and Self-identity: Self and Society in the Late Modern Age*, Oxford: Polity Press.

Gosselin, L. (1994) Throwing caution to the wind. *Women's Sport and Fitness*: 56–61.

Henderson, M. (2001) A shifting line up: men, women and *Tracks* surfing magazine. *Continuum: Journal of Media and Cultural Studies*, 15: 319–332.

Henio, R. (2000) What is so punk about snowboarding? *Journal of Sport and Social Issues*, 24: 176–191.

Humphreys, D. (1997) 'Skinheads go mainstream?' Snowboarding and alternative youth. *International Review for Sociology of Sport*, 32: 147–160.

Humphreys, D. (2003) Selling out snowboarding: The alternative response to commercial co-optation in *To the Extreme: Alternative Sports, Inside and Out* (eds, Rinehart, R. and Sydor, S.) Albany: State University of New York Press.

Jackson, P., Stevenson, N. and Brooks, K. (2001) *Making Sense of Men's Magazines*, Cambridge: Polity.

Jameson, F. (1991) *Postmodernism or the Cultural Logic of Late Capitalism*, London, New York: Verso.

Lash, S. and Urry, J. (1987) *The End of Organized Capitalism*, Cambridge: Polity Press.

Lewis, J. (1998) Between the lines: surf texts, prosthetics, and everyday theory. *Social Semiotics*, 8(1): 55–70.

Lewis, J. (2003) In search of the postmodern surfer: Territory, terror and masculinity in *Some Like it Hot: The Beach as a Cultural Dimension* (eds, Skinner, J., Gilbert, K. and Edwards, A.) Oxford: Meyer and Meyer Sport.

Messner, M. (1992) *Power at Play*, Boston: Beacon Press.

Messner, M. (1995) Boyhood, organised sports, and the construction of masculinities in *Men's lives* (eds, Kimmel, M. and Messner, M.) Boston: Allyn and Bacon.

Messner, M., Dunbar, M. and Hunt, D. (2000) The televised sports manhood formula. *Journal of Sport and Social Issues*, 24: 380–394.

Messner, M. and Sabo, D. (1990) *Sport, Men and the Gender Order: Critical feminist perspectives*, Champaign, Illinois: Human Kinetic Books.

Midol, N. and Broyer, G. (1995) Towards an anthropological analysis of new sport cultures: The case of whiz sports in France. *Sociology of Sport Journal*, 12: 204–212.

Miller, T. (2001) *Sportsex*, Philadelphia: Temple University Press.

Mort, F. (1988) Boy's Own? Masculinity, style and popular culture in *Male Order: Unwraping Masculinity* (ed, Rutherford, J.) London: Lawrence & Wishart.

Mulvey, L. (2000) Visual pleasure and narrative cinema in *Film and Theory :An Anthology* (eds, Stam, R. and Miller, T.) Oxford: Blackwell. Originally published in Visual pleasure and narrative cinema. *Screen*, 16. (1975)

Nixon, S. (1996) *Hard Looks: Masculinities, Spectatorship and Contemporary Consumption*, London: UCL Press.

Nixon, S. (1997) Exhibiting masculinity in *Representation: Cultural Representations and Signifying Practices* (ed. Hall, S.) London: Sage.

Noll, G. and Gabbard, A. (1989) *Da Bull: Life over the Edge*, Berkley: North Atlantic Books.

Pennie, R. (1981) Why gays don't surf, or do they? *Tracks*: 4.

Profile Sport Consultancy survey (1994). *The United Kingdom Windsurf Report*. A joint publication between the Profile Sport Market Consultancy and the Royal Yachting Association; March

Pronger, B. (2000) Homosexuality and sport: who's winning in *Masculinities, Gender Relations, and Sport* (eds, McKay, J., Messner, M. and Sabo, D.) Thousand Oaks: Sage.

Stedman, L. (1997) From gidget to gonad man: surfers, feminists and postmodernisation. *Australian and New Zealand Journal of Sociology*, 33: 75–90.

Tomlinson, A. (2001) Sport, leisure and style in *British Cultural Studies: Geography, Nationality, and Identity* (eds, Morley, D. and Robins, K.) Oxford: Oxford University Press.

Wenner, L. (1995) Riding waves and sailing seas: Wipeouts, jibes and gender. *Journal of Sport and Social Issues*, 19: 123–125.

Whannel, G. (1993) No room for uncertainty: Gridiron masculinity in North Dallas Forty in *You Tarzan: Masculinity, Movies and Men* (eds, Kirkham, P. and Thumim, J.) London: Lawrence & Wishart.

Whannel, G. (2002) *Media Sport Stars: Masculinities and Moralities*, London: Routledge.

Wheaton, B. (2000) Just do it: Consumption, commitment and identity in the windsurfing subculture. *Sociology of Sport Journal*, 17: 254–274.

Wheaton, B. (2002) Babes on the beach, women in the surf: Researching gender, power and difference in the windsurfing culture in *Power Games: Theory and Method for a Critical Sociology of Sport* (eds, Sugden, J. and Tomlinson, A.) Routledge.

Wheaton, B. (2003) Lifestyle sports magazines and the discourses of sporting masculinity in *Masculinity and Men's Lifestyle Magazines* (ed. Benwell, B.) Sociological Review, Blackwell.

Wheaton, B. and Beal, B. (2003) Surf divas and skate betties: consuming images of the 'other' in lifestyle sports in *New Leisure Environments: Media, Technology and Sport*, Vol. LSA Publication No. 79 (eds, Fleming, S. and Jones, I.) Eastbourne: Leisure Studies Association.

Wheaton, B. and Tomlinson, A. (1998) The changing gender order in sport? The case of windsurfing. *Journal of Sport and Social Issues*, 22: 252–274.

Whelehan, I. (2000) *Overloaded: Popular Culture and the Future of Feminism*, London: Women's Press.

Whitson, D. (1990) Sport in the social construction of masculinity in *Sport, Men and the Gender Order: Critical Feminist Perspectives* (eds, Messner, M. and Sabo, D.) Human Kinetic Books: Champaign.

Whitson, D. (1994) The embodiment of gender: Discipline, domination, and empowerment in *Women, Sport and Culture* (eds, Birrell, S. and Cole, C.) Champaign, IL: Human Kinetics.

Willis, P. (1982) Women in sport and ideology in *Sport, Culture and Ideology* (ed, Hargreaves, J.) Routledge & Kegan Paul Ltd.

8 'Mandatory equipment'

Women in adventure racing

*Joanne Kay and Suzanne Laberge**

> A forest trail made slick from rain. Elina Maki-Rautila falls hard off her mountain bike. Petri Forseman, Jukka Pinola and Mika Hirvinen, her three [male] team-mates on Team Nokia, stop and briefly check her condition. Winded by the shock, the young Finnish woman wipes away a tear and quickly moves on. In this brief expression of distress just as quickly overcome, the future adventure racing world champion, after 460km of trekking, canyoneering, mountain biking, rafting and glacial traverse, from September 3–7 in the Swiss Alps between Saint-Moritz and Zermatt, perhaps embodies the singular conduct of women in the sport.
>
> (*Le Monde* 2001)

Adventure racing (AR) is a sport in rapid transformation driven by participants' thirst for innovation. By its very character, it therefore resists strict definition and so is here only cautiously described: AR is a non-stop, self-sufficient, multi-day, multi-discipline, mixed-gender team endurance competition that takes place in the wilderness over a designated but unmarked course. AR combines sports such as trekking, climbing, mountain-biking, paddling, and horseback riding, practised in a remote natural environment, into a competitive and paradoxically collective journey of 'self-development'. The sport is illustrative of trends in 'new' sport culture[1] described in terms of 'lifestyles', whereby the personal is valued over the institutional and the natural over the artificial.

Though the term 'adventure racing'[2] has been applied to the beginner's urban sprint-distance multi-sport race as well as the exclusive, elite and geographically remote expedition epic, the latter holds the greatest prestige. 'Expedition racing', as multi-day (usually 5–10 day) AR epics are often called, requires individuals to form teams months – sometimes a year – in advance. In preparation for the race, teams must finance, equip and train all members. They must have specific skills certified in high-risk activities such as horseback riding, abseiling, orienteering and even scuba diving. They must train up to twenty hours per week

* This chapter is written in the first person to be consistent with the personalised methodological approach. The analysis is based on fieldwork and data collected by the first author.

while balancing (sometimes sacrificing) work and family life. Once on course, athletes are required to endure sleep-deprivation, weight loss, illness, injury, extreme weather, and harsh terrain. Athletes must manage and transport days' worth of food, water and equipment and to progress continuously through unfamiliar isolated areas with minimal rest and/or sleep. Most importantly, for 'finisher' status, each athlete must complete the race with his or her team.

The Discovery Channel Eco-Challenge, the focus of this study, grew not only into one of the most acclaimed adventure races in the world, but also into a yearly 'documentary' sold to TV networks world-wide. Its success as both competitive race and popular show has been built on its reputation as an 'authentic' adventure[3] – a test of mettle and perseverance on a journey into the unknown.

Despite the evident physical 'toughness' such a gruelling, athletic endeavour demands, the general *discourse*[4] of AR – and specifically that of the Discovery Channel Eco-Challenge – touts *teaming* as the sport's key tenet and as AR's measure of success. Mark Burnett, founder of Eco-Challenge, explains the race's philosophy:

> It's not like other sports where you can muscle your way through. It's about working well as a team. Of course the race itself is physically gruelling. I've heard it described as the most difficult physical and mental human test on the planet. But the best teams – even the ones you think are just these incredible jocks – they know that teamwork is the key.
>
> (Mark Burnett, personal communication)

AR discourse simultaneously vaunts the physical toughness required to participate in the sport while privileging teaming as the norm of AR success. Further, unlike other sports associated with (male-biased) physical strength, AR discourse implies there is an opportunity to subvert the 'gender regime in sport' (Connell 1987; Messner and Sabo 1990; Laberge and Albert 2000). For example, AR discourse offers the widely implemented 'gender rule', which requires teams to be co-ed, not only as proof of women's toughness, but as a demonstration that women's specific teaming 'expertise' is a sought-after strength:

> The co-ed idea is good. I think girls in general are better at working in teams. Some of the girls are really strong, but I think it is their teamwork that is their biggest strength. And, in fact, teamwork is the most important thing in this kind of race.
>
> (M, aged 44)

The discourse both asserts women's toughness and suggests that their (teaming) specificity is valued over male-associated physical strength. Similarly, while risk-taking is considered to be a key demonstration of toughness in AR, a quality most often attributed to men, AR discourse gives priority to risk-management, a quality most often attributed to women as a 'natural' teaming skill. Therefore, by privileging teaming over physical toughness, women's specificity over men's, and risk-management over risk-taking, AR appears, *at the level of discourse*, to constitute a site of egalitarian – if not female biased – sport.

Indeed, Susan Birrell and Nancy Theberge (1994: 361-76) have discussed non-traditional sport as an important site for fighting gender oppression and contesting gender relations, suggesting that opportunities outside the mainstream of institutionalised practice 'hold greater promise for the realisation of alternative and resistant sport forms' (371). AR discourse, then, suggests that the sport might act as a 'springboard for the transformation of gender relations by dislodging the gender hierarchy that sport helps preserve' (366).

But at the level of practice,[5] AR's promise does not hold true. Teams are made up almost entirely of three men and one woman, in minimum compliance with the gender rule, demonstrating that women's specificity, prudence and teaming skill are valued far less on the race course than discourse would suggest. More importantly, while references to 'mandatory equipment' pepper descriptions of women's team role, participants still uphold the contradictory discourse that would purport an egalitarian terrain. How, then, can one account for the dissonance that exists between the discourse and the practice of AR? And how can one account for the 'dual' participation in a discourse and a practice that contradict?

To answer these questions, I use Pierre Bourdieu's conceptions of symbolic power (Bourdieu 1991) and field (Bourdieu 1993b) to explain AR as a social process and symbolic system – constructed simultaneously by discourse and practice – that legitimates masculine domination not despite but because of the dissonance that is produced.

This chapter begins with a brief summary of Pierre Bourdieu's notions of symbolic power, field and strategy, then draws on the concepts to examine AR discourse (see Note 4) and practice (see Note 5). I suggest that the naturalisation of women's difference/weakness, and the privileging of physical toughness as the dominant capital in the field, serve to legitimate masculine domination in AR. Lastly, I examine women's strategies to accumulate different forms of symbolic capital, demonstrating nevertheless women's practical complicity in their own subordination.

Theoretical framework

Though Bourdieu's theory of social practice has been criticised for its inattention to gender, his work on symbolic power and masculine domination offers an effective counter-argument to this claim.[6] Further, his concepts of field and capital – which have not yet been extensively exploited in sport studies – are usefully exercised in the study of not just social class, but all unequal power relations, including those anchored in gender.

In line with Bourdieu's social theory of practice (1984, 1998a) and his analysis of sport practice (1993a), my study considers AR as a site of cultural practice manifesting symbolic value, which is the outcome of its particular history and social dynamic. AR practice is thus understood to constitute a symbolic system of social classification, serving as an instrument of domination, legitimating social ranking by encouraging, as Bourdieu explains, the dominated to accept the existing hierarchies in the social field.

Symbolic power and masculine domination

Bourdieu (1998b, 1998c) explains the process of male domination: 'Socialisation of the biological and biologisation of the social' combine to naturalise notions of gender and male domination. This naturalisation becomes 'the basis both of reality and of the representation of reality' (Bourdieu 1998c: 28). Distinctions made between male and female, according to Bourdieu, are more social constructions than biological facts, the qualities attributed to women's 'nature' corresponding trait for trait to the social domination of the male gender. Further, it is Bourdieu's claim that women, as a social group, participate in masculine domination and contribute to the construction of the categories that privilege men. Women's subordinate status is conditional upon their adoption of the categories presented in taken-for-granted discourse.

For Bourdieu, then, taken-for-granted assumptions, practices and discourses are the means used by dominant groups to misrepresent their interests and to 'impose' a hierarchical vision/division of the world. The exercise of domination therefore requires a 'misrecognition' of its arbitrary and interested, or biased, character. Accordingly, I suggest that it is the misrecognition of the arbitrariness and male bias inherent to AR's 'legitimate' form of practice, which maintains and reproduces masculine domination in sport.

Field and capital

Elsewhere, I have applied Bourdieu's sociocultural theory of practice to the sport of AR (Kay and Laberge 2002a, 2002b) specifically using the concepts of field and capital to understand the social dynamics and power relationships fuelling the sport's evolution. Because the concepts inform an understanding of the internal and external interests and struggles animating the continual transformation of a social structure, emphasising its dynamic character, the concepts have proven especially useful to the examination of an emerging, rapidly shifting lifestyle sport culture like AR.

Bourdieu's notion of field can be defined as a social arena – simultaneously a space of conflict and competition – within which struggles take place for the accumulation of different forms of symbolic capital (physical, social, cultural, economic, etc.) valued in it, i.e. as a source of prestige, distinction, power, influence, etc. (Bourdieu 1993b: 72–7; Bourdieu and Wacquant 1992: 7). Social agents' struggles take place not only over particular forms of capital effective in the field, but also over the very definition of which form of capital is most valued. In this sense, fields are arenas of struggle for 'legitimation' (Bourdieu and Wacquant 1992: 84), or recognition of the legitimacy of the power associated with a specific form of capital. The symbolic capital which is dominant in a given field is, accordingly, that which is most efficacious, its legitimacy and value tacitly agreed upon and reified by participants 'playing the game' (Harker *et al.* 1990: 7, Bourdieu and Wacquant 1992: 98).

To explain internal field dynamics, Bourdieu identifies different strategies deployed by social agents striving to maintain or improve their current position in a field (1993b). According to Bourdieu, although these strategies are interest-driven, they are not the result of conscious choice or rational calculation. They are, rather, generated by what Bourdieu calls a 'practical sense' or a 'feel for the game' – the practical dimension of action whereby social agents respond to the opportunities and constraints of a given circumstance according to their position, and thus power, in a field (Bourdieu 1990). Bourdieu recognises three main strategies at work in a field. Conservation strategies tend to be pursued by those who hold dominant positions and enjoy prestige in the field. Succession strategies are attempts to gain access to dominant positions in a field. And subversion strategies are pursued by those who expect to gain little in the struggle for the accumulation of the dominant symbolic capital and who are, in fact, 'condemned' to challenge the legitimacy of the dominant capital in order to improve their position in the field. Accordingly, I use these conceptualisations of 'field' and 'capital' to understand the relative value of *physical toughness* and *teaming* symbolic capitals in the field of AR, as well as women's strategies for position taking in relation to them.

Research methods

Much of my research took place while training for and competing in a 36-hour Raid the North adventure race in Quebec, Canada in September of 1999. I was recruited – based on my athletic record – to be the only female member of a four-person team. In preparation for the race, I participated with my team in daylong hikes, paddles and mountain-bike rides as well as overnight trekking and orientation sessions. This experience not only helped me relate better to athletes' perceptions and judgements, but also permitted a privileged and welcomed entry into the AR community. In December 1999, I travelled to Patagonia, Argentina to conduct a three-week field observation of Discovery Channel Eco-Challenge. In my capacity as a journalist/feature writer for the *National Post*, I was given complete access to competitors, the course and race organisation, including media production facilities and crew, access that would have been denied to me had I gone in any other capacity such as racer, volunteer or spectator. In addition to many informal exchanges – before, during and after the race – I conducted 37 semi-structured interviews with AR participants who took part in the event.

I also relied on an analysis of Discovery Channel Eco-Challenge broadcasts from 1996–1999. This proved invaluable to identifying media rhetoric, as interview respondents often recited the script from previous years' broadcasts in their comments about AR values and anticipated rewards.

Naturalising women's weakness and the misrecognition of bias

In this section, I present the assumptions most embedded in the Eco-Challenge discourse, juxtaposing them against participants' descriptions, perceptions and judgements of practice, highlighting contradictions. I suggest that dissonance naturalises women's weakness through the resulting misrecognition of: first, the bias of male strength; second, the bias of dominant capital; third the bias against women's specificity, and last, the bias against women's dramatic appeal.

The bias of male strength

In AR discourse, the very fact that women participate in the sport is a demonstration of their capacity for physical toughness equal to that of men:

> You have to be strong. A 6'4 guy has no more chance than I do to finish.
>
> (F, 29, Cat 2)[7]

> If you're going to be a female competing at this level, you have to be as strong as the guys are.
>
> (F, 40, Cat 3)

Conversely, in practice, women are clearly perceived as the physically weaker sex. For example, they are considered to be less willing to take risks (or more 'prudent'), less competitive ('less egotistical') and more prone to breakdown or injury ('more fragile'). Though the gender rule implies men's inclusion is mandated along with women's, only women are referred to as 'mandatory equipment':

> Women are sometimes considered as mandatory equipment. It is true. It's not a big spread joke but it's known. I didn't say it. I heard it. I found it funny.
>
> (M, 26, Cat 2)

> We all had to get down beside her and warm her up. Keep in mind that we disliked her intensely and it was only because we could only finish the race if she survived.
>
> (M, 49, Cat 2)

When a woman performs well physically, it is often attributed to good team management of her weakness, rather than to her relative strength. While maintaining the discourse of women's toughness, one team referred to their female member as the team 'barometer,' or the one most likely to tire first:

> In our case, [she] was the barometer. If she was sleepy, there was no question about it, we would sleep. And if she was not sleepy, well the guys would keep going until she wanted to stop.

> *Interviewer: Why was there no question?*
>
> Well, because she's the girl. It's just logical that the girl has to have some privileges.
>
> *Interviewer: Why?*
>
> It is a good question. There was just no discussion about it. If she says she's exhausted, there's no question that she's exhausted. And if she's at her limit, there's no sense in pushing her even further because the next day she would have to sleep a lot more. But actually, [she] was the one who had the best race, if you look at it. Probably because she was essentially, we agreed, the barometer.
>
> (M, 26, Cat 2)

Despite the claims embedded in discourse, treated as the 'barometer', the woman represents the team's baseline strength.

Similarly, whereas men who get injured are perceived to be risk-takers or 'tough', a double standard dictates that a woman's injury is due to overcompensating for her 'natural weakness' rather than an inclination to take greater risks:

> Women get injured more than guys, probably, because they push harder. Team-mates push them because they may at times be the weakest link, and the women have to try to keep up.
>
> (M, 32, Cat 1)

This contradiction highlights a catch-22 of female participation in AR whereby a demonstration of toughness only serves to affirm a lack of strength; women push hard to compensate for their assumed weakness, but when pushing hard results in injury, it is seen as proof of exactly that.

The inclination towards management of assumed women's weakness is clearly evident in the practice of helping the female team member before she displays any evidence of breaking down, even if she appears to be physically stronger than a male member of her team:

> They tow me all the time whether I feel good or bad. It evens us out. It's like a lifeline.
>
> (F, 35, Cat 2)

> We tried not to give her as much of a load in her pack. But [she] was in better shape and could carry as much load as I could.
>
> (M, 38, Cat 3)

> We had to carry a lot of her gear, of course, but except for that, they're just as strong.
>
> (M, 32, Cat 1)

Trivialising women's inability to carry as much weight as men in discourse – and men's simultaneous inclination to take on women's loads in practice – serves, in effect, to naturalise women's relative lack of strength.

And while exceptionally physically strong women – who, for example, carry packs equal in weight to those carried by men – appear to be admired in the AR discourse, they are often criticised, suspected of deviancy or taking drugs, their strength downplayed or attributed to men if they appear 'too strong'. While Team Rubicon was made up of three women and only one man, for instance, their high competitive ranking was frequently attributed to the single male member:

> Rubicon's success may be attributed to a number of factors: The main one is Ian Adamson [the only male member]. He is an excellent athlete, one of the best navigators racing and an excellent communicator. If he had been unable to navigate for any reason and if the navigation had been harder, then they would not have been successful. Next, I have concerns regarding the use of illegal substances with the women. Nevertheless, the three women are very good athletes, not the best, but good. They also had a point to prove. The whole reason the team was put together was for sponsorship and exposure.
>
> (F, 44, Cat 1)

> I would like to race with other women that are strong. Rubicon women intimidate me though. They look and race like men. They could beat me to a pulp!
>
> (F, 25, Cat 2)

Moreover, while Team Rubicon's strength was extolled in discourse, for example, as a model for women entering the sport, Rubicon women were also dubbed 'Ian's Angels' – an obvious allusion to the 1970s TV drama, *Charlie's Angels*.[8] In contrast to the label 'mandatory equipment' that the mandated woman on an otherwise male team would assume, the recurring reference depicts the only male team member, Ian Adamson, as the team's invaluable leader and mastermind. The women are accordingly compared to the 'angels', the obeisant 'field agents' exploiting femininity – not physical toughness – to achieve team success. Women's physical ability, then, can be simultaneously lauded and disputed, naturalising difference and masking the arbitrariness of masculine domination. This process helps explain the apparent paradox embedded in judgements and perceptions about practice:

> With a woman on the team, you might have to slow your pace or even carry more equipment so she can race lighter. It's not because she is not physically capable. Women are stronger in the long run but cannot afford to carry much equipment. The gender rule is good. She can massage my feet [laugh]. I think it's more challenging – women and men together. If we were only men, the teams would be stronger, that's for sure.
>
> (M, 44, Cat 3)

Therefore, though AR discourse implies women's capacity for toughness is equal to that of men, the practice contradicts this claim through consistent reliance on the assumption of women's inescapable difference.

The bias of dominant capital

Cautionary tales about military teams feature heavily in AR discourse in support of teaming (versus toughness) as the norm of success. This discourse can largely be credited to the 1999 Discovery Channel Eco-Challenge documentary, which focuses on the mounting problems and eventual disqualification of a dysfunctional team of Navy Seals. Their bad performance is explained in the narrative: 'They lack flexibility and communication skills. They don't talk when they get in trouble. They shut down.' This lesson has been absorbed by the discourse, which mirrors the narrative's rhetorical claim that 'without teamwork, even the "world's toughest" can't muscle their way through'.

But objective descriptions of practice – as well as the competitive classifications that measure practice – contradict suggestions that teaming is the dominant capital in the field. The top teams at Eco-Challenge, for example, are strictly made up of elite-calibre and professional athletes who expressly exploit physical toughness to achieve high ranking. Top teams are consistently those who aim to sleep the least and progress the fastest, demonstrating the highest capacity for endurance, risk-taking, stamina and skill. Top teams are perceived by participants to 'push their bodies the hardest' and to take more physical risks in the pursuit of a high competitive ranking – symbolic capital that can be later converted into economic capital in the form of sponsorship, prize money and entry fees.

Those who conform to the discourse with their practice, pursuing teaming – not toughness – claim to value personal and lifestyle satisfaction over victory. However, as the notion of competition is crucial to AR's social signification, and as the symbolic capital of teaming is not convertible into high objective ranking and therefore economic form in the AR field, it is inevitably treated, in practice, as a relatively powerless capital in the sport.

Women's legitimation of physical toughness as the dominant capital in the field is achieved through the 'alternate' pursuit of teaming as the more important measure of their personal success. For example, the majority of women indicate that although the teams, which achieve high competitive ranking, occupy more powerful positions in the field, a 'successful' race – for them – is one in which their team worked well together. Women, accordingly, demonstrate a relative privileging of teaming over toughness by valuing participation over competition:

> At one point I said, 'we have to trust each other and it would be nice if we could be friends and like each other,' and he said, 'we don't even know each other. We just have to be tolerant of each other.' That was his vision of teamwork. I was so disappointed by it all. I had watched the Australia coverage and Mark [Burnett, Eco-Challenge founder] talking incessantly about teamwork, and I was so into that. I wanted that so badly.
>
> (F, 33, Cat 3)

Women thus often give priority to teaming, even while acknowledging that it is not transferable to the improvement of one's position in the power structure. As physical toughness is both associated with men and acknowledged as the dominant capital in the field, women's perception of teaming as a means to team success – and a worthwhile end in itself – serves to legitimate masculine domination in the field.

The bias against women's specificity

In AR discourse that touts commitment to the collective through autonomous distinction, specificity is valued among both men and women. Women are accordingly attributed specific qualities that are allegedly invaluable to team success. Teaming, already touted as the measure of AR achievement, is associated with women's 'nature' and specific skill:

> Physically, is the woman typically as strong as the men are? Maybe not. But that's not what makes a successful adventure racer. Teamwork ability is as – if not more – important than physical ability, and that, in a sense, is what women have always been really good at.
>
> (M, 29, Cat 1)

> Good teamwork is trying to make your team laugh and be happy. Cutting a piece of salami and giving it. Little things that probably the guys don't think about because they act so tough. But I find those things very important. I'm emotional. It's not like guys who are tough. It's kind of a good balance.
>
> (F, 29, Cat 2)

> Without women, males are really macho, and if you would have four males, you would have so many teams that would just burst because they would never sleep. There would be too much testosterone and the teamwork wouldn't be there. We're too macho. We push ourselves and we don't want to say to the others that we need a break. So I think it's actually a plus that there are girls.
>
> (M, 26, Cat 2)

It would seem logical, then, that as 'teaming experts', women recruited onto AR teams would be chosen as frequently as, if not more often than, men. However, in practice, men rarely recruit more than one woman onto their team.

What becomes clear through the analysis is that the teaming skill attributed to women takes on a specific but inferior value. Women's teaming expertise is considered more important as a serviceable factor in the management of her 'natural weakness' than it is as a valuable trait in itself:

> If the woman is ever the weak link on the team, it's not because of the physical. It's the attitude that she is unwilling to admit that she needs help. She

> should say, 'I am unable to maintain this pace.' Do your best, is all we ask. It's how you deal with things that matters. Just being honest about if she's having trouble or whatever can be a really big contribution to the team.
>
> (M, 29, Cat 2)

Other traits that appear to be specific to women's teaming ability, are 'emotion', 'prudence' and 'maternal instinct' – traits that expose by corollary a lack of (male) reason, boldness or ego. Although their 'natural' women's qualities are often described as a 'necessary' and 'supportive' counterbalance to typical 'aggressive' male behaviour, they are treated in practice, simply, as weak.

For example, as risk management or 'calculated' risk-taking are seen as effective and necessary to success, whereas risk-taking without foresight is considered irresponsible, women are described positively in discourse as 'more responsible', 'prudent' or 'more safe':

> Women are definitely more responsible. Those guys were fooling around in the kayaks, and I was getting really pissed off. It's fine that they wanted to have fun, but they were pretending to tip, and all our stuff was tied down so if they had really tipped, it would have been a major ordeal. I think they weren't thinking about 'what if'.
>
> (F, 33, Cat 2)

It is clear, however, that in practice, 'prudence' is both associated primarily with women and understood as a detriment to success:

> [She] just wouldn't follow us on the bike because she was scared. We would have made that section in an hour if she wasn't so scared of falling. But then all the teams had at least one woman and were probably in the same situation.
>
> (M, 37, Cat 2)

Further, the discourse of woman's specificity implies that motherhood builds physical and mental strength and is therefore an asset to the team. One of the main 'stories' featured in the 1999 Eco-Challenge broadcast, for example, concerned the return of a new mother to the sport of AR:

> I am back doing AR after giving birth eight and a half months ago. Motherhood has definitely prepared me for this race. Sorry men can't do it. In terms of endurance, sleep-deprivation, balancing time, having a sense of humour, and letting things go.
>
> (Discovery Channel Eco-challenge broadcast)

However, in practice, motherhood was not considered to be an asset. Rather, it was assumed to deter women from taking requisite physical risks:

> Some athletes take bigger risks than others. I don't think a mother of four would take a huge risk or anything but sometimes you need to push really hard to stay up at the front.
>
> (F, 29, Cat 2)

It was also assumed that, in practice, mothers might be distracted with concerns of children left at home. While 'fatherhood' is relatively non-existent in description of practice, the responsibility of 'motherhood' appears as an ongoing theme:

> We're married and we have kids. I'm always asked things like 'as a mother, how do you feel about leaving your kids and going into this sort of race?' Or, 'if a serious accident happened to you, how do you handle that? When there was that big storm, and we were all safe in the tents, I really wanted to call my kids to let them know we were safe and warm and not out in danger. He just couldn't wait until the storm ended so we could continue. Our minds were on different things.
>
> (F, 40, Cat 3)

While women's specificity as 'naturally' emotional and prudent is touted in discourse both as teaming skill and as a criterion for team success, women's 'natural' weakness is simultaneously legitimated in practice through associations with motherhood and maternity.

Lastly, the gender rule itself is described in the discourse as being a positive demonstration of the value of women's specificity:

> Eco's values were originally that gender differences do not limit performance.
>
> (F, 44, Cat 1)

However, in practice, participants understand the rule to act less as a demonstration of 'Eco' values than as a necessity to ensure female participation, which would otherwise not be the norm:

> The gender rule is great because otherwise it's sexist not to have women there. You can't just exclude women.
>
> (F, 29, Cat 2)

> Without the gender rule, I think we would have made the mistake of choosing an all-male team.
>
> (M, 26, Cat 2)

> The mixed gender rule is good for AR. It forces men and women to work together. Also the rule is necessary to maintain strong female involvement, otherwise, I feel that most teams would comprise only men. This would restrict the opportunity of women to race and to be seen racing which not

> only encourages other women to race (and/or extend themselves in other areas) but also provides important role models for women and girls around the world.
>
> (F, 33, Cat 1)

Therefore, while the gender rule is described in discourse as an attestation to women's value, it is treated, in practice, as an equity mandate, naturalising women's weakness and legitimating masculine domination in the field of AR.

The bias against women's 'dramatic appeal'

In the case of Eco-Challenge, the media narrative is inextricably linked to discourse, feeding – if not mainlining – tightly-scripted rhetoric into collective understandings of the sport. But while the 1999 Discovery Channel Eco-Challenge clearly highlights women's weakness through the practice of production, in discourse, participants argue non-complicity in the media-bias on the basis that their 'race' is detached from the 'show'. In practice, however, participants share with the media the assumption that, due to their relative weakness, women hold 'natural' dramatic appeal.

A content analysis of the 1999 Discovery Channel broadcast illustrates that all stories centre on women and, with the exception of Team Rubicon racers, all women are treated as the weak link. In addition, all the injuries that are highlighted are those of women and are treated as either threatening or destroying team success. Early on in the broadcast, for example, the viewer is introduced to Team Vail:

> Mike is the strongest person on the team. We try to be like Mike. André is a freak of nature. He is 48 years old and he is faster than most 20-year-olds. Ellen just has this sparkling attitude. Never hear a bad word out of her mouth. Everything is positive that comes from her.

The visual accompanying these remarks is of Billy Mattison who, the viewer is told, is the strongest paddler on the team, propelling a two person kayak from the rear while Ellen sits motionless in the front, holding a makeshift kite. Mattison smiles for the camera and says, 'just giving Ellen a rest'. Ellen is portrayed as the physically weaker member of the team whose contribution is emotional support.

Next, the viewer meets Team Aussie, another elite team, and sees that Jane Hall is carrying paddles while the men team up to portage both kayaks one at a time. The voice over explains that 'carrying fully loaded kayaks tests teamwork as well as strength'. Hall, shivering as she watches her male team-mates struggle with the kayaks, exclaims, 'I'm starting to wonder what I'm doing here. Gosh, I hate the cold.' Hall, like Ellen, is portrayed as the weakest of the four. Teamwork, in this case, is evidently managing Hall's weakness.

After Team Rubicon's three-woman team is introduced as 'bucking Eco-Challenge tradition', their main rival, Team Greenpeace appears on screen. John

Howard, team captain, describes the team dynamic: 'As a team, we're fairly spread out in how we think. Andrea is good at feeding me when I'm hungry. Keith is good at carrying heavy loads. Neil is a good navigator. We're trying to bring out the best in everyone.'

Tier One is made up of three males from an all-male Airforce pararescue unit and Carrie Lewis, a female airforce survival and escape instructor. Lewis is shown in an unlikely role for a woman as the team navigator. However, within seconds of taking out her map, Lewis exclaims to her male team-mate: 'you can navigate if you want to. I'm pretty sick of it.' Tier One is soon shown again, lost, being led by rescuers out of the bush. 'Carrie Lewis', the voiceover remarks, 'is the team navigator'. Lewis continues: 'Yeah, it's a confusing area. It's a confusing map…' The only highlighted female navigator in the 1999 Eco-Challenge costs the team a disqualification.

Lewis's difficulties navigating are contrasted with Team Halti's effortlessness at the task. Dominic Arduin, the female member on the team boasts, 'we don't have any problems in navigation. The guys are world champions. It's not a problem.' Although the team makes a serious navigational error that costs them several hours, the media focus is on Arduin's battle with bone cancer and chronic pain. Subsequent clips of Team Halti show Arduin in tears, struggling. It is made clear that Arduin is the weak link and 'managing' her weakness is the team's strategy for success. This same strategy is made evident when South Africa's Lindy Bradshaw almost quits the race and disqualifies her team due to her fear of heights and her unwillingness to embark on an uncomplicated rappel.[9]

But while the Discovery Channel producers clearly maintain a male bias, participants distinctly recognise the manufactured character of the TV product, arguing detachment from the process of production and thus from the male-bias:

> I had the impression that certain teams had been invited to make money for Discovery so [Burnett] could sell the Discovery package to their country. When I understood that, I said: 'I'll do it for fun, for myself and enjoy it, and they can do their show'.
>
> (M, 38, Cat 1)

> For sponsorship, it's appealing to have both women and men in the same team because it attracts TV. We do the race while they worry about making a big show. But it doesn't help us in the race when the girl starts to cry, even if the Discovery people get off on it.
>
> (M, 26, Cat 2)

> The cameras always focus on women getting injured. It's expected, but we ignore it.
>
> (F, 29, Cat 2)

Yet even while participants claim detachment from the production process, they actively recognise women's dramatic appeal to the media based on their 'natural' weakness:

> It's Mark Burnett's strategy. Women and men don't react the same way. Men get frustrated and they hit each other. Women tend to cry. It sells more.
>
> (M, 38, Cat 3)

> Of course it's more interesting for TV to see people having a hard time and crying and falling down. If a man is saying 'this is easy' and a woman is saying 'this is the hardest thing I've ever done', of course [the media] will focus on the woman. It's sometimes men who cry or can't finish; that I've seen a lot. But I think it's always easier to find the woman doing that, and it's good on TV.
>
> (M, 33, Cat 3)

Therefore, while participants' 'media savvy' and self-reflexive discourse is posited as a challenge to suggestions of their complicity, validation of the media's male-biased strategy serves to naturalise women's weakness:

> We'd tease [her] and try to make her cry because we noticed that all the girls would cry and they'd get all the attention. So we wanted to get [her] to cry a bit [laughs].
>
> (M, 26, Cat 2)

While participants' apperception of media exploitation and marketing strategy is recognised as non-complicity in the masculine domination process, it is, in effect, the recognition of women's value to media drama – and thus recognition of their 'natural' weakness – that acts along with the documentary rhetoric to naturalise women's weakness.

'Playing the field': women's struggles and strategies in the field of AR

The dissonance between discourse and practice highlights several competing symbolic capitals in the field of AR that are assigned a less valuable women's form, thus defining the field's specific 'gendered' capitals. Physical toughness and risk-taking emerge as the forms of symbolic capital that produce the most relevant differences among female athletes, but which are valued most highly in men. Teaming capital, though touted among both genders as AR's norm of success, similarly takes on less value when accumulated by women (associated with emotional support, good following skills and the ability to arbitrate dissension rather than with leadership, navigation and strength). Media attention also emerges as an important gendered capital, associating women with drama – in contrast to men's more customary link to performance – and thus with a less valuable form. And lastly, competitive ranking appears to take on less value when accumulated by women, explained by a lack of strength or competitive instinct when ranking is low, and explained by the leadership, navigation and physical toughness of male team members when it is high.

Women participating in AR, however, do not constitute a homogeneous group in the field, either with regard to ways of 'playing the game' or to position-taking in relation to gendered forms of capital. Drawing from Bourdieu's conceptualisation of strategies that underpin dynamics in a field, the current discussion explores the different 'practical logics' fuelling women's practice. I thereby demonstrate how women's strategies are linked to their positions in the hierarchy of AR attested ranking – classified, for the purpose of my analysis, into three categories that represent calibre of ability and experience: elite (Cat 1), above average (Cat 2) and average/novice (Cat 3). As described earlier, these strategies are not the result of rational calculation. They are, rather, generated by what Bourdieu calls a 'practical sense,' that is the practical dimension of action whereby social agents respond to the opportunities and constraints of a given circumstance according to their position, and thus power, in a field.

Despite the evidence that the majority of women in AR recognise teaming as the most frequently pursued 'women's' capital in the field, a very small minority of Cat 1 women (approximately five per cent of women participants), in contrast, does not share this recognition. It is, rather, in the interest of Cat 1 women to pursue, like men, physical toughness capital in order to maintain and/or improve their position in the field. Accordingly, Cat 1 women censor emotion, carry heavy loads, take risks and push their bodies to capacity. Cat 1 women's strategy, aiming to minimise any appearance of weakness, can be considered as a conservation strategy of their dominant position among women. Accordingly, as an extraordinarily 'tough' minority, they hold a value of 'rarity' (Bourdieu 1984: 226–50) in the field, a value preserved by demonstrating high levels of physical toughness and by encouraging the existent minority female ratio in the sport.

As women generally do not assemble their own teams and depend on a previously formed team of men to select them as 'the woman', the more physical toughness capital a Cat 1 woman has, the more likely she is to be recruited onto a top-performing team. She can then earn sought-after profit in the form of sponsorship, prestige and 'star' status in the AR community as well as gaining more racing opportunities. Physical toughness capital – and thus rarity value – also gives Cat 1 women leverage, allowing them to act as 'free agents' and even to command payment or, at minimum, reimbursement for their expenses. Most Cat 1 women are able to sustain AR as an all-consuming lifestyle, racing with several different high-calibre teams throughout the year, earning prize money, sponsorship and 'signing bonuses'. The accumulation of physical toughness capital then leads to profit in the forms of symbolic and economic capital.

However, as Cat 1 women acknowledge that without the gender rule Cat 1 men would most often select an all-male team, they accept characterisation as 'mandatory equipment'. Accordingly, they acknowledge that Cat 1 men most often seek only to fulfil the mandated minimum on a team, thus securing Cat 1 women's position as a (subordinate) minority in the field. The accumulation of rarity value, however, ensures a better position in relation to the field's dominant capital. Therefore, though appearing subversive in the AR field through the pursuit and accumulation of male-dominated capital, Cat 1 women legitimate 'men's capital' as that which is dominant, thus naturalising women's weakness in the field.

In contrast to Cat 1 women's conservation strategy, it is in the interest of Cat 3 women (approximately 80 per cent of women participants) to pursue a subversion strategy, suggesting an intentional rupture with the 'traditional physicality of sport' (Hargreaves 1994; Theberge 1989). The strategy to pursue teaming capital appears as a subversive challenge to the legitimacy of physical toughness as the defining standard of AR. However, it is according to their 'feel for the game' that Cat 3 women recognise – but do not challenge – the dominant capital in the field, expecting to gain little in the struggle for the accumulation of physical toughness, and pursuing the subordinate capital instead.

Cat 3 women, accordingly, tend to accept and reinforce their weakness relative to men, downplaying their competitiveness and 'toughness', setting low expectations and emphasising their emotionally supportive role on the team. Although Cat 3 women emphasise inequality and physical weakness through their practice they, in complete contrast to Cat 1 women, by pursuing an 'alternate' capital, reject the label of 'mandatory equipment'. In fact, for Cat 3 women, dysfunctional team dynamics will often make the race experience personally unsuccessful, regardless of competitive ranking:

> I kept my mouth shut most of the time. I didn't care about the team because they didn't care about me. I personally wanted to finish so that I would never have to see these people again, and I was sad the whole time because I had seen what some of the other teams were like. Everyone kept congratulating me because we actually did pretty well, but that just made it worse for me because I knew how it was.
>
> (F, 33, Cat 3)

The interests sought by Cat 3 women differ greatly from those sought by Cat 1 women. Unlike the 'free agent' status pursued by elite women, Cat 3 women race infrequently (their lifestyles usually reflect more general outdoor pursuits and risk recreation than they do AR specifically), but usually with the same team-mates, who are often husbands and/or friends. They consider emotional investment as equally important as their financial investment, and generally expect long-term loyalty from a team. Cat 3 women who acquire teaming capital, then, achieve a protected position on their team and do not have to continually vie, like their elite counterparts, for selection onto different teams throughout the year.

> When we were looking for a replacement last year, she was the one who insisted we look for a guy. She likes the dynamics the way they are – being the only girl. We have to respect that because dynamics are so important.
>
> (M, 32, Cat 3)

Importantly, in contrast to Cat 1 women who pursue symbolic and economic capital within the AR field, Cat 3 women seek to accumulate social profit in external fields (in the form of friendships, alliances and physical capital):

> I never really feel that great about my performance in comparison to everyone else. But when I go home, everyone treats me like I did something incredible. Then I feel strong.
>
> (F, 34, Cat 3)

> We were all pretty close anyway because we work together and we're friends. But after this, I know I can count on them for anything.
>
> (F, 31, Cat 3)

Cat 3 women, aiming to accumulate symbolic profit, not economic capital also take advantage of reduced pressure, recognising a certain freedom – even power – in assumptions about their weakness:

> I cry a lot and they just let me get over it. And then I'm fine. It's liberating. After I cry, everything is relative again. The guys don't let themselves. I'd hate to be a guy doing this. I'm allowed to be the weakest. They're not.
>
> (F, 35, Cat 3)

Finally, Cat 2 women (approximately 15 per cent of women participants) often aim to acquire both forms of capital, but privilege physical toughness over teaming capital as their position in the field – based in increasing ability and experience – improves. A Cat 2 woman, for example, may value her emotional or maternal contributions to the team dynamics while simultaneously recognising her competitive and athletic strengths. One woman with top-ten ambitions going into the 1999 Eco-Challenge competition illustrates Cat 2 women's characteristic strategy of *succession* – to value both women's specificity along with their strength:

> I am different being a woman because, like, when [he] was sick, my maternal side came out. He was like a little child. He would just snuggle and I would put his hat on or rub his back. But I think I was the one who had the least problems. I don't have anything to prove. We're competitive, but we go for a good time. If we start fighting with each other, it's not worth doing it. That's our philosophy.
>
> (F, 29, Cat 2)

Therefore, Cat 2 women, in an attempt to improve their position in the field hierarchy, pursue *succession* strategies to either accumulate *physical toughness* capital or to exploit teaming capital – as the moment dictates. Further, Cat 2 women accumulate both physical toughness and teaming capital, and they, accordingly, accrue both of the resulting forms of profit. Cat 2 women most often maintain loyalty to, and priority with, a specific team, but accept opportunities to race with other (usually Cat 2) men looking for a 'good woman' to complete their team for a specific race.

I have explained how AR's internal field dynamics are underpinned by the interest-driven strategies deployed by participants struggling to maintain or improve their current position in the field. Women from all categories, accordingly, demonstrate a 'practical sense' for the field's dynamics, responding strategically, according to their position in the field hierarchy, to the opportunities and constraints of given circumstances. However, despite the heterogeneity of the participants and strategies deployed, none of the women's position-taking or practices can be considered subversive or transformative to the gender regime in sport. Their strategies – whether based in the pursuit of teaming or physical toughness capital – all act to legitimate masculine domination in AR.

Concluding thoughts

This study has aimed to highlight the symbolic value of sport practice, in the construction/affirmation of individuals and in given social orders such as the sport and gender regimes. AR discourse's emphasis on the value of teaming, and of women's specific teaming ability, suggests that AR might constitute a site of subversion, and thus transformation, of the gender hierarchy sport traditionally helps preserve. However, through a study of participants in the 1999 Discovery Channel Eco-Challenge, AR is presented, rather, as a symbolic system that naturalises women's weakness and legitimates masculine domination.

However, while women have not yet subverted masculine domination in the sport of AR, the data suggests that women do accumulate – by virtue of participation in a 'tough' sport – a form of physical capital only recognisable as such in external fields. Therefore, this accumulation of capital – and thus power – in the social structure may have indirect impacts on transformations in other fields, ultimately, perhaps, influencing gendered dynamics in sport. In other words, though the analysis challenges the feminist inclination to emphasise 'the creative agency of individuals and the instabilities of power relations rather than their recuperative qualities' (Bordo 1993: 294), it allows for Messner's (1996: 229) view of sport as 'a political terrain characterised by internal contradiction and paradox that leaves room for the play of oppositional meanings, and potentially for the organisation of collective resistance and institutional change'.

The study has also uncovered the struggles and strategies that underpin gender dynamics in a specific (sport) field. It has thereby highlighted the shortcomings of research that emphasises discourse as the basis of social reality, ignoring the material, structured relations of power that shape language and ideology (Messner 1996: 227). Most importantly, perhaps, it has demonstrated the impact that gender dynamics have on the definition and constitution of a field – its hierarchy of power and its struggles for valued forms of capital. The study of gender relations in sport is particularly relevant to the exploration of new and emerging lifestyle sport cultures, most often theorised as promising alternative values and structures to those of traditional sport.

Notes

1 The definition of 'new' sport culture is historically relative and the object of debate. I use the term only to designate those sports which ideologically or practically provide alternatives to mainstream sports and their values (Beal 1995; Loret 1995; Rinehart 1998; Wheaton, 1997).
2 As Martha Bell (2003: 228) describes, there is no consensus on the use of terms. New Zealanders, for example, tend to use the term 'multisport', while Americans use the term 'adventure racing'.
3 Kay and Laberge (2002a) describe 'authenticity' as one of the two key forces constituting the specific forms of capital that define the AR field.
4 I use discourse in the anthropological sense referring to culture or ideology (Sawyer 2002) defined here as the expressed collective understanding of the sport's 'legitimate' form.
5 Defined here as personal reflections on participation based in experience.
6 Points of convergence between a feminist approach and Bourdieu's social theory, as well as the potential for the integration of gender as a structuring principle in Bourdieu's theory, have been explored by Laberge (1995) and McCall (1992).
7 Respondents were classified according to ability, experience and past performance: Category 1 = elite caliber; category 2 = above average caliber; and category 3 = novice or average caliber.
8 At the time of data collection, the movie of the same title had not yet been released.
9 Rappel means descend a cliff or mountainside by means of a double rope wrapped around the body.

References

Beal, B. (1995) 'Disqualifying the official: An exploration of social resistance through the subculture of skateboarding', *Sociology Of Sport Journal*, 12: 252–67.

Bell, M. (2003) '"Another kind of life": adventure racing and epic expeditions' in R. Rinehart And S. Sydnor (Eds) *To the Extreme: Alternative Sports, Inside and Out*, New York: SUNY Press. 219–56.

Birrell, S. And Theberge, N. (1994) 'Feminist resistance and transformation in sport' in D. M. Costa And S.R. Guthrie (Eds) *Women and Sport*, Champaign, IL: Human Kinetics. 361–76.

Bordo, S. (1993) *Unbearable Weight: Feminism, Western Culture and the Body*, Champaign, IL: Human Kinetics.

Bourdieu, P. (1984) *Distinction: A Social Critique of the Judgement of Taste*, Trans. R. Nice, Cambridge: Harvard University Press.

Bourdieu, P. (1990) *The Logic of Practice*, Stanford: Stanford University Press.

Bourdieu, P. (1991) *Language and Symbolic Power*, Cambridge, MA: Harvard University Press.

Bourdieu, P. (1993a) 'How can one be a sportsman?' in P. Bourdieu, *Sociology in Question*, London: Sage.

Bourdieu, P. (1993b) 'Some properties of fields' in P. Bourdieu, *Sociology in Question*, London: Sage.

Bourdieu, P. (1998a) *Practical Reason: On the Theory of Action*, Cambridge, UK: Polity Press.

Bourdieu, P. (1998b) *La Domination Masculine* [Masculine Domination], Paris: Seuil.

Bourdieu, P. (1998c) 'On male domination' in *Le Monde Diplomatique*, October.

Bourdieu, P. and Wacquant, L. J. D. (1992) *An Invitation to Reflexive Sociology*, Chicago: University Of Chicago Press.

Connell, R.W. (1987) *Gender and Power: Society, the Person and Sexual Politics*, Cambridge: Polity Press.

Hargreaves, J. (1994) *Sporting Females: Critical Issues in the History and Sociology of Women's Sports*, London and New York: Routledge.

Harker, R., Mahar, C., and Wilkes, C. (1990) *An Introduction to the Work of Pierre Bourdieu: The Practice of Theory*, London: Macmillan Press.

Kay, J. and Laberge, S. (2002a) 'Mapping the field of "AR": Adventure racing and Bourdieu's concept of field', *Sociology of Sport Journal*, 19: 25–46.

Kay, J. and Laberge, S. (2002b) 'The corporate habitus in adventure racing', *International Review for the Sociology of Sport*, 37: 17–36.

Laberge, S. (1995) 'Toward an integration of gender into Bourdieu's concept of cultural capital', *Sociology of Sport Journal*, 12 (2):132–47.

Laberge, S. and Albert, M. (2000) 'Conceptions of masculinity and gender transgressions in sport among adolescent boys: Hegemony, contestation, and social class dynamic' in J. Mckay, M.A. Messner, and D. Sabo (eds) *Masculinities, Gender Relations, and Sport*, Thousand Oaks, London, New Delhi: Sage Pub. 195–221.

Le Monde, 'La femme, avenir du raid' ['Women: the future of AR']. 20 September 2001.

Loret, A. (1995) *Génération Glisse: Dans L'eau, L'air, La Neige… La Révolution Du Sport Des «Années Fun»* [The 'Glide' Generation: On Water, Air and Snow…The Sport Revolution of the 'Fun Years'], Paris: Edition Autrement.

McCall, L. (1992) 'Does gender fit? Bourdieu, feminism, and conceptions of social order', *Theory and Society*, 21(6): 837–67.

Messner, M.A. (1996) 'Studying up on sex', *Sociology of Sport Journal*, 13: 221–37.

Messner, M.A., and Sabo, D. (Eds) (1990) *Sport, Men and the Gender Order: Critical Feminist Perspectives*, Champaign, IL: Human Kinetics.

Rinehart, R. E. (1998) *Players All: Performances in Contemporary Sport*, Bloomington: Indiana University Press.

Sawyer, R. K. (2002) 'A discourse on discourse: An archeological history of an intellectual concept', *Cultural Studies*, 16 (3): 433–56.

Theberge, N. (1989) 'Women's athletics and the myth of frailty' in J. Freeman (ed) *Women: A Feminist Perspective*, 4th edn, Mountain View, CA: Mayfield. 507–22.

Wheaton, B. (1997) 'Consumption, lifestyle and gendered identities in post-modern sports: The case of windsurfing', unpublished thesis, University of Brighton.

9 'Anyone can play this game'

Ultimate frisbee, identity and difference

Andrew Thornton

Introduction

> Anyone can play this game.
>
> (Will/Interview)

It is a common claim made by 'Ultimate frisbee' players that 'anyone' could play their game. In this chapter I explore Ultimate players' struggles over their (athletic) embodiment and identity. My research shows that although Ultimate players reject and limit identifications with dominant sporting ideals they also continue to embrace some of their qualities. This process of identification suggests that maybe not 'everyone' will be able to become part of the Ultimate community.

Before examining the identity construction process, I give some background about Ultimate frisbee, the basis structure of play. I will then show that Ultimate players are concerned with presenting a new and 'different' sporting and cultural identity: one that is gender sensitive even egalitarian, rejects extreme competitiveness and physical aggression, and is all-inclusive. Yet, despite their claims, and ideals, Ultimate largely fails to produce practices and meanings that are beyond the dominant structures, ideals and practices of existing sports.

Historical development of Ultimate frisbee

'Ultimate frisbee'[1] is a sport that was invented late in the 1960s by a group of white, middle-class American High School males in the suburb of Maplewood, New Jersey.[2] They named themselves the 'Columbia High School Varsity Frisbee Squad' even though they, 'had not played any games, had no formal team or rules and someone's mother had made their team jerseys' (Zagoria 1998). Ultimate[2] was originally one part of a larger frisbee culture (Johnson 1975), but it is now the leading form of 'disc sport', except for perhaps disc golf.[3] The sport of Ultimate and culture originates in 1967–68 at a time of social turmoil in the United States. It was the time of the Vietnam War, the Civil Rights Movement and broader transformations in world politics, such as the heightening of the Cold War with the Soviet Union. It was a time of 'high anxiety' for American and sporting ideals (Edwards 1973; 1970). This anxiety is reflected in the guiding principle(s) that players are expected to embody:

> *Spirit of the Game:* Ultimate relies upon a spirit of sportsmanship [sic] which places the responsibility for fair play on the player. Highly competitive play is encouraged, but never at the expense of mutual respect among players, adherence to the agreed upon rules of the game, or the basic joy of play. Protection of these vital elements serves to eliminate adverse conduct from the Ultimate field. Such actions as taunting of opposing players, dangerous aggression, belligerent intimidation, intentional fouling, or other "win-at-all-costs" behaviour are contrary to the spirit of the game and must be avoided by all players.
>
> (Ultimate Players Association 2002b)

The 'Spirit of the Game', and its significance in the formation of Ultimate identities, is the focus of extended discussion later in the chapter.[4]

Ultimate is primarily played in Euro-Western countries, but is also quite popular in Japan. In total there may be as many as 150,000–200,000 participants worldwide. The United States contains the largest number of players, teams and leagues, though the Canadian cities of Toronto, Vancouver[5] and Ottawa all contain very large well organised leagues. There is a range of local, national and international competitions comprised of men's ('open'), women's, 'mixed', youth, and masters divisions. Ultimate is largely self-funding through the payment of league membership and tournament fees.

The Ultimate community's process of identification is in part accomplished by projecting what are broadly considered to be the 'negative' aspects of sport onto other players and identities such as American football and or ice hockey. For example, direct physical aggression and intimidation is rejected, in principle, and Ultimate players are expected to not taunt other players as is common in these 'other' sports. These 'unsporting' behaviours and other qualities are supposedly outside of Ultimate identities and culture. The chapter will show that Ultimate players' identities sublimate or suppress those characteristics that are normally associated with stereotypes of working-class and or black sporting bodies and identities. Ultimate players appear both to reject and celebrate the physical aggression of what are nominally working-class and 'black' sports.

One way of analysing Ultimate could be to compare it to historical precedents in mainstream sports and ideals. For example, the 'Spirit of the Game' seems to reflect the idea of a 'gentleman's [sic] agreement' that is similar to the early rules of English football:

> It was never even thought that a player would intentionally do anything to hurt an opponent. Such conduct would be 'ungentlemanly', and that was an unpardonable offence; [...] the lowering of self-control to depths of ungentlemanly conduct was something which could not be tolerated.
>
> (Elleray cited in Collwell 2000: 202)

Another way of analysing Ultimate would be to situate it in previous research on the nature and meaning of 'alternative' sport. In an age when sport cultures are supposed to be increasingly commercialised, 'McDonaldised' and globalised (McDonald and Andrews 2001; Miles 1998; Maguire 1999) it is important to note that Ultimate was founded on and continues to be defined by rejecting or going against the flow of these broader cultural processes. Beal's (1995) research on skateboarding shows how another (sport) culture was formed through the rejection of standardisation and corporatisation. Beal suggests that skateboarding has been transformed from what was essentially an aesthetic play form, defined by its anti-establishment ethos, into a competitive and corporate sport and commodity. However, the activity of skateboarding as Beal points out has not been entirely co-opted by standardisation and corporatisation (see also Beal and Wilson , this volume). However, its commercial form does interestingly cash in on the 'style' and 'attitude' which made skateboarding an 'alternative' activity in the first place. Ultimate though was established as a sport and as such represents a different social form, but does contain a similar ethos of 'being alternative'.

However the central purpose of this chapter is not to draw comparisons with other sports, but rather to draw attention to the ways in which players are struggling to position themselves within and against not only sporting ideals but broader cultural ideals and issues. Where Gruneau (1983) has argued that sport mobilises middle-class biases in the formation of social relations I would extend his argument to suggest that sport simultaneously mobilises racial, sexual, bodily and gender biases.

Constructing identity and difference

In this chapter, I will draw attention to three dominant aspects of Ultimate culture. The first is gender politics, which has been an open and ongoing concern in Ultimate. The second is the 'Spirit of the Game', which is a code of conduct that is intended to separate Ultimate players' from extreme competitiveness. The last section will address the meaning and importance of Ultimate players' celebration of 'laying out' or 'going ho' which is a phrase used to describe the physical act of diving to the ground to either catch or intercept the disc. Gender equality has always been an important issue in Ultimate and is one sign of its anti-establishment 'alternative' character. However, it will become apparent through an analysis of Spirit of the Game and 'going ho' that Ultimate identifications express a concern with more than gender.

The focus of the chapter is on the *processes* of identity construction and thus if I were to produce a typology of 'different' sports and identities it would suggest a stability of identity that does not exist. As this chapter contends, Ultimate identities don't fit neatly into any existing categories, histories and discourses. They are 'mix and match', and are culturally and historically contingent. In order to understand the ambivalence that structures Ultimate identities I begin from the position that we engage with sporting forms in constrained ways because sport forms are always *already* structured through practices and notions of social difference.

Difference is understood here as an organising feature of how we know about the world and how relations of power and identity are organised. Identity is based on the construction of difference. In the process of marking the limits, boundaries and 'inside' of an identity we also construct its outside. What is outside is not considered as part of the identity. However, it makes sense to argue that the construction of the 'outside' is a constitutive or defining aspect of identity. The construction of an 'inner' and an 'outer' can be seen as a binary opposition. Jacques Derrida (1974) argues that one side of a binary opposition is usually the dominant one, the one that includes the other in its field of operation. For example, 'rational' and 'irrational' appear as obvious opposites, but we can see that the rational has the power to define and position the irrational as an external, extraneous, aberrant feature of the dominant identity. For example, in Western cultures the irrational is rarely granted the power to define the rational (Hall 1997).

Identity then must always be unstable as what is outside or beyond it is virtually endless and cannot be pre-determined. Thus identity formation is always a process not only of inclusion, but active ongoing exclusion and the drawing and policing of boundaries. Jacques Derrida (1974), Homi Bhabha (1986) and Stuart Hall have all noted that the processes of identification are structured in ambivalence.

> Difference is ambivalent. It can be both positive and negative. It is both necessary for the production of meaning, the formation of language and culture, for social identities and a subjective sense of the self as a sexed subject [...] and at the same time it is threatening, a site of danger, negative feelings, of splitting, hostility and aggression towards the Other.
>
> (Hall 1997: 238)

In the formation of any identity those ideals, bodies, embodiments which are constructed as different, as Other are also embraced and rejected in a process of *disavowal*:

> [Disavowal] ... is a non-repressive form of knowledge that allows for the possibility of simultaneously embracing two contradictory beliefs, one official, one secret, one archaic, one progressive, one that allows the myth of origins, the other that articulates difference and division.
>
> (Bhabha 1986: 168)

Thus I will focus on those words, ideals, images and actions that seem to engender moments of ambivalence and disavowal as they arise in Ultimate culture.

This chapter is based on my continued participation in Ultimate as well as interviews, conversations and observations that were part of my doctoral dissertation (Thornton 1998). The research was conducted based on the theory and methods of 'critical ethnography' (Thomas 1993). I have participated in Ultimate as a player for over ten years in Canada, America and the United Kingdom. However, the majority of the empirical data presented here is from the

Canadian Ultimate scene. A number of researchers have conducted critical ethnographies on other sport cultures, bringing similar theoretical and methodological commitments to the analysis of sport cultures. (Klein 1993; Beal 1995; Fine 1987; Hilbert 1997; Polsky 1967; Wheaton and Tomlinson 1998).

How the game is played

Ultimate is a non-contact disc sport normally played by two teams of seven players. Ultimate players use the term 'disc' to describe the 'frisbees' that they play with. Although widely used in common vernacular frisbee is a registered trademark that refers to a range of flying (sports) discs. The discs that are normally used by Ultimate players are not actually 'frisbees'. The standard disc Ultimate players use – the '175 Gram Ultra-Star Professional Sportdisc' – is similar in design to the original trademarked frisbee (Ultimate Players Association 2002a). This is one reason why players regularly drop the frisbee half of the name and call the game 'Ultimate'. Players distinguish themselves from people who merely 'play with a frisbee' in their back yard or on the beach by the use of the term 'disc'. Ultimate is generally played outdoors on grass fields similar in size to American football, but can be played on any flat open space and is played indoors as well. The first games of Ultimate were played on a paved parking lot (Johnson 1975).

The object of the game is to score goals or points. A goal is scored when a player catches the disc in the end zone that the player is attacking. End zones are rectangle like areas at each end of the playing field that are marked either with boundary lines and or small orange plastic cones. The disc must be passed through the air from player to player. Players cannot hand the disc to their team mates as is done in rugby and American football. Nor can they use their feet to pass the disc and they cannot intentionally re-direct (or 'mack' or 'tip') the disc to a team mate. Like basketball and netball, players are not allowed to run while holding the disc. Throwing or passing it to another player moves the disc around the field.

The disc may be passed in any direction. Any time a pass is incomplete, intercepted, knocked down, or contacts an out-of-bounds area, a turnover occurs, resulting in an immediate change of the team in possession of the disc. This is similar to how play proceeds in basketball and soccer. Thus the game has a continuous flow to it. Players make their own 'calls' and interpretations of infractions of the rules. They also make decisions on whether or not a player has gone out of bounds in order to catch the disc. Players do not wait until the 'whistle blows' as is the case in sports with referees and line judges. They make calls from within the flow of the play.

There are no referees in the game of Ultimate. The major reason why there are no referees is that the originators of the sport were consciously rejecting their use and meaning because referees are a central feature of mainstream sports. The sentiment that is popularised in Ultimate circles is that referees open up the way to *not playing fair* because one can get away with breaking the rules *if it is not seen by a referee*. Thus, in ideal terms, Ultimate players put the burden of responsibility for fair play squarely in the lap of each and every player.

Ambivalence in gender difference

I want to begin the discussion of gender difference by examining the ways in which gender comes into play in the interpretation and structuring of the seemingly mundane aspects of playing a game of Ultimate. Ultimate players' awareness of gender tends to conflate gendered (social) limitations and biology as the bases of difference(s) in male and female athletic performance. Although I focus on the 'lay out' in relation to gender identification here, it carries significance beyond just gender identity. I will return later in the chapter to an analysis of the meanings attached to the lay out to illustrate that class and race differences, in particular, are also central features of Ultimate players' identities.

One of the most important signifiers of an Ultimate player is their ability to throw 'the flick' (also called a 'forehand'). The ways in which it is talked about in Ultimate culture suggests it is an act where dominance and gender difference is embodied. It is, I would argue, an act of locating the unacceptable, the inadequate, and the undesirable: the Other of Ultimate:

> [...] more difficult to master than the standard backhand beach-bimbo toss, this tiny little wrist movement can take years of repeated practice to perfect. But is essential both in the game and otherwise. Once it is learned, the player can go to a park and signal to other disc owners that he or she is not just a casual Frisbee catcher, but also an Ultimate player.
>
> (Lind 1992: 12; female Ultimate player)

Although written with considerable sarcasm by a female player, this is an insightful point about Ultimate players' identifications and sporting embodiment and the ways in which gender norms are operating in Ultimate culture. The label of 'beach-bimbo' positions non-players and 'non-flickers' as weak, silly feminised (i.e. 'bimbo') subjects. And within Ultimate circles (in games and tournaments) one of the first things that players watch for is how well someone throws their flick. 'He's got no flick' is a comment I often heard on the field at least among less skilled teams. More generally, at all levels of competition, one assesses the entire make-up of opponents' throwing skills. This practice is used both as a strategic ploy, and as a way of locating others in their lack of experience of playing the game. It is quite clearly a way of *identifying outsiders* to the Ultimate community. Thus an act of athletic skill is not merely a matter of technical precision, it is always also a sign of one's position in a hierarchy of power, and the creation of an (abject) Other. In this instance, the Other of Ultimate identity then is prominently signified as an un-athletic form of feminised embodiment.

It has been observed that there has been considerable change, even in the last ten years, in terms of what is, broadly speaking, possible and 'acceptable' in feminine embodiment. Today, 'athletic', lean and even muscular female bodies have come to be seen as socially acceptable, even desirable, while not necessarily destabilising hegemonic notions of femininity. Athletic female bodies are challenging notions of thin, white, heterosexual feminine attractiveness, but continue to be framed by such stereotypes (Birrell and Cole 1994; Lenskyj 1994; Hall 1996; Cole and Hribar 1995). A closer look at the mundane aspect of guarding or 'marking' opponents in an Ultimate game will demonstrate that this struggle over gendered embodiment is an important issue in this culture.

Normally there are seven players against seven opponents on the field. The general rule for 'co-ed' (later changed to the term 'mixed') Ultimate was that a maximum of five players per team of any 'one' gender were allowed to be on the field at once or the '5-2 rule' in vernacular. (This proportion has changed to 4-3 in recent years across North America.) In the vast majority of 'co-ed' games I observed this was interpreted as five men and two women. This issue and practice continues to be the subject of considerable controversy in Ultimate culture in Canada and the United States (Haman 1994; Price 1994).[6]

During one of my league games a woman on my team was asked to 'play as a man'. That is, she was to guard a male player and substitute in for other males on our team. Generally, women only substitute for other women and men do the same. Women normally guard or mark other women and men mark other men. However, I have never heard anyone say, 'You play as a woman', to a male. Jennifer said she enjoyed doing this because the males that she ends up guarding are usually the slower or least skilled male players on the team and she 'surprises them with her ability to cover them'. She felt that they were somewhat embarrassed at being guarded by a woman, even though she usually had better skills and more experience. Jennifer also told this tale with some pride. She was a very experienced athlete having played basketball and baseball throughout her life. I have heard her variously described as 'tall, for a woman' and having 'a deep voice' which both regulates her out of dominant ideals of masculinity and femininity at the same moment. She is too tall to *really* be a woman, yet still feminised by the last half of the phrase, 'for a *woman*'.

This sequence of events (which is a dominant feature of 'co-ed' Ultimate games) also suggests that men want to avoid playing directly against females because they might be shown to be less capable than a woman. It might be okay to be outplayed by another man, but to be outplayed by a woman would throw serious doubt onto one's status as a competent (masculine) player. Thus, it may be that the issue of *men's competence in comparison to women* is skirted around by the general acceptance that same gender guarding is 'only in the Spirit of the Game' (i.e. only fair and reasonable). The practice of men guarding men pits them against their equals, so to speak, and avoids potential 'embarrassment'. It maintains a fairly rigid boundary between direct male and female competition that reinforces the broader cultural notion that women are categorically incapable of equalling men's physical performance.

A regular part of Ultimate player's conversations is that men and women can never be equal physically. Many will accept that 'some women' are good athletes but that men are just 'bigger and stronger'. However, we cannot interpret physical and biological capability outside of social norms and conventions that suggest that women are 'naturally' or inherently biologically incapable of the same physical feats as men. (Hall 1996; Birrel and Cole 1994; Whitson 1994). Feminist scholarship has provided convincing evidence that the differences between men and women in their physical capabilities are far less significant than the social forces that limit women's and encourage men's engagement with sport. Many have argued that the *overlap* in physical capabilities of males and females is far greater than the differences (Fausto-Sterling 1985; Dyer 1986; Cahn 1994; Hargreaves 1994).

Ultimate as a physical activity seems to assume a 'sportasized' identity and body (Harvey and Rail 1995) in its parlance and practice. The sportasized identity and body is one that already understands the necessary and seemingly 'obvious' features of physical movement and social interaction required in sport. This identification includes assumptions about playing in a team, 'field awareness' and accepting the idea of competition as the only form of play. The sportasized body it has been argued references a stereotypically masculine embodiment (Birrell and Cole 1994). Thus participation in sport, and Ultimate, for women, generally means a transgression of dominant feminine identities.

Most players, at least on my team, were somewhat aware of the social and historical nature of why women generally do not play as much sport as men. *Both male and female players*, at times, seemed to reject the ideas of biology as destiny, and a woman's supposed 'natural' inferiority. They rejected the notion that it was fundamentally a problem of one's biology, but rather that access, practice and previous experience were the keys to one's success and enjoyment:

> I think that's the nature of our socialization. More men are pushed to play team sport, whereas women aren't and I mean for me I was afraid of it. I mean I played tennis and I danced and I didn't even play doubles [tennis]. That's not a team sport.
>
> (Rhonda/Interview)

One important point at which Ultimate players reveal a more ambivalent relation to athletic performance and gender difference is the attention paid to female players 'laying out' (i.e. aggressively diving on the ground) for the disc. Rhonda's comment below is quite typical as she expresses some glee at the sight of a female 'laying out'.

> I saw a woman at the Worlds lay out. She was so awesome. It is hard for a woman to do a lay out because she has breasts. She dove for the disc and just before she hit the ground she would do a front flip. It was wild. She was a gymnast.
>
> (Rhonda/Interview)

It might be argued that if women are seen to be able to embody masculine/athletic power they may potentially subvert and expose the myths of gender being solely determined by biology (see Fausto-Sterling 1985 for an extensive review).

> Women stay away from laying out, but when they do it's great and enjoyable to watch. Guys throw their bodies; girls there's a block. They just won't do it.
>
> (Lucy/Interview)

Lucy's statement on the other hand is an argument for an essential gender difference based on physiology, and as such stands in fairly stark contrast with Rhonda's more socially based explanation. Lucy's later comments also demonstrate the intense focus on women's capabilities which simultaneously constructs men's behaviours and skills as the norm:

> Girls don't catch hammers; seem to be afraid of them. If a girl lays out everyone is excited, but if a guy does it is appreciated. If a girl does it, everyone is high.
>
> (Lucy/Interview)

It is interesting to note that Rhonda and Lucy posit, at different points, women's physiology as the major reason why women do not lay out, then both give examples of a woman doing a 'lay out' with the same body. A lot of men don't 'lay out' either, and men's genitals are every bit as exposed (if not more so) in laying out as women's breasts! So self-protection may be one reason for not laying out, but it is not essentially a biologically-based gender difference. Arguably a male's jock strap provides less protection than a sports bra, though Ultimate women now have access to something called 'tortoise shells'[7] (Canadian Ultimate Players Association 1996). What seems apparent from the evidence I've presented here is that the relation between sport performance and the body is based more in how women and men relate to their bodies than the 'type' of body one possesses. This problem, as I have been suggesting, is a sign and central feature of the ambivalent relation that Ultimate players have to gender difference and sport. The ways in which we perceive the relative 'frailty' – and as Lenskyj (1986) has shown the supposedly delicate nature of women's physiology – is an enduring discourse.

One key to 'laying out' is previous Ultimate play and other athletic experience. It may seem obvious to suggest that athletic skills are developed through repetition and over time. Laying out is quite obviously a developed athletic skill and the elite players with little exception, both male and female, 'lay out all the time' (field notes, Buffalo, October 1993). However, gender norms about the body are so deeply entrenched among Ultimate players and in Euro-Western culture that we are still faced with the notion that 'women don't lay out'.

> ADT: Do men react differently to women when they make a difficult play?
>
> Yes. Because it is expected of men, which is silly. But *when women go ho*, it is astonishing to most guys, especially because most women don't do it. Most guys play rougher because they are used to it from other contact sports. Women are not expected to hurl their bodies through the air.
>
> (Frank/Interview)

> [...] *But* if you come to know players and know this woman is really good at this, then it is diminishing returns. You don't get as excited.
>
> (Sharon/Interview)

It seems that women who 'lay out' transgress essentialised gender discourses of biology and nature, and men who do it are considered exemplars of athletic prowess. These examples show that some women, not surprisingly, are every bit as ready to throw themselves to the ground as men. More interesting is the finding that the location of this gender difference apparently stems from two places: in previous similar athletic experience and in some 'natural' physical difference between males and females. Thus there is a high degree of ambivalence in players' understanding of gender and athleticism. Players have seen and reported on females laying out, but they still can't quite accept it as 'normal'. It is also interesting to note that as some women come to be understood as able and willing to lay out their actions become less notable. Therefore, women who 'lay out' move closer to the subject position of the (supposedly) non-gendered 'Ultimate player'. However, it is apparent that the meanings attached to laying out are not neutral, but rather suggest that the 'correct' and normal gender of Ultimate embodiment is masculine.

Ambivalence in the 'Spirit of the Game'

> Spirit of the Game is to 'be cool.' Play hard, be better, but don't be an asshole. NO deliberate fouling... Be considerate about misunderstood rules, not cocky. No spiking, no trash talking (unless they're friends like that), no dangerous play and make your own calls fairly. And it's 'contest' or 'no contest' no yelling and spitting about it.
>
> (Ultimate Players Association 2002c)

The 'Spirit of the Game' is an important aspect of Ultimate players' claims to being 'different from other sports'. The bases for the claims made by Ultimate players to difference and their (apparent) subversion of sporting norms is defined by the Spirit of the Game in combination with the ways in which it and the rules structure the culture. It emerges in my research as central to the formation of collective and individual Ultimate players' identities. Similar to Canadian and American 'amateur' sport clubs of the early twentieth century (Kidd 1996; Crossett 1990) Ultimate players use the Spirit of the Game clause to construct a distinction between themselves and their Others. The notions of intentional cheating and flagrant violations are generally considered to be features of sports that have referees and lots of direct and constant physical contact like boxing, American football and ice hockey. In comparison to Ultimate these sports are arguably differently racially and class coded in their play and rules (Cole and Andrews 1996). Therefore, they stand in opposition – or at least in competition with – Ultimate ideals. In 'contact' sports, such as ice hockey or American football, players often commit 'intentional' or 'smart' fouls as a competitive strategy. However, this is theoretically, at least, not possible in Ultimate because it would, 'not be in the Spirit of the Game'.

During the beginnings of Ultimate in the late 1960s sport in North America was undergoing profound and wide reaching changes. All of the major professional sport leagues in North America were expanding and beginning to pay athletes huge sums of money to play games. The crass money making and exploitation by the owners and managers of sport institutions were also being widely exposed. Arguably, these are some of the cultural issues that Ultimate originators were responding to. They felt they were going to develop a game 'with no rules, no boundaries and no star system' (Ultimate Players Association 1988). The ambivalent relationship to corporate sponsorship and competition that has developed, and continues to be a major unresolved issue, has a fairly clear grounding in the origins of Ultimate.

For example, the accepted history of Ultimate suggests a constant and broad based struggle over the way to conduct oneself within sport and beyond. Ultimate players regularly draw on the dubious[8] alterity of 'flower power' and 'hippies' to make claims about its uniqueness and difference from more mainstream sports. However, at the same time many players' actions and words tend to refute the associations with the stereotypes of 'skinny guys', 'stoners and acid freaks' (Zagoria 1998). All of these stereotypes seem to suggest connotations of certain types of whiteness and white bodies personified in the MTV characters 'Beavis and Butthead'. This struggle has developed, in part, due to the history of most of the 'originators', who came out of the late 1960s and are often associated with 'hippy culture' (Ultimate Players Association 1988). One of the few vestiges of this identification are the numerous tie-died t-shirts that are often present at Ultimate tournaments and parties, and the many debates over how to do or embody the Spirit of the Game. It is also common to see team names like 'Purple Haze' that reference the music and culture of the 1960s.

Strictly speaking Spirit of the Game *is not a rule*. Intended to limit 'overly aggressive' and or 'dangerous play' it enshrines an idealised notion of fairness and 'respect for opponents and team-mates', which players are supposed to demonstrate in even in the most intensively competitive situations.

> ADT: How does the Spirit of the Game operate in relation to the rules?
>
> I saw it live and then I saw it on TV. In the championship game played this year a player made a spectacular play, a lay out to catch the disc in the end-zone, but, there was some discussion whether he landed in bounds… He made a great effort to touch down the tips of both feet in the end-zone and then rolled over onto the cinder track. A wonderful play. Looking at it in slow-motion replay he may have just been out. My memory of it was the guy himself went, 'I'm not entirely sure'. And the defender came in and said, 'It was a tremendous play, let's score it', and it went as a score. And that's the type of spirit I like to see. Unfortunately, it doesn't always happen.
>
> (Eric/Interview)

There is a form of self-regulation, as seen in the above quote, which seems to arise due to the lack of external referees. There are no referees or line judges at any level of play.[9] And significantly the Spirit of the Game does not identify *specific* acts that contravene its limits (except for 'taunting of opponents'). It works more as a broad interpretive device which players use to assess the moral and legal acceptability of one or a series of plays and players. Thus, Ultimate players are intended to be entirely self-regulating in their play and organisation.

What is interesting here is *the struggle* that Ultimate players are contending with and less so the comparison to other sport histories and contexts. Perhaps the struggle over the ideals of 'fair play' represents a deeper issue concerning the nature of sport. It is more interesting to suggest that perhaps sport cannot be played 'fairly'. 'The Spirit of the Game' in Ultimate is intended to function as a moral and ethical guide to the game and its meaning is interpreted in a variety of ways. It is not the sheer variety of interpretations, but rather the *cycle of not being able to decide* on any clear definition that is most revealing.

Another facet of this identification is the notion that Ultimate players are enterprising and stretching the boundaries of sport. There is an almost heroic stance of some of the local and international organisers as they set out to promote a game that rejected the nastier parts of institutionalised sport:

> *Ultimate is not like life* where losses haunt you forever, there's always another game. It is true Ultimate is a Field of Dreams, where you pursue excellence and glory…Ultimate is a flower child, invented by skinny guys who strove to create a truly new game with new rules…You were pressed again and again to go all out, and then if you failed to catch the disc, to exercise your moral sense in calling the point. And *the measure was not some arbitrary boundary, net or goal, nor was it the judgment of some official, but rather your own maximum effort and potential.*
>
> (Quote from 'The Field of Dreams', Ultimate Players Association 1988)

This notion of being 'enterprising' is one that is at work in this quote and in Ultimate circles. Dissatisfied with mainstream sports being corrupted by competition and elite structures and unwilling to submit to external regulation, the 'ancient' heroes of Ultimate set out to invent 'the Ultimate game' (Zagoria 1998). A game beyond all games, yet, 'made up of all the best aspects of all other games' (Lewis 1994; Ultimate Players Association 1988).

There are a number of connected identifications that are suggested by the quote above and the Spirit of the Game, which include self-regulation, rationality, and an entrepreneurial spirit. The Spirit clause in the rules suggests that the subject of Ultimate frisbee is intended to be rational, aggressive but fair, willing to negotiate, have an equal respect for all concerned, to accept that they may have made an error and to accede to a rule structure.

Spirit of the Game as used by Ultimate players is arguably founded on the underlying assumption of rational thought and universal good will. This philosophy could easily be construed as a re-enactment of the Enlightenment project of the modern Western world (Dyer 1997). The premise of Euro-Western science and knowledge is that humans are capable of identifying the specific nature of the world. There is supposed to be a one to one correlation between the objects of human perception and the categories (or symbols) that we apply to those objects. This would include *the meaning* of 'fair play' in sport as an object constructed by human beings. Theoretically, humans are supposed to be capable of identifying and pinning down the exact meaning and causality of human action. Once the meaning of an object or relation is identified it is presupposed to be consistent across space and time (Seidman 1994). In this case, there is an (unrealistic) assumption that the Spirit of the Game is a predefined set of meanings that everyone agrees upon in different places and different times. One of the clear messages in the rules is that one is supposed to call a foul on ones self even if the person who was fouled does not (i.e. be fully self-regulating).[10]

Another, perhaps a more revealing approach is to see the Spirit of the Game, in Foucault's (1995) terms, as a panoptic mechanism of power. It works to construct a pervasive form of moral control and thereby, a broad form of behavioural regulation (Harvey and Rail 1995). Players awareness of this regulatory device serves to define and constrain their behaviour by internalising 'the gaze' of the unseen 'Spirit' in the same way that Foucault's (1995) prisoners reacted to their unseen guards in the centre of the Panopticon (prison). The widespread and ongoing discussions over the definition of the 'Spirit of the Game' serve as the 'regulatory mechanisms' (Foucault 1995) through which players actively participate in their own regulation. There is no agreed upon definition of the Spirit of the Game, but there is a *pervasive sense that one should play by it*. The Spirit of the Game is the Police inside Ultimate players' heads.

Players are supposed to discuss infractions of the rules, which can include asking other players for clarification. This is very different from other sporting environments, where a referee or judge makes all decisions and there is virtually no possibility of players changing or affecting a decision. Thus, in mainstream sport *decision-making power is removed* from the control of the athletes *from the outset of play* (Collwell 2000). This is a crucial difference as Ultimate players empower themselves with the right of 'making their own calls'.

The Spirit of the Game clearly has power as both a symbol and a structure and appears to signify a relation *among equals*. Nevertheless, there is an implicit hierarchy in Ultimate, as in most sports, which is similar to that of modern Euro-Western patriarchal capitalist colonialism (e.g. team captain, assigned positions, rules and committees). Part of this structure is the obeying of orders and obedience to 'one's betters' that signifies a deferral to 'survival of the fittest' ideology. Walvin (1987) argues that this colonial identity formation was intended to illustrate masculine, British (racial) superiority. Thus, *those who lead in sport* were the embodiment of a classed, gendered and racially superior identity.

The Spirit of the Game is a guide used by players to organise a similarly superior identification. Ultimate players' embodiment of the Spirit of the Game seems to represent a desire for moral purity and the negation of social difference. Ultimate asks players to abide by 'the highest standards of fair play', which is similar to other sporting ideologies of the past and the present. However, notions of 'fair play' tend to ignore difference in attitude, ability, access and commitment to an activity. What is different is that Ultimate assumes that everyone can and will abide by the Spirit of the Game *because there is no question of difference from the outset*. 'We' are among equals here and a 'true sporting gentleman' would never cheat another or question their judgment! *It is not in the Spirit of the Game*. The ideal subject of Ultimate is a judge and jury, a referee, a team player, and a leader, all at once. No one could possibly embody these ideals as they lie in contradictory relations of power that imply incompatible positions in a hierarchy of authority.

Ambivalence in the play: 'laying out'

> It is the responsibility of all players to avoid contact in every way possible.
>
> (Ultimate Players Association 2002b)

> Guys are not as intimidated ... they dive for the disc. Guys catch better because of football.
>
> (Lucy/Interview)

As noted earlier, 'laying out' and 'going ho' are phrases used to describe a particular action and way of playing the sport of Ultimate frisbee. 'Going ho' is short for 'going horizontal' and is synonymous with 'laying out': diving headfirst and extending one's body fully to catch a 'disc' or knock it down. To 'lay out', is considered by many Ultimate players to be a sign of one's 'Ultimate commitment' to the sport and team. It is also a spectacular and difficult athletic feat to perform and observe. Despite the fact that the rules state that players are to 'avoid contact at all costs', the lay out is only accomplished by making contact with the ground.[11] Laying out and the meanings that Ultimate players attach to it is another example of the ambivalence that structures identities in this community, ambivalence that goes beyond sport and the Spirit of the Game.

> AT: Are there similar problems for men and women in learning the game?

> Yes, but they're not gender specific problems. One of the reasons I like it so much is that it is something you can do competitively in a mixed setting. Unlike football, it would be more difficult to have a competitive game. *Ultimate skills are not gender specific* which makes it easier to have a competitive game.
>
> (Frank/Interview)

There is an inconsistency in Frank's comments here and his comments referred to earlier (see page 185). His comments point to ambivalence about gender. Frank concedes (earlier) that it *should not* be surprising to see women layout, but he then states that men and women could not play (American) football together. He says that women would not be able to handle the physical contact of football, a 'skill' *not required or desired* in Ultimate. So while it is okay in Frank's interpretation for women to play Ultimate, they are rejected as possible football players. When examined together, these two statements are powerful exemplars of the ambivalent desires within Ultimate identity. Frank's statement is significant because it is also, I suggest, a racial and class coding due to the association of contact sports, like American football, with black and working-class bodies (Messner 1991; Cole and Andrews 1996). The association of the working-class and blackness with the body and not the mind has a broad cultural resonance (Holmlund 1994; Dyer 1997; Fleming 2001). By de-emphasising the body as the site of physical and or social dominance Ultimate players are emphasising skill and intellect, and in their own terms 'Spirit'. Thus the feminisation of Ultimate, or as Frank says elsewhere in his interview, 'something my wife and I can do together', elides non-physicality with femininity and middle-class whiteness. If we apply a binary logic to the racial dimension it would seem that Ultimate is something that non-physically aggressive middle-class *white men* can do, too!

Going ho is an embodied knowledge of one's limits and then testing those limits. Desire, Butler has suggested is 'in some sense always a desire for recognition' (1992: 89). The recognition of others and self forms a community, and thus desire forms the boundaries of that community. Desire is always related to difference in the sense that what is desired also simultaneously constructs and suppresses what is detested (Hall 1990). Thus what is by implication, and by action, constructed as detestable in Ultimate is *overt physical contact and aggression*. However, Ultimate players seem to demand that the act of 'laying out' be celebrated, yet overtly reject those other sporting embodiments that are defined precisely by physical violence such as boxing, American football or ice hockey. Working-class and black bodies practically and symbolically populate these sports.

Laying out is s a signifier of 'going all out', one's commitment to the game and to 'sacrificing one's body' which are central to dominant bodily ideals of mainstream sport. The desire for physical evidence of *Ultimate's athletic legitimacy* is further established by the way in which bruises and scrapes are shown and talked about on a regular basis. These marks are 'badges of honour' among all Ultimate players. Though physical contact is openly rejected the markers of physical contact or injury are celebrated (as documented in other lifestyle sports, see Chapter 1). Knee braces and surgery scars are a regular topic of conversation (I should know I have had my own knee operated on due to an Ultimate injury). One of the regular prizes sometimes given out at tournaments is for 'worst injury'.

It appears as though the abject category of direct physical aggression is a necessary part of the formation of the Ultimate identities. Not able to knock people down, wrestle or punch, 'laying out' recuperates vestiges of extreme physical aggression and reassures Ultimate players that they too are 'real athletes'. Other forms of athletic prowess are admired, like running speed and jumping ability, but the most praise is reserved for 'laying out'. Certainly, no one is given the same type or amount of recognition for being able to catch, which is definitely more important than the occasional spectacular dive in terms of winning.[13] It is in this celebration of 'laying out,' Ultimate players preferred image of themselves, where we can see the intersection of a series of points of difference.

I heard it regularly repeated, 'This is not [American] football!' on plays where someone made contact with another player. I also had more than one player say to me, 'Oh sorry, I'm used to playing [ice] hockey', after they had run into me. These statements are crucial to the construction of Ultimate's difference to other sporting identities. Ultimate players have a general disdain for overt physical contact and American football in general. The rules on contact also highly constrain potential bodily harm to everyone concerned. Some of my female team-mates have specifically identified the 'non-contact' rules of Ultimate as one of the most important reasons that they were attracted to the sport:

> The physical contact in a game might cause women to shy way from the game, unless they are somewhat used to it. Maybe all-women's ultimate would attract more players. *Some women would never play a sport with a man on the same field without a referee.*
>
> (Lucy/Interview) [emphasis added]

I take this philosophy and practice of non-contact to be fairly unique and central to understanding the game and players of Ultimate.[12] It defines an identity that is productive of different bodies and relations to one's body and the bodies of others within and beyond sport. The important aspect of this difference as I have shown is how it relates to common or dominant sporting ideals.

Yet, ultimate embodiment is also clearly about exhibiting physical dominance over an Other. Within the play of the game the forceful occupation of space and aggression against others is prominent. The exemplary act of 'Going ho' is about mastery of the individual body (another side of discipline), which reveals the individual body to be enmeshed in relations of power and domination with other bodies. There is a sense that I as an 'Ultimate player' can control my body so well that I do not need to knock someone down in order to accomplish my objectives. This conception evokes the arms length, yet deadly, control processes of modern capitalist governance and military organisations (e.g. 'surgical strikes' or 'collateral damage' in the double-speak of American military language). The central point here is that one can and does assert force and dominance on the bodies of others without placing one's own body in direct physical jeopardy. There is some danger in Ultimate of physical injury to oneself in 'laying out', but it is of a fairly limited type.

There is a progressive value in the non-contact nature of the game, however, the emphasis that Ultimate players place on showing off scrapes and bruises, seems to serve as a reminder that this is a 'real' (manly) sport where one does get hurt: Ultimate players are not 'hard', but neither are they 'soft'!

Theoretical reflections

There is a deep ambivalence that resides in Ultimate players' images, talk and behaviour. This ambivalence is expressed in the rejection of overt physical contact in Ultimate and the desire to keep the flow going in games via the 'Spirit of the Game'. It is also the case that physical prowess and dominance are still encouraged, but is obscured by the emphasis on avoiding contact. The readings of 'going ho' that come from my informants show that the act is always read through the normative lens of aggressive sporting masculine physicality of contact sports which are also coded as working-class and black (Carrington 1998; Dyer 1997). This issue deserves much more attention in the social and cultural study of sport than I have been able to provide here.

Lucy's statement, 'Women tend to shy away from laying out', represents a gendered reading of athletic bodies. However, women and men who 'go ho' are accorded the highest praise for their physical abilities. Thus the most extreme act possible is also worthy of the most praise. Therefore, Ultimate players talk and rules suppress physical aggression, but then in the final analysis, celebrate it.

The abject qualities of physicality and physical violence associated with 'other' sports returns as the most desired ways of being in Ultimate culture. Richard Dyer (1997), Stuart Hall (1990) and Frantz Fanon (1967) have all shown us that the demonisation of physicality and aggression are the foundations of white male, bourgeois, heterosexual identification. Dominant (white) masculine identities rest on the repression of physicality and the assertion of spiritual purity/superiority. The Spirit of the Game, the non-contact rules and the celebration of 'going ho' signify a circle back to the knot of anxiety that founds Euro-Western masculine sporting embodiments.

This knot of anxiety is manifested in the way the game is played and the ambiguous relation to physical aggression in Ultimate. It may be a different sporting activity but the desire for competitive individualism and self-autonomy is what seems to drive the players. The *desire* to continue to resurrect failed (colonial) modernist figures of the 'good sport', like those that are evoked by the idealistic versions of the Spirit of the Game, are perpetuated in Ultimate culture. It is at the moment of indecision between play and pleasure, and dominance and competition that 'ultimate masculinities' (Thornton 1998) might be seen as a sign of the struggle between the modern and the postmodern (Lyotard 1986; Seidman 1994). The *fear* of ambiguity is a cornerstone of modernist science, knowledge and identity (McRobbie 1994). Ultimate players' *identifications* express a profound uncertainty: How much or how far can we go with broad inclusion, non-violence and competition before Ultimate looks like every other sport? Or it could be more incisive to argue that players are more concerned with how far they can go before Ultimate is not considered a 'real' (masculine) sport. Frank's comment above about football and, in another part of his interview, 'playing a game with his wife' are informing here. Thus, Ultimate is centrally concerned with how and what it is *to be*: a body, to be masculine or feminine, to be spiritual, to be an athlete.

I contend that the play, rules, and meanings of Ultimate represent a broader cultural formation of identity and difference. In a world where dominant groups are claiming that social regulation has broken down and social *difference* has run amok, difference and heterogeneity threaten disorder (For a review of conservative fears see Fiske 1993; Grossberg 1992; Marqusee 2001). In Ultimate, this fear is expressed in the practices of insisting on collective decision-making, gender egalitarianism and constrained competitiveness. However, in practice women are largely excluded, except when they conform to masculinist standards. It is also the case that mainstream competitive ideals and structures are firmly entrenched in this culture, and decision-making tends to be in the hands of a small group of individuals. Many female players express every bit as much competitive drive and fear of feminisation as many male players. However, it is the subtle, but nonetheless obvious negation and fear of feminised characteristics (e.g., 'slow play', 'weak throws', 'fear of laying out') that delineates the boundary maintenance of Ultimate identities. Ultimate players are unable openly to embrace extreme physical aggression, as it is inconsistent with their rules of play and their rejection of dominant sporting embodiments.

'Real' players 'lay out' and don't throw like 'a beach bimbo'. The fear of not being seen as a 'real' sport I argue is most profoundly expressed in the regulation of the boundaries of physical aggression. Players do not want be physically violent, but they still express a desire for physical dominance and experience pleasure through physical exertion. This identification is expressed by Ultimate players' reservation of the highest praise for those who 'go ho'. So in this way they are embracing a broader, more common concept of sporting masculinities in spite of their desire to maintain a distinction between themselves and the stereotypical images of physicality associated with working-class and black identified sports.

The corruption and duplicity of athletes have disrupted and unsettled modernist notions of 'the good sport' (Andrews 1996). Ultimate was formed in response to models of vicious competition and greedy athletes (Lewis 1994). It is arguable that Ultimate players came along to reassert the possibility of 'fair play' and 'good sportsmanship'. Ultimate players' rules and slogan of 'Spirit of the Game' suggests a strong tie to this sense of nostalgia for a (non-existent) mythic time of untainted free play. Long-term Ultimate players and organisers constantly invoke 'the Sixties' as a reference point for their origins and they pine for the supposedly lost idealism of those days. Many other players reject much of this idealism and are openly more interested in winning and dominating (Lewis 1994). Those days, I would argue, were only the glory days for middle-class straight white men, or more accurately, they were one of the last points at which such an identity could be assumed without question.

Conclusion: an unfinished project?

Ultimate players claim to be developing and living new forms of (gender) embodiment and identification. Do these new identities express or exhibit changes in existing gender, race, class, and body dominance? Butler (1990) argues that it is in the situationality and repetition of parodies of the ideals of gender (and identity) that possible transformation exists. Ultimate players play around with sporting embodiment. However, for any parody to be transformative it must, 'produce a set of meanings that the structures they appear to be copying would preclude' (Butler 1992: 87). Ultimate largely fails to produce practices and meanings that are beyond the dominant structures, ideals and practices of existing sports. Generally, in Ultimate, when identities are marked or signified it is for purposes of differentiating them from the unnamed general reference group of heterosexual, white able-bodied males. Ultimate frisbee represents an interesting, if unrealised, potential for the subversion of dominant sporting identities. Despite Ultimate players' best intentions their own performances may not be so much politically transformative or progressive so much as *the production of a new space* in which to play around within established boundaries of identity.

Notes

1 Throughout the rest of the chapter I will use the abbreviated term 'Ultimate' when referring to Ultimate frisbee. This is common practice among Ultimate players who generally only use the full phrase 'Ultimate frisbee' when talking to cultural outsiders.

2 For more detail on the history, rules and current state of Ultimate visit the Ultimate Players Association website <http://www.upa.org/> or World Flying Disc Federation <http://www.wfdf.org>

3 Disc golf sources claim that world wide up to 500,000 people play on a 'regular' basis and that there are approximately 6000 members of the Professional Gold Disc Association. About 90 per cent of the disc golf courses as of the year 2000 were located in the United States. See http://discology.co.uk/pdf/DiscGolfDemographics.pdf (accessed November 18, 2003)

4 The Spirit of the Game is a very important aspect of the culture and I discuss it elsewhere in more detail (Thornton 1998).

5 The Vancouver Ultimate League claims to be the largest in the world. Go to: www.vul.bc.ca

6 It is not hard to find ongoing debate about the issue of the 'problems' with men and women playing Ultimate on the same field. See, for example, 'rec.sport.disc' which is the longest running internet newsgroup for disc sports in North America. There are many 'threads' which deal with this issue, but the follwing comment is representative of how the issue is framed within the Ultimate community:

> Subject: Coed vs women's: marginalizing women:
> Many women I have spoken with have said they feel utilized and less important in coed, as opposed to women [only games]. These women were good players, often on good coed teams, playing with men who valued their abilities and wanted to utilize them as assets on the field – it wasn't a gut reaction from women caught in a swilly male huckfest.
>
> (rec.sport.disc/Date: 1999/09/28)

7 These are little plastics cups that fit inside of a sports bra to help protect women's breasts while playing.

8 The so-called 'hippies' of the 1960s went onto become the 'yuppies' and 'entrepreneurs' of the 1980s. Essentially commodifying their 'alternative' experiences in the form of art, poetry and film, not to mention taking up positions in Universities. Thus, the alterity or anti-establishment characterisation of hippies is suspect.

9 However, there are now pools of 'official observers' for some high level competitions like the World Championships and UPA Nationals. To this point though these 'observers' can only be 'invited' to make clarifications of the rules. But they can make 'active' calls on whether or not players are in bounds.

10 This raises questions such as: could we ever be so fully conscious that we could do that? How do we account for difference and interpretation inside such a world? Is the point that one calls a foul or that one should avoid making an infraction?

11 If pushed, one might argue that laying out is a foul on oneself!

12 Even a cursory review of the many Ultimate websites and newsletters will reveal the prominence of images of players 'laying out' for the disc. Follow the various hyperlinks to see the many images of laying out on World Flying Disc Federation home page at http://www.wfdf.org

13 Other sports such as Korfball and Netball have similar rules on contact. However, players in these sports are highly constrained to specific zones of play and Netball is not, as far as I know, a 'mixed'/'co'ed' sport. Thus there is a much larger chance of players running into each other on in an Ultimate game.

References

Andrews, D. (1996) 'The fact(s) of Michael Jordan's blackness: Excavating a floating racial signifier', *Sociology of Sport Journal*, 13(2): 125–58.

Beal, B. (1995) 'Disqualifying the official: Exploring social resistance through the subculture of skateboarding', *Sociology of Sport Journal*, 12(3): 252–67.

Bhabha, H. (1986) '*The Other Question*' *in Literature, Politics and Theory*, London: Metheun.

Birrell, S. and Cole, C. (eds) (1994) *Women, Sport, and Culture*, Champaign: Human Kinetics.

Butler, J. (1990) *Gender Trouble: Feminist Subversions of Identity*, New York: Routledge

Butler, J. (1992) 'The body you want: Liz Kotz Interviews Judith Butler', Artforum, (November): 82–9.

Cahn, S. K. (1994) *Coming on Strong: Gender and Sexuality in Twentieth-Century Women's Sport*, Cambridge: Harvard University Press.

Canadian Ultimate Players Association (1996) 'No more duct tape', *Spirit: The Sport of Ultimate in Canada*, (Spring): 8.

Carrington, B. (1998) 'Sport, masculinity and black cultural resistance', *Journal of Sport and Social Issues*, 22 (3): 275–98.

Cole, C. and Andrews, D. L. (1996) 'Look…It is NBA showtime: Visions of race in the popular imaginary', *Cultural Studies Annual*, 1: 141–81.

Cole, C. and Hribar, A. (1995) 'Celebrity feminism: Nike style: post-Fordism, physical transcendence and consumer power', *Sociology of Sport Journal*, 12(4): 247–69.

Collwell, S. (2000) 'The 'letter' and the 'spirit': Football laws and refereeing in the twenty-first century', in J. Garland, D. Malcolm and M. Rowe (eds) *The Future of Football: Challenges for the Twenty-First Century*, London: Frank Cass.

Crossett, T. (1990) 'Masculinity, sexuality and the development of early modern sport' in M. Messner and D. Sabo (eds) *Sport, Men and the Gender Order: Critical Feminist Perspectives*, Champaign: Human Kinetics,

Derrida, J. (1974) *Positions*, Chicago: University of Chicago Press.

Dyer, K. (1982) *Challenging the Men: The Social Biology of Female Sporting Achievement*, New York: University of Queensland.

Dyer, R. (1997) *White*, New York: Routledge.

Edwards, H. (1970) *The Revolt of the Black Athlete*, New York: The Press.

Edwards, H. (1973) *Sociology of Sport*, Illinois: Irwin Dorsey Ltd.

Fanon, F. (1967) *Black Skin, White Masks*, (Translated by Charles Lam Markmann). New York: Grove Press, Inc.

Fausto-Sterling, A. (1985) *Myths of Gender: Biological Theories about Men and Women*, New York Basic Books.

Fine, G. (1987) *With The Boys: Little League Baseball and Preadolescent Culture*, Chicago: University of Chicago Press.

Fleming, S. (2001) 'Racial science and South Asian and black physicality' in Ben Carrington and Ian McDonald (eds) *'Race', Sport and British Society*, London: Routledge.

Foucault, M. (1995) *Discipline and Punish: The Birth of the Prison*, (Translation by Alan Sheridan) New York: Vintage Books (Second Edition).

Grossberg, L. (1992) *We Gotta Get Out of This Place: Popular Conservatism and Postmodern Culture*, New York: Routledge.

Gruneau, R. (1983) *Class, Sports and Social Development*, Amherst: The University of Massachusetts.

Hall, M. (1996) *Feminism and Sporting Bodies: Essays on Theory and Practice*, Illinois: Human Kinetics

Hall, S. (1990) 'Culture, identity and diaspora' in J. Rutherford (ed.) *Identity, Community, Culture, Difference*, London: Lawrence and Wishart.

Hall, S. (1997) 'The spectacle of the "Other"' in S. Hall (ed.) *Representation: Cultural Representation and Signifying Practices*, Sage, London

Haman, A. (1994) 'Coed Ultimate sweeps the West Coast', *Spirit: The Sport of Ultimate in Canada*, (August): 3–4.

Hargreaves, J. (1994) *Sporting Females: Critical Issues in the History and Sociology of Women's Sports*, London: Routledge.

Harvey, J. and Rail, G. (1995) 'Body at work: Michel Foucault and the sociology of sport', *Sociology of Sport Journal*. Special Issue: Sociology of Sport in 'la Francophonie', 12(2): 164–79.

Hilbert, C. (1997) 'Tough enough and woman enough', *Journal of Sport and Social Issues*, 21(1)(February): 7–36.

Holmlund, C. (1994) 'Visible difference and flex appeal: The body, sex, sexuality, and race in the pumping iron films', in Susan Birrell and Cheryl Cole (eds) *Women, Sport and Culture*, Champaign: Human Kinetics.

Johnson, S. (1975) *Frisbee: A Practitioner's Manual and Definitive Treatise*, New York: Workman Publishing Company.

Kidd, B. (1987) 'Sports and masculinity', in Michael Kaufman (ed.) *Beyond Patriarchy: Chapters by Men on Pleasure, Power and Change*, Toronto: Oxford University Press.

Klein, A. (1993) *Little Big Men: Bodybuilding Subculture and the Construction of Gender*, New York: SUNY Press.

Lenskyj, H. (1986) *Out of Bounds: Women, Sport and Sexuality*, Toronto: Women's Press.

Lenskyj, H. (1994) 'Sexuality and femininity in sport contexts: Issues and alternatives', *Journal of Sport and Social Issues*, (November): 356–75.

Lewis, S. (1994) 'The Ultimate sport', Paper presented at The Canadian Sociology and Anthropology Sessions, Canadians Learned Societies, June (Calgary, Alberta).

Lind, L. (1992) 'Spin out with the Ultimate cult', *EYE Magazine*, (6 August): 12–13.

Lyotard, J. (1986) *The Postmodern Condition: A Report on Knowledge*, Manchester: Manchester University Press

Maguire, J. (1999) *Global sport: Identities, Societies, Civilizations*, Cambridge: Polity Press.

McDonald, M. and Andrews, D. (2001) 'Michael Jordan: Corporate sport and postmodern celebrityhood' In Andrew, D. and Jackson, S. (eds) *Sport Stars: The Cultural Politics of Sporting Celebrity*, London: Routledge.

McRobbie, A. (1994) *Postmodernism and Popular Culture*, Routledge: London.

Marqusee, M. (2001) 'In search of the unequivocal Englishman', in B. Carrington and I. MacDonald (eds) *'Race', Sport and British Society*, London: Routledge.

Messner, M. (1991) *Power at Play: Sports and the Problem of Masculinity*, Beacon Press: Boston.

Miles, S. (1998) 'McDonaldization and the global sports store: Construction consumer meanings in a rationalized society' in M. Alfino and J. S. Caputo and R. Wynyard (eds), *McDonaldization Revisited: Critical Essays on Consumer Culture*, London: Praeger.

Polsky, N. (1967) *Hustlers, Beats and Others*, Chicago: Aldine.

Price, J. (1994) 'Women in Ultimate: Looked off or not looking?' *Tour: The Ottawa Ultimate Review*, Summer: 12.

Seidman, S. (1994) *Contested Knowledge: Social Theory in the Postmodern Era*, New York: Routledge.

Thomas, J. (1993) *Doing Critical Ethnography*, Newbury Park: Sage Publications.

Thornton, A. (1998) 'Ultimate masculinities: An ethnography of power and social difference in sport', unpublished PhD thesis, University of Toronto.

Ultimate Players Association (1988) 'UPA Newsletter, 20th Anniversary Issue', (September) Colorado Springs, Colorado.

Ultimate Players Association (1992) UPA Newsletter, 12 (5) (November).

Ultimate Players Association (2002a) Homepage of the Ultimate Players Association available online http://www.upa.org/ (accessed 21 March 2002).

Ultimate Players Association (2002b) The Rules of Ultimate Frisbee. Available online http://www.upa.org/ultimate/rules/rules.shtml (accessed 20 January 2002).

Ultimate Players Association (2002c) Comments posted by players on the Spirit of the Game. Available online: http:www.upa.org/ultimate/sotg/sotg.shtml (accessed 20 January 2002).

Walvin, J. (1987) 'Symbols of moral superiority: Slavery, sport and the changing world order, 1800–1940' in J.A. Mangan and J. Walvin (eds) *Manliness and Morality: Middle-Class Masculinity in Britain and America*, 1880–1940, New York: St. Martin's Press.

Wheaton, B. and Tomlinson, A. (1998) 'The changing gender order in sport? The case of windsurfing', *Journal of Sport and Social Issues*, 22 (August): 252–274

Whitson, D. (1994) 'The embodiment of gender: Discipline, domination, and empowerment' in S. Birrell and C. Cole (eds) *Women, Sport and Culture*, Champaign (Illinois): Human Kinetics

World Flying Disc Federation (2002) WFDF homepage. Available online: http://www.wfdf.org (Accessed March 20, 2002).

Zagoria, A. (1998) 'Ultimate spreads from maplewood to the world'. Available online: http:www.upa.org/upa (accessed 21 June 1998).

10 Extreme America

The cultural politics of extreme sports in 1990s America

Kyle Kusz

Introduction

> [...] the early 1990s seemed like the epicenter of 'toxic masculinity'... a categorical shift had occurred and it threatened bedrock concepts of American manhood.
>
> (Faludi 1999: 42–43)

> So where can men go to feel like men?
>
> (Kimmel 1996: 309)

> [...] extreme athletes... with their unwavering cool in the face of extraordinary circumstances, resemble the romantic heroes of spaghetti Westerns or Indiana Jones-style adventures and thus pique the imaginations of those secretly wishing to put that Man With No Name swagger in their step – if not full time, at least for a few brief moments on Saturday or Sunday
>
> (Koerner 1997: 59)

The 30 June 1997 *U.S. News and World Report* cover story about extreme sports modifies the conservative pundit George Will's famous adage about baseball to proclaim: 'If you want to understand America, you must know extreme sports' (quoted from Koerner 1997: 56). Throughout the article, extreme sports are introduced through dramatic images and narratives of white everymen performing supra-normal athletic feats in high-risk sporting activities like B.A.S.E jumping[1] and sky surfing. Extreme sports are also portrayed as sporting activities that have revived a set of traditional American masculine values and pursuits: rugged individualism, conquering new frontiers, and achieving individual progress. Two years later, *Time* magazine offered a remarkably similar cover story about extreme sports (Greenfeld 1999). Like the *U.S. News and World Report's* story, *Time* depicted extreme sports as activities which were resurrecting traditional American ideals such as pushing boundaries, taking risks, and being innovative. Both articles even went so far as to connect the white male participants in these sports to a peculiar fraternity of American icons (both real and fictional) like William James, the American frontiersman, Indiana Jones, and the *Old Spice* sea captain.

For those who have followed extreme sports[2] since their formation in 1995, this favourable and distinctly patriotic Americanised portrayal of these sporting activities might be more than a bit surprising. Upon their initial creation, extreme sports were primarily imagined in American media culture as a radical new collection of non-traditional sporting activities like skateboarding, BMX bike riding, street luge, and in-line skating which were associated with a (sub-)urban street culture and performed mainly by 'alternative' young white male athletes (in their teens and twenties) (Stouffer 1998). Extreme sports were popularly represented as the preferred sporting activities of that so-called lost, apathetic, and nihilistic younger generation of slackers popularly known as Generation X (Rinehart 1995). In the early 1990s, this allegedly notorious X-generation, as they have sometimes been called, was demonised across American media culture as living proof of all that was said to be wrong in the United States in the early 1990s (Leland *et al.* 1993).[3] But by 1995, corporate America discovered that Gen Xers, despite pronouncements of their bleak economic present-futures, actually controlled $700 billion in individual and familial spending power per year (Greenfeld 1998). ESPN, armed with this knowledge, created extreme sports primarily as a means of tapping into this much-coveted young demographic and attracting them to its then fledgling station: espn2 (The *Economist* 1994).

Because of these dynamics, many American sports fans and pundits initially dismissed extreme sports as made-for-TV pseudo-sports created solely to peddle products to the much coveted teen male demographic. Additionally, these sporting activities were publicly derided as the sporting outgrowth of the short-attention spans, nihilistic desires, and aberrant world views of wayward Generation Xers (*Sports Illustrated* 1999). Thus, the American general public's dismay of Generation X was projected onto these new and different sporting activities upon their creation. But only a few short years later, an astonishingly new image of extreme sports was constituted in cover stories by *Time* and *U.S. News and World Report;* gone was the image of extreme sports as suburban street activities performed by a misguided younger generation of slackers. It was replaced by a depiction of extreme sports as adventurous activities involving substantial risks that were increasingly enjoyed by uniquely different, but 'average' middle-aged white men (ranging in age from 20 to 40) in pristine and majestic pastoral settings. Notably, within these two mainstream magazine cover stories extreme sports were largely distanced from their 'Generation X' roots and dramatically re-constituted as symbols of all that was right in *fin de siècle* United States.[4]

So then, my interest in this chapter lies not in examining the lived experiences of the participants of any of the activities that have been articulated together under the term: 'extreme sports,' but rather in interrogating the representational politics of this dramatic re-articulation of the American mainstream image of extreme sports in the late 1990s as it can be evidenced through the *U.S. News and World Report* and *Time* magazines cover stories referenced above. The questions that broadly frame my inquiry are: How do we make sense of this radical re-articulation of the identities of extreme sports and its participants on the pages of these mainstream magazines in late 1990s America? How are these 'different', non-traditional sporting activities, which had previously existed on the margins of American sporting culture and were largely ridiculed by the American mainstream, suddenly embraced by the American mainstream and re-articulated as symbols of a contemporary reaffirmation of American ideals in the late 1990s? And finally, what sense are we to make of the concomitant 'Americanisation' and masculinisation of these extreme sports activities as they are mainstreamed?

In order to provide provisional answers to these questions, these representations of extreme sports must be situated within the socio-historical context of their production. More specifically, I argue that this particular re-codification of the identity of extreme sports and its participants must be read within a post-1960s United States context of a perceived crisis of white masculinity where the meanings articulated with white masculinity are struggled over within various sites of American popular culture. I will also make visible the cultural politics of the white masculinity being constructed and valorised in these celebratory stories about extreme sports, showing how these stories about extreme sports participate in this cultural struggle over the meanings articulated to white masculinity in late 1990s America. Stated a bit differently, I show how this masculinised and patriotic representation of extreme sports can be read as a symptom and imagined solution to this post-1960s perceived crisis of white masculinity.

Post-1960s crisis of white masculinity

Many cultural observers have identified post-1960s America as a time of a crisis of white masculinity (Cole and Andrews 2001; Davies 1995; Faludi 1999; Kimmel 1996; Pfeil 1995; Savran 1998; Weis *et al.* 1997). This post-civil rights American crisis of white masculinity was produced by a historically specific constellation of social, cultural, political, and economic forces and conditions which Savran describes as:

> the re-emergence of the feminist movement; the limited success of the civil rights movement in redressing gross historical inequities through affirmative action legislation; the rise of the lesbian and gay rights movements; the failure of America's most disastrous imperialistic adventure, the Vietnam War; and, perhaps most important, the end of the post-World War II economic boom and the resultant and steady decline in the income of white working- and lower-middle-class men.
>
> (1998: 5)

One of the key effects of these conjunctural forces and conditions was that they publicly illuminated the largely invisible social, cultural, psychic and economic privileges which white men enjoy in American society. In *Stiffed: The Betrayal of the American Man*, Faludi (1999), echoes Savran's description of post-1960s America above, asserting that the social institutions which formerly revered and nurtured men and reproduced their socially privileged positions have deteriorated during this period. This perceived loss of social supports that valorise men, according to Faludi, also coincides with the rise of an increasingly ornamental culture that further feminises men by valuing a manhood displayed (one based on a look and appearance) rather than a manhood demonstrated (based on one's achievements and civic responsibilities).

This crisis of white masculinity was also exacerbated by some destabilising economic changes which took place in the United States from the 1970s to the 1990s. Due to the related forces of deindustrialisation and globalisation, the American economy underwent significant restructuring during this time period (Messner 1997). From 1973 to 1992 white men experienced a steady decrease in their median income from $34,231 to $31,012 (Wellman 1997).[5] According to Mishel *et al.* (1997) these poor economic trends seem to be continuing into the mid-to-late 1990s:

> [...] despite growth in both gross domestic product and employment between 1989 and 1994, median family income in 1994 was still $2,168 lower than it was in 1989... [So] the 1980s trends toward greater income inequality and a tighter squeeze on the middle class show clear signs of continuing in the 1990s.
>
> (3; cited from Fine and Lois 1998: 17)

Further, these economic restructurings and poor economic climate created tremendous anxiety in many middle- and working-class white men during the 1990s whether they actually experienced real declines in their economic position or merely feared that they might (Faludi 1999; Fine and Weis 1998; Messner: 1997).

The economic fears and anxieties of many white men were expressed and magnified within a number of 'paranoic' (Scott 1995: 112) discourses about such things as the changing racial demographics of the United States (where it is predicted that whites will soon become the numerical racial minority) (Maharidge 1996); affirmative action policies (popularly imagined as unfairly discriminating against whites) (Wellman 1997); or the new cultural logics of multiculturalism and cultural diversity (especially present in advertising discourse and thought to marginalise whites) (McCarthy 1998).[6] Such discourses were popularly read as signs of the 'downward spiral of the living white male' (Gates 1993).

At the same time, the anxieties of many white men were further heightened by related calls to improve minority rights and to re-write American history from the bottom up, not to only recognise the contributions of marginalised groups to American history, but to also bear witness to the racial and gender violences, exclusions and oppressions which were perpetrated in the process of building the United States (Giroux 1997). Such calls to re-write American history challenged many taken-for-granted, mainstream popular narratives and historiographies of U.S. history which reductively articulated whiteness with America, constituted white males as the sole or central determining agents of American history, and effectively erased the contributions of historically marginalised groups.

It was also during the 1990s that whiteness as a racialised identity became increasingly visible and 'came under scrutiny by various social groups as an oppressive, invisible centre against which all else is measured' (Giroux 1997: 286). Evidence of such public criticism of whiteness can be seen in *Newsweek*'s 1993 cover story titled, 'White Male Paranoia'. The public critique of white privilege was often directed at white males who were constituted as its embodiments (Gates 1993).[7] Such criticisms of white male privilege left many white men feeling either guilty, angry, or resentful.[8] The comments of American comedian, David Spade, excerpted from a *George* magazine article tellingly titled, 'White Man's Blues' reveal not only the anxieties of many white males at this time, but also how their anxieties were too easily converted into tales of white male victimisation: 'I'm talking about the disadvantages of being a white guy in America. I'm sick of minorities hogging the good complaints. Whitey's been silent for too long...Whitey's been getting a constant pounding. I've been taking so many lefts, I'm begging for rights' (Spade 1998: 52).

I want to be the minority: contemporary responses to this crisis of white masculinity

During the 1980s and 1990s, symptoms of this crisis of white masculinity ranged from the popularity of Robert Bly's *Iron John* books and his all-male, 'tribal' weekend retreats to the rise of the Promise Keepers; from the popularisation of 'hard bodied' male celluloid figures like Rambo and the Terminator (Jeffords 1994), to the appearance of 'white males-in-crisis' films like *Falling Down*, *The Fan*, and *Disclosure*; from the mid-1990s school shootings in Arkansas, Colorado, Kentucky, Oregon, Mississippi, and Pennsylvania to Timothy McVeigh's bombing of a federal building in Oklahoma City (Savran 1998). These socio-cultural phenomena showcase one frequent response to this crisis of white masculinity – testosterone-dripping displays of male masochism coupled with rage directed at others (Savran 1998).

During this time period a reactionary 'recovery rhetoric' also formed across a variety of sites within American media culture. This recovery rhetoric did not assume a monolithic form, but involved a variety of representational strategies and discursive logics mobilised in complex ways. The implicit purpose of this recovery rhetoric (whatever its form) was to protect and re-secure the central and normative socio-cultural position of white masculinity in the United States (Kincheloe and Steinberg 1998). As exemplified in the comments from David Spade above, one key strategy mobilised within this recovery rhetoric was white males' use of the logic of identity politics[9] to constitute themselves as the latest social victims of American society (whether of affirmative action, feminist and multicultural initiatives, an increasingly feminised American culture, etc.) (McCarthy 1998; Kincheloe and Steinberg 1998).

Another reactionary strategy, as Wray and Newitz (1997) observe through the popularity of television shows like *Roseanne*, *My So-Called Life*, *Married with Children*, and *Grace Under Fire* and music like grunge rock during the 1990s, was the American mainstream's seemingly insatiable appetite for images of whites who were apparently authentically disadvantaged, unprivileged or otherwise 'trashed' (1997). For Wray and Newitz, these representations of 'trashed' whites functioned as a popular means of disavowing the privileges of whiteness.

Similarly, Yudice (1995) observed that many whites (from all class backgrounds) made various 'claims of marginality' at this time (256). By a white 'claim of marginality', Yudice means the practice of a white-skinned person attempting to construct his/her identity in and through various codes which signify cultural difference or a lack of economic or social privileges in order to gain entry into the emergent multicultural system of (market and socio-cultural) value. Yudice's observation highlights how, in the midst of the spread of cultural diversity in 1990s America – where whites were often not imagined as having a seemingly authentic place – this increase in the display of stories of authentically disadvantaged, unprivileged and 'different' whites within the mainstream media can be read as a part of a reactionary white recuperation effort to defuse the counter-hegemonic force of multicultural initiatives by constituting whiteness in codes of marginality, difference and a lack of privilege (which are the moral and political foundation of many of these minority initiatives).

Finally, another strategy employed within backlash efforts to re-secure the privileged position of white masculinity during the 1990s was the use of populist rhetoric about returning to the traditional American values (like individualism, self-reliance, meritocracy) that the nation was founded upon and protecting American families (Giroux 1997). This populist rhetoric – which does not explicitly mention race, gender, or class – was often employed in the 1990s to ratify, protect and reproduce the values, institutional structures and social relations which reproduced the central and normative socio-cultural position of white masculinity. This populist rhetoric often portrays multiculturalist and feminist forces as threats to American families, traditional values and the nation, all of which are coded as white (see Bennett 1992 and Sacks and Thiel 1995 for examples of how this rhetoric operates).

Together, these representational strategies which organised images of whites all across American media culture (magazines, newspapers, popular films, radio, and television shows) implicate these texts as key instruments and effects of such white male backlash politics, which attempt to deny the existence of racialised privileges of whites while masking (and thus ensuring the reproduction of) asymmetrical racial relations of power in the present. Additionally, these strategies were constituted by, and constitutive of, the cultural backlash which attempted to arrest the minimal gains made by historically marginalised groups since the 1960s (Giroux 1997; Kincheloe and Steinberg 2000; McCarthy 1998; Savran 1998).

It is within this politico-cultural context which this mainstreaming of extreme sports – which involves its Americanisation, masculinisation, and implicit racialisation – took place. Thus, in the rest of this chapter, I show how this recent re-articulation of extreme sports as a distinctly 'American' cultural activity in these *U.S. News and World Report* and *Time* magazine cover stories is not only predicated on the racial and gender dynamics of this crisis of white masculinity, but also reproduces the representational strategies of the backlash politics discussed above while simultaneously offering extreme sports and its participants as imaginary solutions to this supposed crisis of white masculinity.

Extreme America: the racial and nationalistic politics of extreme sports

Rodriguez (1998), drawing on the work of Nakayama and Krizek (1995), has argued that, at the level of everyday discourse, one of the ways in which whiteness obtains its largely invisible position as the un-raced social norm in the United States is through the conflation of whiteness with American-ness. Rodriguez submits that equating America with whiteness is, whether intentional or not, a policing of national identity that constructs an essentialist and stagnant view of the nation, one which contests other representations of national identity which would highlight the inevitable 'messiness of overlap' in racialising America's national identity. Conflating whiteness with American-ness relegates 'all individuals and groups in the United States that fall outside of the white equals American paradigm to a marginal role in national life' (Rodriguez 1998: 45–46). Even further, this strategy of representing whiteness as American-ness 'downplay[s] and even remove[s] from history, and thus from memory, the way contributions by people of various races and ethnicities as well as by women and by people of varying sexual orientations have all contributed to the character of what constitutes American-ness' (Rodriguez 1998: 46).

Within the *U.S. News and World Report* and *Time* cover stories about extreme sports, whiteness (more specifically – white masculinity) and 'American-ness' are conflated by articulating the predominantly white male extreme sport participant to America via associating him with a fraternity of American masculine icons and the American mythology of the frontier. The American mythology of the frontier is invoked to produce a nationalistic narrative whereby extreme sport participants are represented as the metaphoric offspring of the rugged white male individualists frequently imagined as founding the United States. Photos of individual white extreme sportsmen located in natural surroundings pushing themselves to their limits are included to visually reinforce this point. The frontier which challenges, yet is ultimately conquered by, white American men is a foundational national trope which reproduces not only dominant ways of how America imagines itself, but also how American manhood is imagined. It is invoked here to articulate extreme sports not only as a contemporary extension of this mythology, but also as a contemporary site where the masculinising practices and values of this mythology are reproduced. Both of these white male figures – the extreme sportsman and American frontiersman – are valorised as ideal American citizens because they are invested in a set of distinctly American values: rugged individualism, self-reliance, personal responsibility and individual/social progress. Further, the white male extreme sport practitioner's representation as an ideal American citizen is authenticated by contending that he, like the American frontiersman, is constituted by an insatiable appetite for risk, a thirst for adventure, and a desire to be the embodiment of strength, coolness and confidence (Koerner 1997). In this way, the narrative constructs an unmistakable whitened, male-centred national genealogy which begins with our country's founding fathers and extends to the extreme sport practitioner.

By articulating the extreme sport participant with the mythic American frontiersman and forwarding them as embodiments of 'traditional' American ideals, a specific image and story of America is produced which privileges the contributions of white men (over and against the contributions of, and structural violences and marginalisations against, Native Americans, African slaves and women). This essentialist view of America positions white males as the central and most important agents of American history (in the past and in the present). These heroic white men are the ones who have risked their lives and pushed themselves to their limits for the collective good of American society. The articulation of the white masculine extreme sports figure with America's national identity comes at a time when changing racial demographics and multicultural initiatives have challenged the often taken for granted connection between whiteness (white masculinity) and America (Kincheloe and Steinberg 1998; Maharidge 1996). Cole and Andrews' (2001) discussion of Tiger Woods' portrayal as an unifying symbol of the United States' multicultural present-future – where his success (both on and off the field) is represented as a measure of contemporary America's (read: white America's) colour-blindness and tolerance for cultural diversity – reveals how sport is a key terrain where the struggle over the racial identity and consciousness of the nation is currently taking place. In contrast to these portrayals of Tiger Woods as a symbol of multicultural America, we can read this celebratory discourse about extreme sports, which casts its exclusively white male participants as the embodiments of a revival of 'traditional' American values as a cleverly disguised version of the contemporary reactionary populist rhetoric about which re-secures and privileges the articulation of white masculinity with America within what McCarthy (1998) calls, 'the Age of Difference, the Multicultural Era' (339).

Constituting America's ethos as being founded upon a proclivity for risk and adventure in and through this extreme sports discourse may seem innocent and apolitical at first glance, but when one looks more closely, this whitening of American national identity resonates with other contemporary reactionary efforts like the rhetoric of Rush Limbaugh (Giroux 1997), the White Patriot movement, and the rise in the White Supremacist movements (McCarthy 1998). In each of these sites, attempts are made to reclaim a whitened image of America by representing white males as America's authentic and most important subjects over and against the other emergent multicultural and non-white representations of American national identity being produced in late 1990s America (see Berlant 1996; Cole and Andrews 2001).

The return of 'the man': extreme sports participant as white masculine ideal

Within this alleged crisis of white masculinity, extreme sports are constituted in these cover stories as a masculinising practice where white male participants can experience a set of affective and bodily pleasures which allow them to reclaim a masculinity which they feel has been lost. The crisis of white masculinity is implicitly signified in these stories by depicting American culture as a feminised 'scaredy-cat culture…that seems hell-bent on expunging risk from every aspect of life', and by constituting men (at least those who do not participate in extreme sports) as feminised subjects experiencing excessive worries about waistlines and corporate bottom lines due to pervasive cultural and economic conditions (Koerner 1997: 56). Set within this context, extreme sports are tacitly celebrated as an imaginary solution – a masculinising corrective – to the apparent cultural feminisation occurring with American white men in the 1990s. Extreme sports are said to appeal to those white men who 'secretly wish to put that Man With No Name swagger in their step – if not full time, then at least for a few brief moments on Saturday or Sunday' (Koerner 1997: 59). Extreme sports are also implicitly figured (through the absence of women[10] and people of colour) as a racially and gender exclusive place, what Kimmel (1996: 309) calls a 'homosocial preserve', where (white) men can un-apologetically perform an ideal masculinity which they covet by taking death-defying risks, enduring the pain of participation, and displaying an unwavering confidence and coolness in the face of apparent danger. Additionally, through the valorisation of the unusual and extraordinary athletic feats which they perform, these white males are portrayed as extraordinary and exceptional individuals who are different from, and superior to, anyone not willing to attempt such potentially dangerous athletic exploits.

In subtle contrast to the familiar sensitive, apprehensive and appearance-oriented (read: feminised) 'new man' (Kimmel 1996), the extreme sportsman is forwarded as an exemplary white masculinity deserving of mass cultural admiration because he is represented as in control, confident, unconstrained, superior, and sovereign over himself (Flax 1998). For example, through performing athletic feats (like B.A.S.E. jumping, extreme skiing[11] and mountaineering[12]) where he risks his health and safety by staring death right in the eye, he is displayed as possessing an extraordinary (imagined) sense of control over himself and his environment. It is this sense of control which American cultural definitions of white masculinity (oriented by liberal–humanist discourses) have taught white males that they are entitled to in their everyday lives. Perhaps then, the attraction of extreme sports for many white men in this era of their 'falling down' (economically, socially and culturally) is that they provide an opportunity for these men to satisfy an inarticulable desire (yet one which I contend many white men 'feel') to experience a sense of control over themselves and their surroundings during a historical moment when this sense of control has been compromised by changing socio-historical conditions. Because the extreme sport participant is one of only a few who are willing to participate in such dangerous athletic endeavours, his participation produces a sense of superiority or extraordinariness about himself in relation to others not willing to take such risks.

These sentiments are best represented in *Time's* description of the feelings of a B.A.S.E. jumper just prior to his jump and immediately after successfully touching down on the ground:

> He [the extreme sports participant] prays that his parachute will open facing away from the dam, that his canopy won't collapse, that his toggles will be handy and that no ill wind will slam him back into the cold concrete…When he lands… he hurriedly packs his chute and then… lets out a war whoop that rises past those mortals still perched on the dam… It's a cry of defiance, thanks and victory; he has survived another B.A.S.E. jump.
>
> (Greenfeld 1999: 29)

Clearly, the experience of B.A.S.E. jumping is represented as an opportunity to test one's fate against the gods. But once the risky athletic endeavour is completed successfully, the participant is able to claim a 'god-like status' for himself and sense of superiority over others (remember, he is immortal in relation to 'those mortals still perched on the dam') (Greenfeld 1999: 29). Thus, the article's description suggests that participation in such dangerous and 'extreme' sports provides men with a practice through which they can satiate a desire to demonstrate an ideal masculinity within an era where it is imagined that there are fewer opportunities to do so.

The appearance of this particular story about extreme sports in mainstream non-sporting magazines indicates a broader-based cultural valorisation (one that transcends the boundaries of sport) of an ideal American white masculinity constituted through this depiction of the extreme sportsman – a white masculinity that is strong, brave, sovereign, demonstrably superior and in control of himself – within this era of a perceived crisis of white masculinity. This transcendent cultural valorisation of white masculinity is further reinforced through the peculiar inclusion of subsections within the *Time* article which feature individuals (all of which, except one, are white males) who are not necessarily extreme sportsmen (firemen, neurosurgeon, options trader, etc.), but who embody the masculine characteristics and values being lauded through this cover story about extreme sports. In one subsection, the story of a New York City fire fighter is mobilised to articulate extreme sports with a heroic white masculinity that sacrifices 'for the greater good [of society]':

> I was in the Marines in Vietnam, and fire fighting is like war. If a life is in there, you go in, you get 'em out – even when it's black and smoky, your body's burning up and you're fighting the natural urge to run. The F.D.N.Y. [Fire Department of New York] trains you to be aggressive and hypervigilant, not to take stupid risks. We don't do this for sport or for thrills or money. You're risking your life to save somebody. That's what makes this job special. We take risks for the greater good.
>
> (Greenfeld 1999: 34)

In another, the first disabled person to climb Yosemite's El Capitan (he was paralysed in a previous climb) is valorised for his optimism, his determined unwillingness to be limited by his disability, and his exceptionality for continuing to climb despite his disability. Finally, another subsection in *Time* on an extreme skier who was caught in an avalanche while filming an extreme skiing video celebrates his extraordinary agency and his ability to keep control of himself which enabled him to survive seemingly certain peril (Greenfeld 1999: 34). Each of these stories highlights the agency, bravery, strength, unwillingness to be constrained, willpower, sacrifice and exceptional abilities of these white male individuals, while they also assert the value of these individuals to the optimal functioning of society. Together the stories are seemingly included to develop a sense of awe and reverence of these conspicuously white and male 'extreme' individuals while they simultaneously constitute the extreme sport participant as a supra-normal individual who is not only a hip, unique, and 'different' individual (the dominant way in which extreme sports figures are imagined), but is, more importantly, *exceptionally* different from and superior to the average American subject.

The invisible man: public criticisms of whiteness, white desire(s) and the mass-mediated extreme sports' white masculinity

We must also situate this mainstream valorisation of the white male extreme sportsman within the context of a 1990s America where whiteness as a racial identity and its structural privileges were increasingly being made visible and undergoing criticism, even in the world of sport (see Price 1997).[13] Situated within this context, an implicit appeal of extreme sports is that they offer a cultural space that is overwhelmingly white, yet is rarely ever imagined as a racially exclusive space. In crude terms, extreme sports is constituted largely as a white sporting fraternal order where membership is predicated on one's investment in recovering an ideal *white* masculinity (one that is lacking any visible signs of material privilege). In this way, extreme sports, as they are mediated in these articles, implicitly serve the interests of a reactionary white male backlash politics by providing a space/practice where white men can not only strengthen their relations with one another, but where, as argued above, they can re-imagine themselves as superior and extraordinary subjects. In fact, in their de facto racial exclusivity extreme sports seem to share something in common with other reactionary men's groups of the 1990s like the Promise Keepers and Robert Bly's 'Iron John' contingent, as well as, the White Patriot and White Supremacist movements mentioned above.

But, as mentioned earlier, extreme sports are also portrayed in these articles as activities which satiate a male desire to put that 'Man With No Name swagger' back in their step (Koerner 1997: 59). In racial terms we might read this desire as a defiant reaction by white men (though one which they probably would not – or could not – articulate) to the increasing visibility of whiteness during the 1990s and the subsequent constraints that having their whiteness made visible and particularised (as opposed to being understood as the 'universal human subject') places on them as racialised subjects. This desire to evade the constraints imposed by the increased public marking of whiteness is also evidenced in the representation of extreme sports as an activity which provides 'an outlet for the kind of creativity and individual expression often squashed in a homogenising culture of chain stores and minimalls' (Koerner 1997: 58). Of course, this desire to evade racial categorisation (where white masculinity is increasingly publicly imagined as always already privileged, oppressive, uncaring and dominant) can not be abstracted from the multicultural age of difference from which it emerged (McCarthy 1998), nor from a cultural context where a pervasive essentialist public equivocation of whiteness with economic and social privilege was prevalent. The desire for individual expression and creativity associated with extreme sports can be read as a desire to evade the homogenising effect (a new social constraint on whites) and derogatory characterisations which the increased visibility of this notion of whiteness places on these white men.

At the same time as this desire to be a 'Man With No Name' expressed in one of the cover stories about extreme sports can be read as a symptom of, and reaction to, the pervasive public criticisms of white masculinity going on during the 1990s. Extreme sports, through the overwhelming whiteness of its participants (as well as norms and values), simultaneously provide a space/practice where whiteness operates as the unspoken norm (thus, is rendered largely invisible) so that the white male participants are not constrained by its categorical logics. Perhaps then, this popular mainstream celebration of extreme sports is at least partially grounded in the way that extreme sports provide a seemingly authentic white cultural space and practice for white men where they can also temporarily escape an American social context rife with public criticisms of white male privilege and a concomitant need to be cognisant of, and sensitive to, issues of cultural difference.

Ironically, the overwhelmingly white and male cultural space/practice of extreme sports also offers its participants an cultural space/practice where its largely white male participants can simultaneously cultivate (and be read as) a seemingly different, marginalised, and unprivileged white masculinity. This depiction of the white masculinity of the extreme sports athlete as different and unprivileged is made possible by the oft repeated notion of extreme sports as activities existing on the margins of the professional American sporting landscape (defined in relation to basketball and football which are implicitly represented as the central and prominent sports of 1990s American culture, as well as sports dominated by African-Americans to the imagined exclusion of whites[14]). Additionally, the values, norms and ideologies of these 'alternative' sports are constituted as new, unique and different from mainstream sports like football, basketball and baseball which are linked with a set of values described as boring and traditional.[15] Consequently, the apparent cultural difference and lack of privilege of the white male extreme sportsman is achieved and authenticated by extreme sports' marginal position within the professional American sports formation. Additionally, the frequent articulation of many of the sports which make up extreme sports with the anti-establishment ethos of the 1960s further solidifies the alternative and seemingly unprivileged character of the extreme sportsman's white masculinity. Once we recognise how the extreme sportsman's white masculinity is also coded through signs of difference and an apparent lack any sort of socio-cultural or economic privilege we can read this white masculinity as an effort to distance and differentiate it from the image of white masculinity as always already privileged, oppressive, and dominating that organised many popular modes of imagining white men during the 1990s. Following Wray and Newitz (1997) these images of seemingly different, alternative and unprivileged white guys within extreme sports implicitly function, like other images of other 'trashed' whites, as seemingly authentic 'evidence' of white non-privilege which is used to disavow and deny the existence of structural white privileges. Thus, this mainstream representation of white male extreme sports participants as unique and 'different' individuals, and extreme sports as an alternative, non-traditional, marginalised sporting practice, can be understood, in Yudice's (1995) terms, as an example of a cleverly disguised white masculine 'claim of marginality'.

Conclusion

Through this chapter I have offered a provisional attempt to make sense of the American mainstream's embracing of extreme sports in the late 1990s as it was registered in the *U.S. News and World Report* and *Time* cover stories (Greenfeld 1999; Koerner 1997). I have rendered visible the complex and overdetermined constellation of social, cultural and political forces that are responsible for this popular valorisation of extreme sports. My analysis has pointed out the identities, values, and desires being endorsed through the mainstream press' praise of extreme sports as the symbol of a new American zeitgeist (understood as the revival of traditional American values like individualism, self-reliance, risk taking and progress) at the end of the 1990s. Namely, I have argued that extreme sports are celebrated in these cover stories because they enable the apparent return of strong, confident, superior white men who are seemingly in control (of themselves and their environs) and no longer paralysed by feelings of anxiety, uncertainty, resentment, and paranoia. The white masculinity of the extreme sports performer is, paradoxically, positioned both as different, marginalised, and unprivileged and as a supra-normal white masculinity. This complex and contradictory depiction of the identity of the extreme sportsman enables the disavowal of white privilege, while it simultaneously allows the resurrection of a superior and privileged white masculinity. Additionally, within this era marked by increasing multicultural images of America, this discourse about the overwhelmingly white extreme sports re-articulates and attempts to naturalise the link between whiteness and America. In each of these ways, this specific mainstream discourse about extreme sports implicates these sporting activities as an important cultural site that is produced by, and productive of, the perceived crisis of white masculinity and the representational strategies and cultural logics of the recovery rhetoric of white male backlash politics.

Notes

1 B.A.S.E. jumping is an acronym for building, antenna, span (bridges), and earth (cliffs) jumping. In most cases these jumps are illegal.

2 By 'extreme sports' I mean the mass mediated construction and articulation of a wide range of physical activities like skateboarding, BMX bike riding, in-line skating, sky surfing, street luge, snowboarding, etc. that was spearheaded by ESPN in 1995 through the creation of the 'Extreme Games'. So, by stating that extreme sports were formed in 1995, I do not mean to suggest that these sport activities did not exist or had no previous history prior to 1995. Instead, I merely want to highlight how these physical activities only became articulated under the sign: 'extreme sports' at this time. In other words, these sports would not have been referred to as 'extreme sports' prior to their construction and articulation in 1995. Thus, I contend that the history of 'extreme sports' extends only as far back as 1995 when this sports formation was constructed (both in material and media terms).

3 For a more detailed discussion of the politics of the Generation X discourse, see Kusz (2001a).

4 Though it should also be noted that by the late 1990s, the popular discourse about 'Generation X' was significantly re-contoured so that this formerly apathetic and wayward generation was now said to be strongly invested in the contemporary American virtues of hard work, family and upward mobility (see Hornblower 1997).

5 It should also be emphasized that this decline in white men's median income does not mean that men lost their earnings advantage over women and people of colour during this time period. So, despite these declines in their median income, on average, men still earned comparatively more money than women and people of colour. Thus, arguments of white men's economic disadvantages in contemporary America are gross over-exaggerations which function merely as backlash mechanisms to protect the social and economic privileges of white men.

6 The comments of women's tennis player Martina Hingis at the beginning of the 2001 US Open regarding the advantages that the (African-American) Williams sisters get in garnering endorsement deals because of their race exemplify the way in which whites perceive the leveling of economic opportunities for African-Americans as a disadvantage to them.

7 It should also be noted that white males were not the only public embodiment of white privilege. Feminist and lesbian scholars like Frankenburg (1997) and Davy (1997) have illuminated how the normativity of whiteness operated even in more progressive pro-feminist and pro-lesbian political efforts. But, in attempting to explain why white males became the most frequently imagined figure of white privilege, perhaps it is because they were often the ones who spearheaded the white backlash against progressive racial initiatives.

8 See Kimmel (1996), or Faludi (1999), or Giroux (1997) for evidence of white men's reactions to the public critiques of their privileged structural position.

9 White men appropriated this strategy from those historically marginalised groups (people of colour, women, gays and lesbians) who had previously employed the strategy not only as a means of identifying the privileges and oppressions structured into the very fabric of American culture and social life (at both an interpersonal and institutional level), but also to expose, challenge and eliminate such structural inequalities.

10 It should be noted that the *U.S. News and World Report* cover story begins with a story about a female 'radical skier' who is highlighted for her perilous cliff jumps and six knee operations. Otherwise, women are excluded from this magazine's representation of extreme sports.

11 By extreme skiing I mean those skiers and snowboarders who are often air-lifted to the summits of mountain ranges to ski on dangerous terrain for the purpose of shooting a for-profit video. Such feats are highly dangerous activities which hold the threat of

producing avalanches or other complications which put the lives of the skier and his accompanying personnel – camera persons, helicopter operators, etc. – in danger.

12 Although my discussion of extreme sports focuses exclusively on how extreme sports and its practitioners are rendered visible in these two mainstream cover stories, I think this argument about the way in which extreme sport athletes symbolise an ideal white masculinity applies also to the way in which skateboarders, BMX bike riders, Motocross riders who perform extraordinary aerial tricks and jumps are also revered in popular cultural sites like ESPN telecasts of the X Games.

13 For a critical analysis of the racial politics constitutive of (and constituted by) the 6 December, 1997 *Sports Illustrated* cover story, 'Whatever happened to the white athlete?', see Kusz (2001b).

14 See Kusz (2001b).

15 Although this categorical difference between extreme sports and mainstream American sports is often asserted, Rinehart (1995) has shown how the mainstreaming of extreme sports has involved a process of incorporating the meanings of these sporting activities so that they better fit the cultural and economic imperatives of the mainstream American sports formation – re-coding the norms, values, and ideologies of these sports so they conform to and reproduce the norms and values of the historically specific hegemonic (white) masculinity of the moment as well as American and capitalist ideologies.

References

Bennett, W. (1992) *The De-valuing of America: The Fight for our Culture and our Children*, New York: Touchstone.

Berlant, L. (1996) The face of America and the state of emergency in *Disciplinary and Dissent in Cultural Studies* (eds, Nelson, C., Gaonkar, D.P.) New York: Routledge.

Cole, C. and Andrews, D. (2001) America's new son: Tiger Woods and America's multiculturalism in *Sports Stars: The Politics of Sport Celebrity* (eds, Andrews, D., and Jackson, S.) New York: Routledge.

Davies, J. (1995) Gender, ethnicity and cultural crisis in *Falling Down* and *Groundhog Day*. *Screen*, 36(3): 214–32.

Davy, K. (1997) *Outing Whiteness: A Feminist/lesbian Project in Whiteness: A Critical Reader* (ed. Hill, M.) New York: New York University Press.

Economist, The (1994) Games plans. March 19, 108.

Faludi, S. (1999) *Stiffed: The Betrayal of the American Man*, New York: William Morrow and Co.

Fine. M. and Weis, L. (1998) *The Unknown City: The Lives of Poor and Working-class Young Adults*, Boston, MA: Beacon Press.

Flax, J. (1999) *The American Dream in Black and White: The Clarence Thomas Hearings*, Ithaca, NY: Cornell University Press.

Frankenburg, R. (1997) Introduction: Local whitenesses, localizing whiteness in *Displacing Whiteness: Essays in Social and Cultural Criticism* (ed. Frankenburg, R.) Durham, NC: Duke University Press.

Gates, D. (1993) White male paranoia, *Newsweek*, 121, 13: 48–53.

Giroux, H. (1997) Rewriting the discourse of racial identity: Towards a pedagogy and politics of whiteness. *Harvard Educational Review*, 67(2): 285–320.

Greenfeld, K.T. (1998, Nov. 9). A wider world of sports. *Time*, 152, 19: 63.

Greenfeld, K.T. (1999, Dec. 6). Life on the edge. *Time*, 154, 10: 29–36.

Hornblower, M. (1997, June 9) Great expectations. *Time*, 151, 28: 58–69.

Howe, S. (1997) *(Sick): A Cultural History of Snowboarding*, New York: St. Martin's Press.

Jeffords, S. (1994) *Hard Bodies: Hollywood Masculinity in the Reagan Era*, New Brunswick, NJ: Rutgers University Press.

Kimmel, M (1996) *Manhood in America: A Cultural History*, New York: The Free Press.

Kincheloe, J. and Steinberg, S. (1998) Addressing the crisis of whiteness: Reconfiguring white identity in a pedagogy of whiteness in *White Reign: Deploying Whiteness in America* (eds, Kincheloe, J., Steinberg, S., Rodriguez, N., and Chennault, R.) New York: St. Martin's Press.

Kincheloe, J. and Steinberg, S. (2000) Constructing a pedagogy of whiteness for angry white students in *Dismantling White Privilege: Pedagogy, Politics, and Whiteness* (eds, Rodriguez, N. and Villaverde, L.) New York: Peter Lang.

Koerner, B.L. (30 June 1997). Extreeeme. *US News and World Report*, 122, 25: 51–60.

Kusz, K. (2001a) Andre Agassi and Generation X: Reading white masculinity in 1990s America in *Sport Stars: The Politics of Sport Celebrity* (eds, Andrews, D. and Jackson, S.) New York: Routledge.

Kusz, K. (2001b) 'I want to be the minority': The cultural politics of young white males in sport and popular culture. *Journal of Sport and Social Issues*, 25(4): 390–416.

Maharidge, D. (1996) *The Coming White Minority*, New York: Vintage Books.

McCarthy, C. (1998) Living with anxiety: Race and renarration of public life in *White Reign: Deploying Whiteness in America* (eds, Kincheloe, J. and Steinberg, S.) New York: St. Martin's Press.

Messner, M. (1997) *Politics of Masculinities*, Thousand Oaks, CA: Sage Publications.

Mishel, L., Bernstein, J. and Schmitt, J. (1997) *The State of Working America*, Washington DC: Economic Policy Institute.

Nakayama, T. and Krizek, R. (1995) Whiteness: A strategic rhetoric. *Quarterly Journal of Speech*, 81: 291–309.

Leland, J., Monserrate, C. and Senna, D. (1993, Oct. 11) Battle for your brain. *Newsweek*, 42–6.

Pfeil, F. (1995) *White Guys: Studies in Postmodern Domination and Difference*. London: Verso.

Price, S.L. (1997, Dec.6) Whatever happened to the white athlete? *Sports Illustrated*, 87(23): 32–51.

Rinehart, R. (1995) Cyber-sports: Power and diversity in ESPN's The Extreme Games, paper presented at the North American Society of the Sociology of Sport, Sacramento, CA.

Rodriguez, N. (1998) Emptying the content of whiteness: Toward an understanding of the relation between whiteness and pedagogy in *White Reign: Deploying Whiteness in America* (eds, Kincheloe, J., and Steinberg, S.) New York: St. Martin's Press.

Sacks, D. and Thiel, P. (1995) *The Diversity Myth: 'Multiculturalism' and the Politics of Intolerance at Stanford*, Oakland, CA: The Independent Institute.

Savran, D. (1998) *Taking it like a Man: White Masculinity, Masochism, and Contemporary American Culture*, Princeton, NJ: Princeton University Press.

Scott, J. (1995) The Campaign against political correctness: What's really at stake in *After Political Correctness: The Humanities and Society in the 1990s*, (eds. Newfield, C. and Strickland, R.) Boulder, CO: Westview Press.

Spade, D. (1998, April) White man blues. *George*, 52

Sports Illustrated (1999, July 5) Importing X Sports. 24.

Stouffer, J. (1998, Nov.9–15) X faithful may be young, but they're smart and savvy about their sports, *Street and Smith's SportsBusiness Journal*, 1(29): 24.

Weis, L., Proweller, A. and Centrie, C. (1997) Re-examining 'A moment in history': Loss of privilege inside white working-class masculinity in the 1990s in *Whiteness: A Critical Reader* (ed. Hill, M.) New York: New York University Press.

Wellman, D. (1997) Minstrel shows, affirmative action talk, and angry white men: Marking racial otherness in the 1990s in *Displacing Whiteness: Essays in Social and Cultural Criticism* (ed. Frankenburg, R.) Durham, NC: Duke University Press.

Wray, M. and Newitz, A. (1997) *White Trash: Race and Class in America*, New York: Routledge.

Yudice, G. (1995) Neither impugning nor disavowing whiteness does a viable politics make: The limits of identity politics in *After Political Correctness: The Humanities and Society in the 1990s* (eds, Newfield, C., and Strickland, R.) Boulder, CO: Westview Press.

Index